Vanishing Jobs

Canada's Changing Workplaces

Lars Osberg
Fred Wien
Jan Grude

James Lorimer & Company, Publishers
Toronto, 1995

James Lorimer & Company Ltd. acknowledges with thanks the support of the Canada Council, the Ontario Arts Council and the Ontario Publishing Centre in the development of writing and publishing in Canada.

Canadian Cataloguing in Publication Data
  Osberg, Lars
  Vanishing Jobs

ISBN 1-55028-483-5 (bound) ISBN 1-55028-482-7 (pbk.)

1. Unemployment - Canada. 2. Labor market - Canada.
I. Wien, Fred, 1943-   . II. Grude, Jan. III. Title.

HD5728.072 1995   331.13'7971   C95-931468-7

James Lorimer & Company Ltd., Publishers
35 Britain Street
Toronto, Ontario M5A 1R7

Printed and bound in Canada

Contents

Acknowledgements

We would like to thank the Social Sciences and Humanities Research Council of Canada for financial support under grant No. 499-89-0022.

Maureen MacDonald deserves a vote of thanks for her exemplary work as research assistant on the case studies, assisted by Mary Kilfoil. Zhengxi Lin did an outstanding job as research assistant on the quantitative side.

A special thanks is also due to Monique Comeau, Jeannie Doyle, Heather Lennox and Cheryl Stewart, who maintained their good cheer through many drafts. We are also very grateful to the many persons who shared their time and knowledge with us in the case study firms and for the policy interviews. Members of our Advisory Committee who helped guide the research project also deserve our appreciation.

Preface

In this book, we report on what we have learned from a wide-ranging series of case studies of workplaces in the early 1990s. Our focus is on the changing structure of employment. Although many books on structural change have been concerned with one sector (often manufacturing) or one type of firm, we wanted to look at the economy as a whole. We selected our case studies to include a cross-section of small, medium-size and large employers in resources, manufacturing and government, in both traditional and knowledge-based service industries. We interviewed workers and managers in a wide range of environments — from high technology aerospace manufacturing to traditional lumber mills, and from computer-intensive architectural firms to domestic cleaning franchises.

Our case studies were selected from Nova Scotia, a province which has the industrial diversity of much of the rest of Canada — both heavy and light manufacturing, both financial and community services — but which also possesses, to a greater degree than average, some of the structural problems of the Canadian labour market. Nova Scotia's economy differs from Central Canada's in the greater relative importance of its rural areas and their declining economic base. In much of Canada, double-digit unemployment didn't arrive until the 1980s, but in Nova Scotia it has a longer history because the employment base of rural areas has been shrinking for a longer time.

Currently, roughly half the labour force of Nova Scotia lives in the Halifax-Dartmouth metropolitan area, which invariably compares well with other Canadian cities in level of average earnings and in unemployment rates (for example, Halifax had less unemployment than Vancouver throughout the 1980s and has had a lower unemployment rate than Montreal every year since the mid 1970s). The difference between Nova Scotia unemployment rates and the average rate in the rest of Canada is entirely due to greater unemployment in rural areas and in Cape Breton.

Nova Scotia was settled earlier than most other parts of Canada, and Nova Scotians have a deep attachment to the small rural communities which grew up on the basis of an earlier technology of small-scale fishing, lumbering and agriculture. Despite this attachment, however, the long-term trends are unmistakable. A comparison of the Census of 1881 and 1986 indicates that the number of farm families in Nova Scotia fell from 55,873 in 1881 (70.2 per cent of the population) to 4,283 in 1986 (1.9 per cent of the population). In the 1880s, most of the Canadian prairies were still unsettled, while many Nova Scotia farms were small (over 20 per cent were under 10 acres in size) and often had marginal land.[1] As larger, more fertile farms became available in the Canadian and American West and as industrialization created millions of urban factory jobs, the rural areas of Nova Scotia were depopulated by emigration, and this process has continued throughout the past century.

Rural Nova Scotia has therefore faced for many years the problems of a declining employment base which places like Northern and Eastern Ontario, Saskatchewan and the B.C. interior have only encountered more recently. The problems and prospects for rural employment in Nova Scotia are highly relevant for many areas of Canada, in part because we have been able to observe the consequences of rural underdevelopment for a longer period. However, although the mythology of life in Atlantic Canada continues to stress the region's historic roots in small-scale fishing, forestry and farming, the reality of economic life in the late twentieth century is that this is not what the vast majority of people in this province actually do for a living — fishermen, for example, number less than 2 per cent of the Nova Scotia labour force. Indeed, the diversified structure of urban employment means that Nova Scotia in 1990 had more accountants (7,510) than fishermen (7,290) and more civil engineers (1,070) than ships officers (440).[2]

We would argue, therefore, that although the trends and policy responses which we observed in our study are of particular relevance for Nova Scotia, they are of general applicability to Canadian society in the 1990s. Although the case studies of this book are all drawn from Nova Scotia, we selected our cases so that most of them could be from "Anywhere, Canada." We interviewed technologically sophisticated multinational companies, innovative small entrepreneurial firms, and some low-tech traditionalists; it would not be difficult to find similar examples in any province. The similarity of economic structure across Canada is not particularly surprising; the speed of technological and market change and the pressure of competition have forced firms in most industries to scan their environment continually for new developments. Regardless of their location, firms selling most of their output in national and international markets now take their bench marks of success from international comparisons, and firms servicing local markets also increasingly recognize that survival depends on being up to date in production technology.

This book reports the results of a three-year research effort, funded by the Social Science and Humanities Research Council of Canada, that has attempted to address the issues surrounding structural change in the labour market. We have tried to bring something new to the debate by combining the insights of different disciplines and by examining different lines of evidence. Our academic backgrounds are in economics, sociology and business administration, and each of these disciplines tends to view the labour market, and the role of public policy, from a slightly different perspective. We have combined the lessons learned from an extensive analysis of over twenty case studies of employers with a series of econometric analyses of survey data from Statistics Canada. And since our underlying concern has been to derive some specific policy suggestions from our analysis, we have taken advantage of the insights and suggestions offered by an advisory board of business people and civil servants.

Because we started with the perspective that many of the emerging trends in the Canadian labour market might be due to the increasing competitive pressures of international trade, especially the opening up of the Canadian domestic market to U.S. competition by the Free Trade Agreement, we tried to ensure that in sectors that were potentially exposed to international competitive pressures, we would interview some firms that depend largely on a domestic market, as well as some firms that are more fully exposed to international competition. In addition, we began the research project with the hypothesis that technological change, especially that associated with computerization, might be largely responsible for the changing employment strategies of firms. We therefore selected our case studies to be as informative as possible, making sure we talked both to highly progressive firms and to more traditional employers in all the major industrial categories, and in small, medium and large size categories.

This book offers us the opportunity to outline the relationships between competition, technology, employment and social policy in the 1990s, and to integrate what we have learned from case studies and from statistical analysis. We realized very early in our research that every single one of our case studies offers a wealth of complexity, but here we want to draw out some of the general lessons that come from specific examples.

Our case studies typically began with an interview, usually of several hours duration, with the chief executive or other senior officers of the firm, followed by interviews with plant managers, personnel administrators and union representatives. In order to obtain the maximum amount of frankness, we promised all our respondents anonymity; this book in all cases refers to companies and individuals by pseudonyms. Each case study is, however, a real firm and all the comments reported in this book are drawn directly from interviews with specific people. Many people will be able to recognize themselves in these pages, but we hope that we have disguised their identities enough that others cannot.

Since we were particularly interested in changes in the nature of employment for low- to middle-income positions, we typically selected, at each employer, two large, low-income occupational groups, and interviewed in depth both new, low-seniority workers and older, high-seniority employees, in addition to our interviews with union representatives, plant managers and senior executives. To be clear about the extent to which our case study firms were typical of the industry to which they belonged, we built up extensive background files on technical and economic developments in each industry. Throughout all this, we obtained excellent cooperation from executives and workers at our case study firms, and much of the credit for this must go to the assistance we received from our advisory board. The notes to interviews were extensive and we did many interviews. Some of the summary reports on our case studies run to fifty or sixty pages; the most difficult problem we faced in doing our case studies lay in deciding when we had enough information. Each industry and each firm offered us its own fascinating reasons for digging ever deeper.

This volume presents only part of the output of the research project. To keep some of the vividness of our case studies, we avoid presenting massive statistical tables, but we do have such data. The research project has also produced a number of Ph.D. and M.A. theses in economics which focus more intensively on specific issues within the general themes addressed in this volume. In addition, the project has supported the preparation of quite a number of conference papers and specialized econometric articles for academic journals.[3]

However, although the qualitative discussion of case studies and the econometric analysis of survey data are dramatically different in vocabulary and methodology, both methodologies share a common problem — how do the pieces of the puzzle fit together? How can one go from a particular case study or the statistical analysis of one type of behaviour to an understanding of the labour market as a whole? Case studies can be a superbly suggestive source of hypotheses and can suggest interrelationships that might otherwise have been overlooked, but it is not possible for a series of case studies to provide quantitative evidence on how important one issue is relative to other potential issues.

Similarly, in statistical analysis of a specific issue, such as estimating a multiple regression which predicts the probability that a single parent will look for a job, the researcher tries to get a precise answer to a narrowly specified question by holding constant the influence of other factors, such as the structure of employment demand. When economists analyze the impacts of social programs, such as unemployment insurance, they usually do so in a "partial equilibrium" context, examining issues on a separate, one-at-a-time basis, and ignoring the interdependence and feedback effects of the real world.

In this book we present the *qualitative* results drawn from our case study interviews, but we have also done a great deal of *quantitative* research. One of the products of that research is a microsimulation model of the Canadian labour market. One of the major benefits of building a comprehensive econometric model is that model building demands quantitative consistency and it forces explicit consideration of the inter-relationships among different behaviours. This research project provided the initial funding for the development of a microsimulation model of labour market behaviour in Canada to analyze the interrelation of behaviours in the labour market and the impact of alternative public policies.[4] The model uses data on a representative sample of all Canadians, and rigorous econometric analysis of the determinants of labour force participation, unemployment, and employment.

However, a computer model has the disadvantage that it cannot examine *qualitative* change. Furthermore, in statistical analysis, one can only test hypotheses about the variables available in existing data from Statistics Canada. This invariably means one can only look at part of past behaviour. This book therefore tries to do what computer simulations of secondary data cannot do — pull together *qualitatively* the implications of our case studies of individual employers, suggest future trends and discuss the appropriate public policy response.

Because this book is based on case studies, it is written in a very different style from conventional articles in academic economics journals. In order to keep the presentation as clear as possible, there are no mathematical equations, few footnotes and not many numbers. We hope that readers who miss these things will take the opportunity to read the technical working papers and journal articles based on our econometric work and microsimulation model.

The most difficult problem we have encountered in writing this book is the problem of selection. Our case study research was fascinating and fun, because the people we talked with were often articulate and insightful, and each had a slightly different perspective on the particular reality of their corner of the economy. Our case studies offer us a wealth of qualitative detail about the actual problems faced, and strategies adopted, by firms and social agencies. Our statistical analyses, and the broader literature on structural change, offer us a vast array of quantitative data on trends in the labour market as a whole. In this book, we have attempted to sift this mass of evidence, while still providing some of the vividness which case studies can provide.

In preparing the original research proposal and handling all the many details of project administration, Osberg and Grude were happy to be able to "leave it to Fred." Grude, Osberg and Wien all participated equally in the case studies (usually two of us participated in each interview.) When it came to writing things up, Osberg took the lead role. Grude, Osberg and Wien all took a hand in the writing of Chapter 3, while Wien did the first draft of Chapter 6 and Grude did the first pass at Chapter 5. Osberg is responsible for chapters 1, 2, 4, 5, 7 and 8 and final revisions to all chapters.

Introduction

What has happened to the jobs that high school graduates used to get? In the 1960s and 1970s, people with a high school education (or perhaps less) could go directly from school into a permanent job. Although that job might not have offered the best pay, or the most iron-clad security, it typically offered some of both. People who worked hard and dependably could expect to keep their jobs for many years. As they worked their way up the ladder, they learned what they needed to know about their job duties by experience and on-the-job training. Whether the jobs were blue collar ones in the resource industries or manufacturing, or white collar ones in banking or insurance, there was enough pay and enough security for people to consider themselves members of the middle class.

Beginning in the early 1980s, however, disturbing trends emerged in Canada. The distribution of earnings became more unequal, more polarized between high-income "yuppie" professional jobs and low-wage services employment. There was a steady increase in unemployment. In the decade of the 1950s unemployment averaged 4.2 per cent in Canada, rising to 5.0 per cent in the 1960s, and 6.7 per cent in the 1970s. The big increase, however, has come in the last fifteen years, as unemployment rose to an average of 9.5 per cent in the 1980s, and over 11 per cent in the early 1990s. The recession of 1981–83 left many people dependent on social assistance, and poverty rates declined only slowly throughout the recovery of the mid-1980s. When the new recession of the early 1990s hit, an increasing proportion of the Canadian population was forced to rely on transfer payments from unemployment insurance or social assistance.

These issues are of crucial importance for Canadian society. Canadians like to think of themselves as belonging to a fair and compassionate community, but that vision is endangered if earnings in the labour market are unable to prevent many Canadians from slipping into poverty. Canadians also want to look forward to rising standards of living, but that hope is diminished if an increasing fraction of the population become permanently dependent on transfer payments. Public policy has to address the changing structure of the Canadian labour market, but there is a wide variety of analyses and viewpoints on why these trends are occurring, and what do about them.

In one view, the basic problem is that ordinary Canadians are too inflexible, too dependent on government and too highly paid. In this view, firms are not hiring because Canadian workers do not have the skills to warrant the wages that they demand and governments have deficits because social programs have been excessively generous. This view recognizes that many jobs have disappeared but contends that "lots" of new jobs are available for those who are willing to retrain, relocate or accept reduced wages. The proposed solution to unemployment and poverty is for ordinary Canadians to reduce their appetites, and become satisfied with less income, less security and a lower level of public services.

In thinking about public attitudes to Canada's economic problems, it is remarkable how successful the last fifteen years of bad economic performance have been in depressing the aspirations of many Canadians. One often hears the phrase, "The jobs are gone, and they're not coming back." Many youths have come to expect economic insecurity and low-wage jobs (when available). Even though Canada has historically been a country of growing affluence, an increasing number of Canadians now expect that future generations will not be as well off as we are today.

In our case studies, we found many examples of the events that have generated this pessimism. It became abundantly clear that many jobs *have* gone forever and that the remaining jobs usually demand more intensive work and often deliver less pay and poorer economic security. The key issues are, however, why this is so and what can be done.

Our analysis of the data does not indicate that Canada's economic problems have arisen because Canadian workers have demanded excessive wages. We find no evidence that the solution to the problems of increased economic inequality and poverty lies in decreasing the wages and working conditions of less affluent Canadians. We do not, therefore, believe that a "race to the bottom," in which Canada attempts to compete with the low wages and abysmal social benefits of Third World countries is either desirable or likely to be economically successful. We do believe that social and economic policies can make a difference, but they have to operate both at the "micro" level of the individual workplace and at the "macro" level of aggregate demand and broad framework policies.

We interviewed some workers in firms whose future depends on trends in the broader economy that are essentially beyond their control. If the fish stock disappears, or if tourists stop visiting Canada, it is inevitable that some fish plants will close and some hotels will go bankrupt. The key issue for Canadians is to distinguish between the trends that are inevitable and the trends that can be influenced. The comparison of fish plants and hotels provides an example, because although Canadian governments may not be able to bring back the cod, government policy *can* bring back the tourists. Aggregate demand in the Canadian tourism sector is heavily influenced by the relative cost of a Canadian vacation, compared to a foreign vacation, and government policy plays a major role. By allowing short-term interest rates to decline, the Bank of Canada can bring down the foreign exchange value of the Canadian dollar. As the Canadian dollar depreciates, Canadian vacations become cheaper compared to U.S. and foreign vacations, and Canadians begin to spend more of their travel dollars at home, while foreigners begin to discover what a good bargain a vacation in Canada can be — and the jobs in the hotel industry which disappeared as hotels went bankrupt begin to reappear as hotels reopen and expand.

In looking, therefore, at the experiences of our case study firms, we want to distinguish between the inevitable and the changeable. Broad trends like technological change and computerization are beyond the control of any nation; the best that Canadians can do is to try to use such trends to our best advantage. But, even though other trends, such as the literacy skills of high school graduates or the level of interest rates, are beyond the control of any individual firm or industry, they *can* be influenced by government policy.

"Macro" policies are therefore crucial, but as well, we want to focus on those "micro" strategies that have helped some firms to swim against the tide. Even when the recession of 1990–93 was at its worst, some firms managed to stay in business, prosper and expand employment. How was this possible?

Throughout this research, we have become increasingly convinced of the interdependence between the "hard" technology of capital equipment and technical skills and the "soft" technology of organizational structure and human relations skills. These organizational choices also have important implications for the success of competitive strategies based on price and quality. Figure I summarizes the four-cornered problem facing firms — a problem whose interdependent aspects often have not been recognized by the individual academic disciplines to which we belong.

Figure 1 **THE FOUR-CORNERED PROBLEM**	
MARKET DEMANDS	**TECHNOLOGY OF PRODUCTION**
Cost	*Hard* - Capital Equipment - Human Capital in Cognitive Skills
Quality	*Soft* - Organizational - Motivational

In using the terms "hard" and "soft" technology, we do not mean to imply that some technologies are hard to change, or that others are soft and gentle. Rather, we are using the term "hard" to refer to technologies that are tangibly embodied in the capabilities of individual workers, or particular machines. By "soft" technology, we mean technologies that are less tangible, and comprise the relationships among people at the workplace, and the organizational strategies that influence their motivation to work.

Economists have tended to focus on the top half of Figure I, i.e. on individual skills, tangible capital and the least costly method of production. Since the time of Adam Smith, over two hundred years ago, economists have emphasized that the training of workers is an investment process and that one can see the increase in workers' skills which training produces as "human capital." Human capital is embodied in individual workers, while physical capital is embodied in individual machines, and economists have tended to think of production as occurring when human capital, physical capital and raw materials are combined at the workplace. But the method of combination is seen as purely an engineering relationship. In most economic models, the emphasis is on the necessity for low-cost production, in markets where competition is based only on price.

The perspective of people in business schools has historically been somewhat different, emphasizing the importance of marketing and *perceived* quality of production, as well as price, in competitive success. In business schools, one learns of the fundamental ambiguity in the idea of "quality" and how important satisfying the customer's definition of quality is to competitive success.

If quality is ambiguous and hard to define, how do firms supply it? Firms have to depend on motivating their workers to want to satisfy their customer's needs. Although economists usually assume that workers only care about their wages, sociologists have a different slant. They have tended to focus much more on the "soft" technology of organizational design, individual motivation and team formation within firms. Each discipline has its own insights and its own blind spots. The focus of sociologists on why some workers put in extra effort for their employers comes at the cost of paying relatively little attention to the "hard" technology of capital equipment and cognitive skills. Economic analyses of profit-maximizing capital investment strategies typically assume that worker preferences for leisure or income cannot be manipulated by employers. Neither perspective provides a full picture.

In the real world, of course, firms have to solve all the aspects of the four-cornered problem of Figure I simultaneously. The "soft" technology of organization design, individual motivation and team building, and the "hard" technology of capital equipment, training and cognitive skills, are very interdependent. Our case studies have convinced us of the importance of perceived quality, in addition to price, for the competitive success of many firms, and of the fundamental ambiguity of "quality." In a world of rapid technological change, "quality" is often ambiguous, but all important. If customers are to be satisfied, workers have to use their initiative and intelligence to solve the problem of how to satisfy them, i.e. workers have to be *motivated*. Organizational success may, therefore, depend as much on the organization and motivation of workers as on their cognitive skills or capital equipment.

In a number of our case studies, we found managers who were highly aware of the interdependence of cost, quality, "hard" technology and "soft" technology. In some firms, a new paradigm of production is emerging, based on information technologies that enable the devolution of authority to the operational level and motivational/organizational strategies that try to lead by consensus and team building. However, in more traditional firms such organizational change requires a fundamental re-thinking of a firm's culture.

The problem of structural change is being faced today by many thousands of individual firms, and their millions of workers, on an individual case-by-case basis. Micro-level solutions to this problem will inevitably be unique, dependent on the particular circumstances of the market pressures, history and technology of each case. Solutions will also, inevitably, be temporary, since there is a continuous need for change in advanced capitalist economies, and the one certainty about structural change is that it will not stop. The responsibility of government is to do what it can to minimize the social costs and maximize the social benefits of change.

Governments must also recognize the interdependencies between "macro" strategies for framework policies, just as firms must recognize the interdependencies between "micro" strategies for their survival. If governments want to encourage firms to adopt particular types of individual strategies to cope with change, governments have to help establish a context in which such strategies make sense, and contribute to firms' profitability. It makes no sense, for example, for governments to preach at firms about the necessity of instituting a "training culture," while simultaneously following a high interest rate monetary policy. High interest rates create high unemployment, which means that firms will not invest in training, because they know a queue of qualified labour is already available. Since government policies set the framework within which individuals and firms must operate, that framework must recognize both the imperatives for change and the reasons why people now behave as they do.

Canadians want an end to high unemployment, stagnant wages and increasing economic inequality and insecurity. If this is to happen, there has to be change at both the "micro" and the "macro" level — at both the level of the individual firm or workplace *and* at the level of the broad framework policies of government. On their own, neither type of change is enough; our case studies provided several examples where firms had done all the "right" things for success — yet failed for lack of aggregate demand. Change has to come at both levels simultaneously. Government policies alone cannot guarantee success, but well-chosen policies can increase the odds of a prosperous future. The aim of this book is to discuss both the broad trends affecting the Canadian labour market and the ways in which individual firms have reacted. The first five chapters outline the situations and the strategies of a cross-section of firms, while the last chapters discuss the role of public policy.

The Resource Sector

Traditionally, the resource sector has provided most of the employment base of rural Canada. Demanding few educational credentials of workers, it relied on on-the-job training for the skills it needed and it provided physically demanding jobs for thousands of male blue collar workers. Although women also found employment in processing occupations (e.g. in fish plants) and although jobs were often interrupted by seasonal lay-offs, the full-time employment of male breadwinners in forestry, fishing, mining and agriculture was the economic basis on which successive generations of rural Canadians were raised. In Nova Scotia, as elsewhere in Canada, the crucial problem facing rural areas today is the large-scale disappearance of such traditional jobs.

Primary industries employed 1,111,700 Canadians in 1951, but by 1991, employment in these industries had fallen to 868,030. Over these forty years, the experienced labour force almost tripled, so primary sector employment as a proportion of total employment fell even more dramatically — from 21.3 per cent in 1951 to 6.1 per cent in 1991.[1] These declines in aggregate employment are mirrored in the firms we studied. The mining firm we interviewed employed 13,000 workers in 1951, but in the mid 1990s, it is expected to employ only 1,700 workers. At the other end of the employment scale, the Annapolis Valley farm we interviewed needed 25 to 30 farm hands as recently as 1971, but gets by today with 3 or 4 permanent employees, plus seasonal contract workers.

The resource sector provides some clear examples of powerful trends that are almost impossible to avoid. Employment in the primary sector has fallen by an order of magnitude, primarily because modern technology has massively displaced labour. In some cases, continued investment has substituted capital for labour; for example, chain saws replaced axes in logging, and then were themselves largely replaced by tree harvesting machines. In other cases, modern technology has economized on the use of both capital and labour; for example, solid state electronics has replaced electro-mechanical switches (and the people needed to repair them) in mining machinery.

In addition, some industries have specific structural problems of resource availability and/or market demand. The recent decline in fish stocks in the Atlantic region has severely affected employment in the fishery. In Western Canada, low wheat prices have imperilled the survival of many farms. Smaller, lighter automobiles need less steel, and reduced steel production has lessened the demand for coal. All this, of course, was magnified in intensity by the early 1990s recession, but even with a general economic recovery, the problems of labour shedding, resource availability and depressed final demand will not go away.

In addition to a general loss of jobs in rural areas, the employment that does remain is increasingly centralized. In farming areas, the consolidation of small farms into larger units means a decrease in the farming population. A decline in the population base implies a decrease in the demand for private services (such as retail trade) and for public services (such as schools or hospitals). Local suppliers, both private and public, no longer have the demand they need to continue to supply such services. As local stores close and schools and hospitals are consolidated, small villages wither away — a process that is accelerated if an improved road network makes it feasible to centralize service activity in a few large rural towns.

Similarly, the Nova Scotia coastline used to be dotted with small fish processing plants, each providing the economic base for its surrounding community. However, technological change (such as the introduction of fish-filleting machines) has increased economies of scale in fish processing, and one large plant can now do more cheaply what dozens of small local plants used to do. In modern fish processing plants, capital has replaced labour and much larger volumes of fish are needed to be profitable.

Throughout the resource sector, transportation costs have fallen, and production has become more capital intensive. The "harvesting radius" of resource industries has therefore increased. Large trawlers in the fishery (like tree harvesters in the forest) now span a larger area from their central base. Fewer people are employed, and those jobs that remain are centralized in a limited number of rural communities.

Together, this combination of job loss and centralization of production has led to a massive erosion of the employment base of many rural communities. Although the emigration of younger families has also left behind a need for employees in homes for senior citizens, these jobs often have significantly lower wages than the primary sector jobs they replace. The disappearance of many traditional "good jobs" in the resource sector has especially affected unskilled male workers, and the loss of such "breadwinner" jobs has placed substantial strains on traditional family expectations.

Does all this imply the total depopulation of our rural areas? Can one look forward to a future Canada of crowded cities separated by uninhabited forests? We think not — for three main reasons.

First, profits in the resource sector come about from the combined inputs of labour, capital and a naturally occurring resource, such as an ore body, forest, fish stock or fertile land. As long as the total selling price of the product exceeds the cost of capital, labour and taxes (in economic jargon, as long as some rents to the natural resource endowment remain), firms can make money in the natural resource sector, and will want to employ labour. Although it is true that increasing labour productivity means that it takes fewer and fewer workers to harvest a given resource, some employment in natural resources extraction will remain.

Second, even if the natural resource sector is still producing the "same old thing," it is not necessarily doing it in "the same old way." Coal from Cape Breton and Alberta now competes in the global market place with coal from Chile, South Africa and Poland. Canadian lumber competes with Swedish and Russian wood for European and Japanese markets. In the past, the Canadian resource base was often so abundantly superior to the resources available to our competitors that Canadian exporters could be successful even at somewhat lower levels of efficiency. Today, international competition is much more intense and our most abundant forests, richest ore bodies and most plentiful fisheries have been harvested — sometimes overharvested. Today, the survival of jobs in the resource sector often depends heavily on raising productivity levels, producing old commodities with new efficiency. Our case studies offered us some object lessons in why some Canadian firms are able, and some are unable, to cope with these new challenges.

Third, even if rising labour productivity is lowering the level of total employment in the traditional resource sector, there is a nontraditional sector which offers some hope for expanding employment. We do not want to pretend that non-traditional niche producers are an easy answer to the problem of rural job loss, since lay-offs at mines and fish plants often affect hundreds of workers at a time, while employment at new start up firms is typically measured in tens and twenties. Nevertheless, in our case studies we interviewed energetic entrepreneurs who are creating new markets in specialized agricultural products, aquaculture and small-scale mining, and our case studies offer some evidence of the barriers they face and the reasons for their success.

"Coal Mine Company" — New Technology, Old Attitudes

High technology has definitely come to the resource sector. Although this is true in almost all industries, our interviews at "Coal Mine Company" were particularly vivid. It used to be common for men to go directly into the coal mines before finishing high school. A strong back and a strong work ethic were the main qualifications one needed for employment. In the 1950s, the mines we visited used a "room and pillar" technology, in which miners drilled and blasted areas of the coal seam, leaving a pillar of coal to support the rock ceiling. Once the coal had been broken loose, it was shovelled manually into trolleys to be taken to the surface. As late as 1962, pit ponies were used underground to pull coal trolleys and deliver supplies. Hard physical labour was the norm.

As one suits up today to go down a coal mine, it becomes clear that a coal mine is still a dangerous and hostile environment, but coal mining is a carefully organized, sophisticated operation. Mine visitors are instructed in the use of their portable breathing apparatus, in case underground ventilation should fail. Matches and cigarette lighters must be left behind, because any underground spark might ignite coal dust or methane. Hard hats and boots must be worn at all times as protection against small underground rock falls. And after a long ride into the underground darkness, the first thing one reaches at the base of the shaft is a permanently manned underground nursing station.

However, inside that nursing station one notices that the wall posters are warning workers about the dangers of heart attacks, not industrial accidents. Although tradition dictates that local restaurants serve meals with heaping helpings of french fries — food fit for a hard day's labour underground — it is in fact now much more efficient to let machines do the work. Physical effort is still involved in coal mining, but it is the intermittent effort involved in shifting machinery and installing conveyor belts, rather than the continuous effort required to shovel tons of coal. Since the collapse of energy prices in the early 1980s, there has been no new hiring in the coal mines (except for specialized trades) and many low-seniority workers have been laid off. Since many older workers have taken early retirement, the vast majority of miners are now in a very narrow age span — thirty-five to fifty. Given the age, diet and somewhat sedentary work of coal miners today, an emphasis on the prevention of heart disease is perfectly reasonable.

Today, Coal Mine Co. uses the "long-wall retreat" mode of mining. Parallel tunnels are driven deep into the coal seam on either side of the main shaft, and the ends of these tunnels are connected. The coal between the connecting tunnel and the main shaft is then removed by an electrically driven shearer which goes back and forth, cutting coal in strips from the coal face. As coal is removed, the mining machinery is moved forward towards the coal face by hydraulic jacks, and the area from which coal has been removed is left to collapse in on itself.

The "shearer" consists of a pair of huge rotating cutting wheels which eat their way along the coal face, depositing loose coal on a drag line, from which it is automatically transferred to the surface by a system of conveyor belts. Although there may be 450 men underground on a given shift, the vast majority of them are involved in boring preparatory tunnels, laying out the conveyor line and the electrical and air systems, or monitoring and repairing machinery. There are only fifteen men working at the coal face at any given time, most of whom assist in moving hydraulic jacks and positioning machinery so that the shearer can cut continuously and the mine roof can collapse safely behind them. The entire underground operation is organized to set up the two men who operate the tiny control panels (which look much like Nintendo controls) so that the Eikhof electric shearer can operate continuously at peak speed.

As the mine manager puts it, "when it's going well, the men don't work hard." Production declines when the coal seam is uneven and rock is encountered, or when bad layout, machinery breakdown or disorganization interrupts production. The nature of the production process has changed fundamentally, since productivity now depends primarily on coordination of jobs and on cognitive and social skills, not on individual physical effort.

In the old days, men used to work in small groups, which were paid on a group piece-rate basis (indeed, work crews were charged for their individual use of supplies, such as gun powder). If one gang fell behind, or messed up, the production of others was not particularly affected. Today, however, all the jobs of a modern mine are interdependent. Production bonus continues to be an important part of total pay, but it is a bonus paid on the production of the mine as a whole. Teamwork in large groups, the anticipation of potential production problems, continual monitoring of machinery, meticulous attention to safety and quality repair work — these are the skills which ensure that machines can mine and extract coal quickly, without interruption.

In the mining industry, many now speculate about the maximum extent to which machinery can replace people. Will robots eventually be able to replace miners entirely on the coal face, or is there always going to be some role for a skilled operator, to deal with the unpredictable events for which the robot has not been programmed? Will miners eventually be able to remain on the surface, operating their machinery by remote sensing and remote control? Does it pay to substitute machinery for labour in maintenance roles? When the workforce is much smaller, and the remaining jobs need more brain than brawn, how can management enlist the active cooperation and involvement of workers? What training will people need to keep the machinery in top running order?

Historically, Coal Mine Co. invested heavily in training and apprenticeship programs — but only in "directly useful" skills. With hindsight it has become apparent that training should have placed more emphasis on abstract principles and general skills, rather than just training in immediately job-relevant skills. When, in the 1980s, solid state electronic controls using microprocessors and embedded logic and diagnostics became common, the limited educational background and highly specific vocational training of the older generation of mine electricians meant many had difficulty making the transition. The company now depends heavily on some of the younger tradespeople, who have a better educational background and training developed through the local community colleges. As well, the company depends on equipment suppliers for training and for servicing — the new shearing machine was, for example, accompanied by a technician to supervise its installation and provide servicing and training for the first year of its operation. However, there is little point now in redesigning training programs, because "Coal Mine

Co." now has little need for training. Since employment declined continuously throughout the 1980s, and another mine closed in the early 1990s, the company has a surplus of skilled tradespeople; as a result, it has largely discontinued its apprenticeship programs and training efforts.

Today, the control room of a modern mine is on the surface, linked to solid state sensors throughout the mine. With its banks of monitors and computer screens, it resembles the air traffic control centre of a modern airport. Throughout the mine, computerized sensors record air flow, gas concentrations, conveyer belt speed, the temperature of individual bearings, and so on. Seated at a central console, miles away from the farthest part of the mine, a pair of operators can control and monitor the entire mine.

The technology of production is impressively modern — yet it is hard for old habits to die in the coal mining industry. Someone who left school for the coal mines in 1958, at the age of sixteen, was only fifty-three years of age in 1995. Senior mine managers and union officials tend to be somewhat older, but they too are "too young to retire, too old to move."

Furthermore, in mining (as in fishing, forestry and agriculture) both workers and management are co-participants in old industries, with a long cultural tradition. Although they may have come to view their struggles from different angles, both middle management and workers have a shared history and a common set of operating assumptions on the basic roles of management and labour. In the executive suite, one may hear talk of employee "empowerment," "total quality," "delayering," and all the other buzz words of modern management, but the attitude at lower levels of the hierarchy is much more traditional.

Managers find it hard to envisage new ways of involving workers in decision-making, and it can be equally difficult for workers to change their habits. In the days when mining was a semi-skilled occupation, work crews were made up at the start of each shift, from among those who showed up for work. When tasks are not highly differentiated, the absenteeism of an individual worker is not particularly important for total productivity. However, a modern mine is a highly complex, technologically interdependent, continuous process operation. Although workers may have inherited the idea that it is no big deal for anyone else if they do not show up for work and lose a day's pay, the interdependence of skills in a modern mine means absenteeism has a significant impact on the productivity of other workers. At Coal Mine Co. the modern reality is that production costs cannot exceed the international market's price of coal, and mine management needs a more dependable work force. But there is also a poisoned history of labour relations in Coal Mine Co., in that management has inherited a style which thinks only in terms of "cracking down on" absenteeism, and workers think of occasional absenteeism as a reasonable thing to do. So far, attempts to change habits have mainly produced conflict.

Attitudes to absenteeism provide just one example of the entrenchment of attitudes and expectations and the limits social attitudes place on the effective operation of modern technology. We interviewed one worker in his thirties, but only one. Overwhelmingly workers, management and union officers are white males aged forty to sixty who have spent their entire working lives in the mining industry. As a metaphor for social attitudes, our visit to the local offices of the union was especially memorable. Up a narrow staircase, on the second floor of a tattered frame building in the decaying downtown core, past fading group photographs of the 1948 and 1956 continental conferences of the international union, one enters an office cluttered with manual typewriters and cardboard file boxes, whose panelling has not changed in forty years. And, as the conversation begins, the talk turns to tales of the old days in the industry — the danger of working conditions, the exploitation of miserable pay, and the thousands of workers who used to be employed.

Management types have nicer, more modern offices, but they are cut from the same cloth. The union president may have started underground in 1953 driving a pit pony, but the mine manager went into the colliery in 1951 at the age of seventeen. Both came from the same neighbourhood and both had worked all their lives in coal mining. Both were of the same ethnic origin and both had a similar level of education. Although they are now on opposite sides of the bargaining table, both share a common set of organizational assumptions on the roles of management and labour. Talking about the union, the mine manager said, "They've got their job to do, and we've got our job to do," — and the comment of the union president was almost word-for-word identical.

The summer before we visited the mines there was a strike over the contracting out of a few dozen trucking jobs. In the months since our visit, there has been a series of work stoppages in protest against disciplinary lay-offs. High production costs have also forced the closure of a major shaft. The mines remaining in operation have a relatively low cost structure but their continued profitability (and the hundreds of jobs they support) depends on whether workers and management can change the attitudes they have inherited from the past.

"Atlantic Fisheries" — Change in a Traditional Firm

For coal mines, it is the decreasing cost of bulk transportation of coal which has increased the pressures of international competition; the product itself is basically the same as it has always been. Fish plants, however, have to compete in an international market which is increasingly differentiated, with a new emphasis on quality and value added. In addition, the East Coast fishery has had to adjust to a sudden collapse in groundfish stocks and a moratorium on the fishing of cod and some other species in 1993. Given these stresses, and the need for change, our interviews with "Atlantic Fisheries" provided a classic example of how much more difficult it is to change the social environment of production, compared to changes in the physical plant and equipment.

Since we had interviewed at one of the same plants in 1979, we could compare production technology in 1979 and in 1991. The change in equipment, lay-out and all aspects of production technology was truly remarkable. In 1979, one entered a large shed, directly from the parking lot. At one end of a conveyor belt, a dozen men were filleting tubs of fish, which were passed directly to a row of women at a long table who trimmed, weighed and packed boxes of fish fillets, ready for the freezer. Standard blocks of frozen cod were the product, and aside from the freezer, capital equipment was minimal. With little investment in marketing or the development of a brand name and relatively little capital tied up in machinery, an entire fish plant could be opened up, or shut down, at very little cost.

Now, each section of the plant is air-sealed and temperature-controlled, to prevent spoilage. All workers must wear white coats (without buttons) and hair nets to limit the chance that something might get dropped into the line. Everyone must "scrub down" with disinfectant before entering the food processing area. In 1979, a fish plant's major capital expenditure was the purchase of its freezer, but in the 1990s rows of $500,000 Baader filleting machines (each replacing a dozen workers, with 4 per cent higher yield) feed the conveyor belts, which are lined with ergonomically designed trimming and packing stations.

Fish quality has been vastly improved by rigorous quality control at sea, i.e., by immediate gutting and icing, combined with much more careful packing. There is also a new emphasis on differentiating markets and adding value. Fresh fish gets the best price, but needs to be carefully handled and speedily marketed. Frozen fish gets a better price if it can be marketed as a fish dinner than if it is sold as raw fillets. Covering fish with a little sauce and packing it in a microwaveable container with vegetables and rice does not really create all that many jobs directly, but it does help to maintain the share of fish in the total food expenditure of consumers. Throughout the industry, it is recognized that the days of producing large volumes of unprocessed "cod blocks" are long gone.

However, social change can be much slower than physical change. The organizational philosophy in Atlantic Fisheries remains very traditional — management is to design the work process and enforce quality standards, while workers are to do their jobs as defined by management. The motivation to work quickly is the cash provided by piece rate payments. At Atlantic Fisheries the piece rate bonus is based on a detailed time and motion study, and is a very significant fraction of workers' pay, but it is also incredibly complex. Because fish are of different species and sizes and may even differ in quality (for example, worminess) depending on when and where they are caught, at Atlantic Fisheries the bonus system recognizes up to 6,000 different combinations of variables which may affect bonus — with the result that almost nobody really understands it.

Quality control is done by sampling the final product and disciplining workers, in the traditional way. No attempt is made to involve workers in decision making — indeed we were told that they are forbidden to talk to each other while on the processing line. Not surprisingly, workers report that being at work is "like being in jail." Very little training is done, at any level of the corporate hierarchy; a symptomatic story was of the production worker who, on her first day on the job, was not told she should put two fish sticks in each box of frozen fish and chips. For an entire day, she only put one fish stick in each box, necessitating the scrapping of an entire day's production run when the error was discovered.

Most of the jobs in a fish plant do not really need much training. The technicians who adjust and repair the fish filleting machines need a mechanical background before beginning an 8,000-hour apprenticeship program, organized by the German machinery manufacturer, but there may be only four such technicians in a fish plant employing 450 people. The cutters size the fish fillets and cut out any scales or other defects. They need manual dexterity, and their speed improves a lot with practice, but much of the length of their six-week training period is accounted for by the fact that it takes that long for them to experience the variety of fish species they need to know how to cut. Packers assemble cut fish fillets in boxes of 500 grams or 280 grams, but since they have electronic scales which flash red if the boxes are over- or under-weight and green if they are acceptable, there is clearly no need for complex cognitive skills.

On the cooked fish line, workers have to ensure that individual pieces of fish are clearly separated, so that they can be completely coated with batter before being cooked, and workers have to pack fish in boxes; conscientious attention to product quality is far more important than education. In addition, the fish plant offers employment for forklift drivers, crane operators and freezer technicians — the local community college offers short-term training programs for these occupations.

For Atlantic Fisheries, the most important parts of education are the attitudes and habits it creates. Corporate executives stress that labour force illiteracy is a real barrier to productivity improvement, but the reason why company management now wants to hire high school graduates is not because fish plant workers typically need Grade 12 Physics or Chemistry in order to do their jobs adequately. Rather, it is because high school graduates are much more likely than non-graduates to have the self-confidence, positive attitude to technical change, and social skills needed to adjust to improvements in technology, and to suggest further ways of increasing efficiency.

During our interviews at corporate head office, one could only admire the view of the harbour. The building was sleek and modern and the executive offices were tastefully decorated. From the corner office suite, there was a panoramic view of the comings and goings of international commerce in the harbour below. Executives had a sophisticated understanding of the evolution of international fish markets, and the need to develop new, high quality products to fit into rapidly changing niches in the consumer market place in different countries around the world. They recognized that alienated, untrained workers will not provide the continual improvements in productivity that are needed.

However, the contrast was sharp between the statements of top management on the need for "empowerment" of shop floor workers, in order to involve them in increasing productivity and improving quality, and the comments of workers that, "here, you do what you are told." There was also a distinct contrast between the recognition by senior union leaders (whose offices also have a nice view of the harbour) of the need for flexibility and fundamental reorganization of the industry, and the concerns of individual workers about preserving their rights to specific jobs within the plant.

"Flexibility" may be something that management would like, but security is something that workers need, and the determinants of their job security can be very complex. Rigidity of job classifications and the seniority system are intimately linked, since there are three different types of seniority within the fish plant — departmental seniority, plant-wide seniority and hire date seniority. The definition of a "department" is a management right and is somewhat arbitrary, but it is important because within departments low-seniority workers bear the costs of any fluctuations in production, since a lack of product to process implies that low-seniority workers are sent home. Lay-offs of less than five days are allocated within departments, but after five days workers can "bump" into other departments on the basis of plant-wide seniority. If lay-offs are anticipated to be more than seven days in duration, they are initially allocated on the basis of plant-wide seniority.

In the fish plant, all jobs are categorized in detail and there is an internal posting procedure for vacancies within the plant. There is considerable competition for vacancies in "desirable" departments, but it is not motivated by base rate of pay (which is set by union scale and does not vary much between departments). Instead, people are concerned that some departments are more vulnerable to lay-off. Since day-to-day job security depends on whether you have been able to work yourself into a high seniority position in a "safe" department, job classification and seniority rights are jealously guarded.

At one plant we visited, management reported that one of their major recent achievements was success in computerizing seniority calculations, so that now they know what seniority is for each worker, by each concept. However, they also noted the union did not always agree with their calculation. A person who transfers between departments can easily have fewer days of seniority in that department than a person with less years of seniority in the plant. As a result of this and the fact that lay-offs are of uncertain length, there are frequent grievances based on the calculation of seniority. Workers universally complained that shortage of work in specific departments can imply that workers with many years of seniority are sent home, while workers with less seniority in the plant are kept on working in other departments, and they saw this as an infringement of basic norms of fairness.

Clearly, the seniority system, and the rigid demarcation of jobs, is a major headache for management — and it is also a major headache for the union. Within the union, there is a recognition that the company has to make money if it is to be able to pay higher wages, and rigid job demarcation and seniority provisions are inefficient. Although this was not expressed with the same polish by top officials and by the shop stewards we interviewed, they did say essentially the same thing — as one shop steward put it to us, "It doesn't make any *sense* today. In the old days, when we were finished up on one end of the plant, we would go down to the other end and help finish up there." Although this shop steward was clearly a man who believed in always protecting the rights of workers against any encroachments of the company, he could also see the practical benefits of job flexibility.

However, despite the evident costs of rigid job demarcation and widespread complaints by both workers and management about the seniority system, the system continues. Jobs are scarce in rural Nova Scotia. The long tradition of the fishing industry is that workers are sent home when there are no fish available to be processed — i.e. the cost of any instability in production planning is borne by low-seniority workers (and partially by taxpayers, as laid-off workers draw UI). Although union leaders may personally think that abolition of the job classification/seniority system would be "better than what we've got," any attempt to change the system would meet the vehement opposition of older workers. And, if one looks at it from the perspective of someone over forty who may have no other type of job experience and who often has relatively little education, one can see the point. Younger workers have better options for mobility out of the fish processing sector; the only security that older workers really have is the protection of their seniority.

Similarly, both top management and union officials dislike the bonus system, but it continues because middle managers swear that "without the bonus, the place would fall apart," and because some workers depend on it financially. For example, although the base rate for a trimmer is approximately $80 per shift, $20 or $30 additionally may be earned in bonus. Anything the mysterious bonus formula calculates to be over "50" receives bonus pay, and production per worker is monitored continuously — indeed, each section of the production line has a clerk whose job is to record individual production, in order to pay bonus and maintain work norms. Although the plant manager feels that bonus pay is essential to maintain the pace of production, workers complain about the pressure caused by an increase in work norms, since trimmers who do not score "50" 80 per cent of the time are called in for counselling (which is, as a union representative put it, "the first stage of punishment"). The problem is that nobody — not the plant manager, not any of the workers, not union representatives and not top management at head office — could tell us what making "50" meant exactly. Workers thought that it meant mainly working as fast as possible, but they were unclear whether, or how, the bonus system also recognized the quality of their work.

In fish plants, 100 tonnes of fish may come in from the dock, but only about 40 per cent goes out the door in the form of useful product. Most of the loss of weight occurs at the filleting stage but, since almost all the costs of the operation of the company depend essentially on the input volume of fish, any increase in the yield of fish product would go directly to increasing the firm's profits. One of the most important variables affecting the firm's profits is the yield of useful fish product, at each stage of the process.

At Atlantic Fisheries, work norms and the bonus system are not part of the collective agreement and are solely under management control. However, plant managers, human resources managers at the plant level and senior management at corporate head office were all unclear about whether bonuses were based on volume of fish processed (i.e. speed of work), or whether they also recognized the impact of yield (i.e. work quality) on firm profitability. Setting work norms and bonus rates has an enormous direct impact on the profitability of Atlantic Fisheries and a enormous indirect influence on morale, the industrial labour relations climate and labour productivity. The production engineer who designed the bonus formula works out of a windowless office behind a rural fish plant. He assured us the bonus system does recognize the importance of yield, even if the 6,000 different possible combinations of factors that might also influence labour productivity in the bonus scheme means that workers (and other managers) had only the foggiest notion of how the bonus system actually operates.

The bonus issue is an example of how middle managers at Atlantic Fisheries see the firm's production problems purely in technical terms, within a fairly narrow understanding of employee motivation.

It is taken for granted that in Atlantic Fisheries workers have nothing useful to say about plant layout, product quality, or other aspects of job design. Presidents and vice presidents may chat with senior union leaders and agree that fundamental change is necessary if the industry is to survive. A high-level consensus may exist on the need to increase productivity, on the importance of high quality and new product development, and on the necessity to involve shop floor workers in operational decisions and productivity improvements. But senior managers have come and gone at Atlantic Fisheries, and middle managers have become cynical about "the flavour of the month" in corporate restructuring. Middle management (and workers) share a perspective that things will go on as they always have, hopefully with a small change in one's personal favour. However, it is hard to see how one can expect labour to participate in the process of continuous quality improvement and productivity enhancement, if workers are simultaneously treated in the same way they always have been — purely as raw labour, a "variable cost" in production.

In the months after we visited Atlantic Fisheries, the moratorium on the cod fishery meant that one of the plants we visited closed, for lack of fish to process. The other plant we visited remains in operation, at a reduced output, by processing foreign fish and the species that remain available. Head office operations were moved from town to one of the plants, in order both to save money and to signal a new style of management. Hundreds of people were laid off from their jobs at fish plants and trawlers, and after aggressive cost-cutting the company (now much smaller) managed recently to post a profit. Even the best-run company could not have avoided most of these layoffs, since their overriding cause was the virtual disappearance of cod and haddock stocks. But one does wonder whether some layoffs could not have been avoided if the company could have made better use of the skills of its workers. One wonders also how safe the jobs that remain are, given the continuation of traditional management practices.

"Family Sawmills Inc." — The Small Business Sector

Both the mining and fishing case studies are examples of large firms, each with a long history and a firmly entrenched "corporate culture." Their size is partly a disadvantage, in that senior management must convince both middle management *and* workers, if change is to be successful. Larger firms may, however, sometimes also find it easier to recognize and to import new ideas. There are some hopeful signs, in both "Atlantic Fisheries" and "Coal Mine Co.," that labour and management are groping toward new patterns of communication; the major question is whether such change will be big enough, soon enough, to protect the jobs that remain.

By contrast, small businesses come and go every day without media attention. The owner is the boss, and he talks directly to workers. The whole place could be changed overnight, but some of these businesses remain very traditional.

Small-scale sawmill operations have long been a staple of the Nova Scotia countryside. With a big round saw in an open shed, a pile of saw logs in the front and a stack of lumber in the back, small sawmills have long provided seasonal employment, at low wages, for unskilled male workers. The jobs and the technology have changed very little over the years. There is still a job for a man with a pole to push logs around in the pond and get them on to the chain drive which pulls them into the mill. Someone still has to clamp the saw log to a travelling dolly, which then runs back and forth, as the saw cuts the log into strips of lumber. And there is still a job to be had stacking lumber in the yard. A laser indicator now shows the sawyer where the saw will cut but, other than that, the mill's machinery would have been easily recognizable fifty years ago. And just as it did then, the mill is still open to the elements and it still lays its workers off every winter.

In short, in pay, working conditions and seasonality of employment, "Family Sawmills Inc." is a surviving example of low wage, low technology employment. Firms like this continue in operation because there continues to be a limited market for rough sawn, air-dried lumber. The family firm we interviewed has followed a consistent strategy for over sixty-five years. In all this time, the major technological innovation has been the replacement of water power for the saw by a diesel engine, and later by an electric motor.

"Family Saw Mill Inc." is run by three brothers who inherited the mill from their father. Total employment is forty-two people, but there is no "middle management." All decisions are taken by one or another of the brothers, each of whom can also fill in working in the mill themselves if the need should arise. The family has always avoided the risk involved in using bank finance to expand capacity or improve production technology. In finance, as in technology and labour relations, they follow a conservative strategy. This conservatism means that the company is debt free, and has remained in business despite the ups and downs of lumber prices which have crushed some other firms under the weight of interest payments.

All that Family Sawmills has to do to stay in business is cover the cash costs of operation from the cash receipts from lumber sales. As a result, they continue in much the same way as they always have. However, the threat is that their domestic markets may be taken by the highly automated, large volume, low cost mills of Western Canada. When U.S. lumber markets turn down, the western mills divert their production to Eastern Canada at prices which Family Sawmills cannot match. The firm's export markets are also vulnerable if the European Community imposes the requirement that lumber imports must be kiln dried. (The brothers never invested in kiln-drying because "we couldn't see it paying off.")

In some respects, Family Sawmills can be seen as a "satellite" company, since much of its timber comes from cutting on the lands of a major multinational pulp producer. The mill depends on the multinational for saw logs for its own production and as a buyer for the woodchips, "hog fuel" (bark and sawdust), and pulpwood which is sold to the multinational. Since cutting on their own land only meets twenty-five percent of the sawmill's lumber needs, the survival of Family Sawmills clearly depends on remaining in the good graces of the multinational.

However, despite the interdependency of the production relationship between Family Sawmills and the multinational, there is no similarity between these two companies in returns to workers. Employees of the multinational are relatively highly paid, with good fringe benefits and a system of clearly defined employee rights. The low pay and poor fringe benefits of workers at Family Sawmills come without any of the protections of a collective agreement — whatever workers have depends entirely on the day-to-day discretion of the owners.

Many would argue that it is not much of a benefit to workers to have seasonal employment at $8.00 per hour, for eight or nine months per year, and to depend on Unemployment Insurance in the off-season. Workers have no pension plan, no supplementary health insurance, no union, and no opportunity for advancement. They face a fair likelihood of plant closure in the near future and their day-to-day job security depends entirely on the owners' whim. However, under current conditions, Family Sawmills cannot afford to provide a much better employment package.

A small scale sawmill producing a standardized, low grade commodity (such as rough cut 2 x 4s) can only compete on price. It is easy to say that if such a firm cannot afford to pay a decent wage, perhaps it *should* go out of business. However, the problem is that Family Sawmills Inc. provides traditional jobs, at a traditional rate of pay, to a traditional type of labour force. There is no need for literacy if your job is stacking 2 x 4s in a lumber yard. The group dynamics of quality control circles do not need to be mastered, if the product is rough sawn, standard size lumber. Employment at Family Sawmills does not demand the high-level cognitive and social skills which high technology firms require, and it is not entirely clear where its workers can go if the firm ceases its sawmill operations.

However, even at this "low-tech" end of the lumber business, some skills are required. The firm has branched out into the manufacture of roof trusses for the local construction trade, and it employs a community college graduate for design and layout. The sawyer is the only skilled person in the sawmill, but his speed and accuracy are crucial to the rate of production of the entire mill. When the old sawyer retired, the firm needed a training course (of five weeks duration), which it was able to get through the Maritime Lumber Bureau, (the local branch of the voluntary industry association of lumber producers).

One of the lessons of this case study is, therefore, that the survival even of traditional jobs depends in part on the services industry associations (and sometimes government) provide to individual firms. At the national level, the Canadian Woods Council promotes the use of wood and participates in the setting of building codes and standards. The regional organization also provides a two-week course in lumber grading and quality control. The owners of Family Sawmills are hard-bitten, penny-pinching small capitalists, but they are also strong supporters of the industry association. As they put it, "the market could not survive" without the grading standards, research and training provided by the industry association.

"Diverse Construction" — An Alternative Strategy for Small Business

Although Family Sawmills is an example of how a family-owned firm in a traditional industry has reacted to the pressures of change by minimizing its exposure to risk, "Diverse Construction" is an example of how another family-owned firm has reacted to change by diversifying its activities — minimizing its risks by not keeping all its eggs in the same basket and maintaining efficiency by emphasizing the flexible allocation of a permanent labour force. Originally, almost all the firm's business came from public contracts for the construction of roads or wharves. Employment was highly seasonal, with as many as 300 workers in the summer when construction activity was at its peak, but only 50 or so in the winter months. However, although the father's picture still hangs on the office wall, the son now runs a very different operation.

Today, there are fewer jobs (about 200), but there is also less seasonal unemployment — only about 50 of the firm's workers are laid off in the winter off-season. Greater employment stability has been achieved by diversification and the flexible allocation of labour between activities. At present, the construction part of the operation remains predominant, but the company also operates a stone quarry which exports construction aggregates to the United States, a cement company for building construction, a machine shop and two surface coal mines. As well, when prices and exchange rates warrant, the company has the capacity to gear up for gypsum mining, and it will shift labour between activities as necessary. Some of the heavy equipment and labour used in road-building can be quickly transferred to open-pit coal mining, or to gypsum mining.

Essentially, the company stays profitable by staying nimble. It has low administrative overheads and a quick response time, so it can easily adapt to changes in world market prices, and it can weather periods of low prices. Within particular operations, the emphasis is on flexible allocation of labour. In the machine shop, for example, where the company's heavy equipment is repaired, work is shifted among the machinists, mechanics and electricians rather than being rigidly divided. Rather than hiring labourers to clean the machine shop, the tradesmen do the necessary sweeping themselves, when work is slow.

One of the coal strip mines also illustrates the flexible-allocation-of-labour principle. At the time when the coal mine was purchased by Diverse Construction, it had been operating for a century as an underground mine. The new owner, motivated in part by employee and community pressures, gave the miners the opportunity to be retrained for heavy equipment operation in the above ground strip mining venture. Of the thirty-five miners involved, those over sixty-five years of age were retired, and about half of the remainder were able to make the transition, especially the younger ones. The conversion involved a good deal of experimentation, with workers trying out different kinds of equipment, and even at the present time (a decade since the transition) there is still a good deal of switching around, by some if not all workers.

There are no detailed job descriptions and all the heavy equipment operators earn the same wage. With the exception of the machine shops, all the workers are unionized, but the union has not placed roadblocks in the way of job flexibility. Wages are in the $15 per hour bracket (somewhat higher in the machine shop) and fringe benefits include a pension plan and drug and dental insurance. Labour relations seem fairly harmonious — there are few grievances and the last decade has seen only two strikes (of three days each). Negotiating the collective agreement is usually a four to five hour affair, since the company pays relatively good wages by local standards and tries to keep up with inflation, while keeping fringe benefit costs under control. There are frequent suggestions from workers for productivity improvements and a fairly relaxed atmosphere at each work site.

In short, Diverse Construction has been able to pay relatively good wages, decrease seasonality of employment, and provide a package of fringe benefits by effectively and flexibly using the skills of its employees *within* the framework of collective agreements with a unionized work force. Not surprisingly, all this tends to produce relatively good morale, and good morale is particularly important for Diverse Construction since the heavy equipment it uses is so very expensive. Workers have to be able to think ahead to use their equipment effectively and they also have to use it carefully if maintenance and repair costs are to be kept under control. There are very few supervisory staff at Diverse Construction, but even if there were a great many, there is no way they could effectively prevent the multitude of foul-ups and small accidents typical of a disgruntled work force.

It is the ability to manage the "soft technology" of job flexibility and worker motivation that is crucial to the success of Diverse Construction. Some of its products are simply bulk commodities (raw gypsum, coal, or stone aggregates), while others (such as road construction) must follow specifications prepared by the customers' engineers — the capacity for research and development, or "product design," is irrelevant for this company. In Nova Scotia, as anywhere in the world, the best new production technology is available off the shelf from any number of multinational manufacturers of heavy equipment. Manufacturers not only embody best practice technology in the design of new equipment, but also provide extensive training in its operation and repair.

Particularly in its mining operations, Diverse Construction is competing with some very large operators. The same "hard technology" of machinery and training is available to everyone, and large operators can also benefit from significant economies of scale. Hence, a small firm can only survive and prosper if the "soft technology" of its workplace organization and worker motivation is good enough to enable a flexible and rapid response to changing market conditions.

"Modern Farms" — New Products in Old Industries

In many industries, it has been clear for a very long time that competition in the production of bulk, low-value commodities is a losing proposition — particularly in agriculture. Canadians have inherited the colder, rockier part of the North American continent and Nova Scotians are particularly poorly placed. Nova Scotia has hilly terrain, scattered pockets of good soil and a short growing season; since the nineteenth century it has been possible to grow bulk grains much more cheaply on the Western plains. Over the last century, the total acreage under crops in farms in Nova Scotia has shrunk from 944,000 acres to 271,000 acres, and the number of farms has gone from 55,823 to 4,283. Those farms which survive must either find a protected local market (e.g. dairy products, for instance) or a very specialized market niche.

Broccoli and cauliflower are, for example, very specialized crops, but there are specific locations in the world where the soil and the micro climate are just right. "Modern Farms" has recognized this potential and has moved to establish a profitable, expanding business, serving the Maritime market and exporting to New England.

In many ways, specialized agricultural crops are "knowledge intensive" commodities. Specialized "niche" crops like broccoli require specialized production technology and specialized marketing. To stay ahead of the California competition, and to keep abreast of agricultural research and harvesting technology, continual innovation is essential.

The image of the farmer as a country bumpkin is an entirely inappropriate stereotype of the modern farmer. Successful farmers must know product markets, soil and plant science, machinery maintenance, accounting and labour law, and much more. A great deal can be learned by growing up in a farming family, but a strong natural science background is also required if new developments in agricultural technology are to be fully understood and utilized. The owner of Modern Farms grew up on the farm and he inherited it from his father, but he has a big modern house on the other side of the road from the old family place, where his mother now lives. He also has an engineering degree and a diploma in plant science. He is linked by fax to international markets on a daily basis and he travels extensively in the off-season (primarily to Europe and California) to observe the latest specialized technology.

The market place demands consistently high quality, which places a premium on careful handling and on harvesting the crop exactly when it is ready for market. The market price also fluctuates considerably, often from day to day. This combination of shifting market prices and the fact that there are only a few days in which to harvest each field places a premium on rapid decision-making ability and a dependable labour force — one which is willing to work hard for long hours to get the crop in when the weather is right. Work days can be twelve hours or more, for as long as fourteen straight days, but the important thing is to get to the crop in the field, in order to pick it at its peak of freshness.

As a result, many of the jobs Modern Farms has created do not go to Canadians. Farmers of labour-intensive crops, such as broccoli or cauliflower, have to face the fact that they cannot get in Canada the labour force they need at a wage they can afford to pay. Since Modern Farms competes in produce markets with California farms, it must be able to meet their prices. Since California farmers have access to a low-wage labour force (i.e. illegal Mexican farm workers), Nova Scotia farmers cannot pay much more than $6 or $7 an hour for labour and still deliver a similarly priced product. At these wage rates, it is hard to attract Canadian workers to long hours and hard, physical labour in the cold and the mud.

In years gone by, the Annapolis Valley did have an agricultural labour force that moved with the seasons from vegetable growing to apple picking to seasonal unemployment. Most of these jobs are now gone, since mechanization has decreased the numbers, and increased the skills, needed for work on the farm. Most of the people also left for the city years ago, since most have found that there are better options in life than seasonal work at low wages, with no fringe benefits, no security and no chance for advancement.

But for Modern Farms to survive, the crop has to be picked exactly when ready, and the farmer has to be sure that the labour force will be there — dependability is essential. Field work also requires a lot of small decisions — the labour force has to be conscientious. Several years ago, Modern Farms came to the conclusion that at the wages it was offering, it could only draw labour from the bottom of the local labour market. Although workers were hired for several years through the local Canada Employment Centre, there was a very high turnover rate. At the wages they offered, Modern Farms could not get the dependability, physical fitness and conscientiousness it needed. These days, four Canadians have skilled jobs as field supervisors and mechanics at Modern Farms, but the field labour is now done by seasonal contract workers imported from the Caribbean.

Interestingly, the owner of Modern Farms does not blame his problems with Canadian workers on the existence of unemployment insurance or social assistance. He commented that on rainy days, people's willingness to come to work diminished once they had qualified for UI, but he did not think that UI disincentives were the major issue. For several years, he hired social assistance clients for field work, but he found that either because they lacked the physical stamina for long days of stoop labour, or because they did not have the mental ability or capability of consistency the job demands, they were unsatisfactory.

In his view, "it is not that they don't *want* to do the work, it's that they *can't*." The type of worker he needs can make considerably more than $6 an hour (seasonally, with no prospects of advancement) in the Canadian labour market. They are simply not attracted by the jobs he has to offer — indeed, it is a measure of Canada's development that most of Canada's population left the life of seasonal farm labour for urban employment several decades ago. By contrast, imported contract workers from less developed countries cost somewhat more, due to the cost of airfare and accommodation, but $6 per hour attracts a much better quality of worker from the Caribbean; as the owner put it, someone "much higher up the ladder," young, physically fit, often with a relatively good education. Until he started to hire offshore labour, the workers he was able to attract were of borderline employability, both physically and socially. With imported contract labour, he now has a ready supply of dependable workers. Workers who slow down or who are otherwise unsatisfactory are simply not asked to return the following year — and there is a ready supply of replacements.

A dependable work force, however, is only part of the problem. In addition, modern farmers have to find the optimal scale of operations, for production and for marketing. Large-scale farming can make effective use of expensive, specialized machinery and can supply the volume and continuity of produce that large supermarket chains demand. Corporate farms can even afford to finance specialized research and development, to further increase their productivity. However, as farming increases in scale, it is extremely difficult to retain the detailed knowledge the family farmer has acquired, over generations, of terrain, soil conditions and micro climate.

Producer cooperatives can be an effective way of pooling the need that several farmers have for expensive, indivisible assets (such as warehousing facilities). By combining their sales, cooperatives can also assure buyers of the continuity and the volume of supplies buyers need, while simultaneously retaining the small farmer's advantages of quick decision-making in production and detailed knowledge of local conditions. But in order to be effective, cooperatives have to be carefully structured, and they rely heavily on mutual trust.

Modern Farms has formed a producer cooperative with several other growers in order to economize on marketing expenses, buy fertilizer and other inputs in bulk, and share usage of a common warehouse. Many cooperatives have failed because their aims are too idealistic or because of dissension among members. Cooperatives can also fail if producers use it only when it is convenient to do so — the reputation of the co-op as a whole suffers if high quality produce is sold privately for top dollar and only low quality produce is sold through the co-op. In the case of Modern Farms, the cooperative works well because it provides tangible savings to each grower, because new entrants are carefully screened for compatibility, and because all growers have to commit to selling all their output (both high quality and low quality) through the co-op.

The bottom line of all this is that a combination of individual entrepreneurship and cooperation with other producers has enabled Modern Farms to survive and to continue to provide some jobs to Canadians. Although most of the employment Modern Farms creates goes to short-term contract workers from abroad, the remaining permanent jobs are better paid and relatively secure. Those jobs, plus the local purchases of the farm's inputs, help to maintain the viability of the local community. None of this was inevitable; if the owner of Modern Farms had tried to stick with traditional crops, he would likely have gone out of business and the problem of rural depopulation would have been that much worse.

"New Tech Fish Farms" — Innovation without Cooperation

Developing new processes and new products may be the main hope for saving jobs in the resource sector, but the fate of "New Tech Fish Farms," an aquaculture operation, was an unhappy demonstration of what happens when cooperation between producers cannot be organized. The aquaculture industry is important, because if aquaculture firms could become firmly established in the thousands of bays and inlets which dot the Nova Scotia coastline, the jobs they generated would be dispersed widely across the province, which would help to limit the centralization of jobs in a few relatively large communities. If fishing could move from the "hunter/gatherer" stage of catching what nature provides to "farming" and the cultivation of the ocean as a food source, total employment in the fishery could well increase dramatically.

However, aquaculture is a new technology. When fish farmers moor their nets and enclosures in bays and inlets, they may interfere with the traditional fishery and they may impede recreational boating. In the old days, there was no need to establish ownership rights in waterways, but fish farming is a use of the waterways that is permanent and that excludes other uses — hence property rights in the waters of bays and inlets have to be established.

Technology also has to be researched and proved out. Just as in land farming, each fish farm has slightly different local conditions. With so many fish penned in such a small space, disease is always a danger, hence fish farmers need both a good technical education in fisheries biology and intimate knowledge of local conditions. Since the product is often new, markets have to be developed and then supplied on a dependable basis. Entrepreneurs have to be able to combine innovative solutions to all these problems with access to the labour and capital they need.

Mr. B of New Tech Fish Farms is a classic entrepreneur. Although brought up in the area, he is, like many other entrepreneurs, of immigrant stock. Despite his setbacks, he remains tied to Nova Scotia by his enthusiasm for its natural beauty and quality of life. His observation that mussels are a delicacy in his parents' native Belgium, and grow easily in Nova Scotia, provided the initial idea behind mussel aquaculture.

Like many other innovations, that idea would never have gone anywhere without a fortuitous combination of events. Mr. B is an avid scuba diver, and he loves to make a deal. After graduating from a local university with an MBA, he turned his hobby of diving into a business, teaching diving courses, preparing equipment and selling scuba gear. And since he loved to go diving and had the business background and all the diving gear, building and tending underwater cultivation trays of mussels was an easy step to take.

Traditionally, there was no market for mussels in Nova Scotia because nobody ate them. New Tech Fish Farms aimed at export sales, but also needed a local sales base. To this end, it developed a series of supermarket promotions to encourage mussel consumption. For the first five years of the mussel business, the firm lost money as it gave steamed mussels away to the curious in supermarket promotions and at trade shows. During this time, the diving business in effect subsidized aquaculture, but in the sixth year a profit appeared and in the seventh and eighth years, good money was made in mussels.

Mr. B had big dreams (he showed us architect's drawings and promotional material for a proposed processing facility and a chain of fast food outlets featuring "McMussels"), but he also had the good sense to use his periods of peak profits to pay down debt and re-invest in his diving shop business. In 1987, a food poisoning scare involving cultivated mussels hit the headlines. Although the mussels in question were from Prince Edward Island, consumers did not discriminate and sales went from boom to bust overnight — as Mr. B put it, "we got our heads kicked in."

Markets have gradually recovered but the industry as a whole is now plagued with over-capacity and fragmentation. Once supermarkets had become interested in stocking fresh mussels, they needed a dependable source of quality production. For a time, New Tech Fish Farms could meet this supermarket demand by buying raw mussels from other mussel growers and providing a grading and wholesaling service. However, in grading mussels there is inevitably some rejection rate and a weight loss as the mussels are cleaned. There is always a substantial margin between wholesale prices to growers and retail prices in the supermarket. In a new industry, there is not much experience as to how much weight loss is "normal" and what amount of wholesale margin is "fair." Individual growers did not trust New Tech Fish Farms; since they thought they were being exploited, each began, individually, to invest in grading machinery and to market directly to supermarket chains.

Fragmentation of an industry can be costly if buyers need assurances of quality control and of dependability of supply. Individual, small scale growers cannot offer assurances of the dependable, large volume production supermarket chains demand. When each grower invests in their own grading and processing machinery, their operations become over-capitalized, and they cannot offer the same assurances of quality control as central processing facilities could provide. The industry can then become very vulnerable to shocks.

Some authors have used the term "extra market social infrastructure" to refer to the framework of cooperation small firms need in order to prosper. In the Prince Edward Island mussel industry, the government worked to develop this social infrastructure by providing incentives (in the form of low-cost financing for a central processing facility) for producers to join together in a processing cooperative. The Nova Scotia government had a different model in mind — one of individual competitors in a sort of "cottage industry," and it provided assistance to individual growers, with the view that by so doing it was encouraging a competitive industry.

However, some elements of cooperation can also be a prerequisite to competitive success. In the mussel example, small scale individual producers in Nova Scotia were hurt by their inability to attract a reputation for the dependable delivery of a quality product. By banding together in a producer cooperative, Prince Edward Island producers were able to create such a reputation, cope with the shock of a sudden decline in demand, rebuild their reputation and still survive. Their cooperation in achieving their common interest was a prerequisite for their long-term survival as competitive individual producers.

Meanwhile, New Tech Fish Farms has sold its mussel equipment and gone out of the business. Bay scallops are the new thing for Mr. B ("A beautiful product," as he says). As we interviewed him at his Halifax office, he was juggling phone calls from across the eastern United States, selling packets of live cultivated scallops for air freight delivery to upscale seafood restaurants. Since he has a ready supply of skilled labour available from the B.Sc. programs of local universities, as well as great growing conditions and plenty of contacts in a wide open North American market place, Mr. B remains optimistic about the future.

Conclusion

A common denominator of the firms we interviewed in the resource sector is that they employ fewer workers today than they have in the past. In some cases, the job loss has been dramatic, as mines and fish plants have closed, eliminating hundreds of jobs and threatening the livelihood of entire communities. Should we conclude from this that Canada's rural hinterland is doomed? Can the resource sector only generate jobs if it is heavily subsidized (which seems highly unlikely to happen)?

The future of Canada's rural areas depends heavily on the prosperity of Canada's resource industries. That prosperity depends, in large measure, on events beyond the control of any individual firm. When fish stocks disappear, trawlers are tied up and fish-processing plants are closed. When energy prices are high (as in the early 1980s), even high-cost coal mines make money and mining companies plan expansions; but when oil prices collapse, the price of coal follows, high-cost mines close and even low-cost coal mines must struggle for survival.

Although we think some of the trends that have hammered resource sector employment are hard to avoid, we still think that something can be done.

The "resource sector" is composed of a wide variety of firms of different sizes, using different types of labour, with very different technologies, and facing very different markets. Each firm confronts its own specific problem and has its own specific opportunities. Yet there is a common theme that emerges from our case studies of success and failure within the resource sector — a theme that can be summarized in terms of the importance of the "social relations of production."

The fishing and mining case studies can be seen as examples of the fact that substantial change in the capital equipment and technology of production does not imply, necessarily, a corresponding degree of change in the social attitudes and patterns of work organization that have been inherited from the past. It is not difficult, if funds are available, to buy the most modern machinery and have it installed and serviced. In a technical sense, it is not particularly difficult to institute training programs for machine operators — even if it may be hard to convince management of the profitability of investing in training and equally difficult to convince labour of management's motivations. But in a long established industry, it can be very hard to shake off old attitudes about the work process and to discard old suspicions about the motivation, sincerity and future behaviour of others.

In the resource sector, as in other sectors, almost every firm we interviewed emphasized the rapidity of technical change in their particular industry. As technology changes, some of its potential can be achieved even within old organizational structures. But in an extremely competitive global environment, it may not be enough to achieve part of potential. Survival often depends on modernizing both the "hard technology" of capital equipment and the "soft technology" of organizational culture and workplace relationships.

Within large firms, organizational change can only come about if shop floor workers, union leaders, middle managers and senior executives all come to share, and to support, a common vision of change. The process of organizational change is necessarily a complex one of persuasion, reassurance and coalition building. At Atlantic Fisheries and at Coal Mine Company, senior executives may come and go, but middle managers remain. Their experience is needed for ongoing production, and without their cooperation, talk of organizational reform will be empty rhetoric. But middle managers also have the most to lose from changes in the "soft technology" of production. If employee "empowerment" ever became a reality, managers would have to operate more by persuasion and less by command. Fewer of them would be needed, if decision-making were effectively decentralized. Some would have the people skills needed for the new ways of doing business, but others would not — hence, the shift to a new mode of operation would be difficult and threatening. And union organizers may also find it easier to repeat traditional patterns rather than try to think through a new relationship with management.

In small firms, there may not be any intermediary between owners and individual workers — organizational change can be very direct. However, our case studies of Diverse Construction and Family Sawmills provided examples of owner-operated firms which have, and which have not, made the internal organizational changes necessary to cope with a new, more competitive environment. Although both firms were small players in risky markets, one had reacted to the pressures of the changing economy by minimizing its exposure to risk through a low investment strategy, with a low wage, contingent labour force. Over the years, this strategy has made the firm more and more marginal, to the extent that its continued survival is now in question. The other firm reacted by diversifying its activities and developing a work force that can be shifted between operations to match the shifting tides of the international market place. Although the firm now provides fewer jobs than it used to, the ones that remain are relatively stable and relatively high wage — and they depend crucially on the "soft technology" of workplace organization.

However, small firms are also very dependent for their survival on the social infrastructure of cooperation and support among firms. Standard models of the economy tend to emphasize the virtues of competition. The "ideal type" of economics textbooks is the heroic entrepreneur who single-handedly enters the market, competes aggressively against all comers and emerges victorious. But in practice small firms have both a common interest in the prosperity of their industry and a competitive individual interest in maximizing their share of that prosperity. Our case studies of small businesses provided several examples of the benefits to small firms of cooperation — and the costs to an industry where it does not occur.

Economics textbooks rightly caution against cooperation among firms that takes the form of price-fixing or other restraints on trade. However, there has been too little recognition that cooperation among producers can also be socially productive. Small firms may not have the resources to afford, by themselves, expensive, indivisible pieces of capital equipment. Individually, small entrepreneurs cannot take the time to design a training program for the skills they need, and individual firms always face the danger that other firms will poach the skilled labour whose training they have financed. Small firms cannot, by themselves, guarantee continuity of supply or uniformity of quality standards. And in selling to an international market, the reputation of individual producers can be tarnished by their proximity to low-quality producers in the same region.

Our case studies in agriculture and aquaculture illustrated the important role for cooperation, as well as competition, in the building of the "extra firm social infrastructure" on which individual innovators depend. To a large extent, we have to expect that the resource sector will, overall, continue to lose jobs — but to the extent that such job loss can be offset, it will be by new firms developing new products, within a new context of industrial support.

2

The Manufacturing Sector

Although the resource sector has provided the employment base for rural Canada, it is manufacturing that has provided much of the employment on which Canada's towns and cities were founded. Across Canada, hundreds of small towns have grown up around, and still rely on jobs in, the local textile factory or pulp and paper mill. Cities such as Hamilton and Sydney have depended on the thousands of jobs created by iron and steel mills or engineering work. Historically, these jobs demanded a basic education, a strong work ethic and the experience gained by on-the-job training. These jobs have been the mainstay of Canadian working-class families, but they are now under threat. Between 1989 and 1992, 338,000 jobs in manufacturing in Canada disappeared, a decline of 16 per cent in employment. Although 1993 and 1994 saw a partial recovery, many economic forecasters do not see manufacturing employment returning to the levels of 1989 anytime soon.

Workers in the resource sector can console themselves with the knowledge that some Canadians will always remain employed in the extraction of resources, because the resource employment that survives is inherently tied to a Canadian location. Since the output of the resource sector is produced by the combination of capital, labour and a geographically immobile resource base, as long as the total costs of resource production remain sufficiently low that capital inputs receive a normal profit, labour will continue to be employed. However, manufacturing jobs do not have the protective buffer of resource rents as a shield from the pressures of international competition.

Manufactured goods are produced when technology combines the use of capital equipment with human skills and effort. Both technology and capital are internationally mobile. The jobs which manufacturing creates are *not* inherently tied to a Canadian location. In many manufacturing industries, the production plant can be anywhere in the world, and (depending on transportation costs) the firm can still compete effectively in Canadian markets.

Although manufacturing output has always been potentially exposed to foreign competition based on cheaper labour or more productive technology, it could, for many years, count on the shelter of tariff barriers. Although Nova Scotia (and the Western provinces) long complained that these tariff barriers, from the days of the National Policy of the 1870s on, primarily favoured the development of central Canadian industry, tariffs did provide some shelter from international competition to everyone. However, those days are gone — the manufacturing sectors of all provinces now have to deal with the loss of tariff protection produced by the 1988 Free Trade Agreement with the United States and the 1993 North American Free Trade Agreement (NAFTA) with the United States and Mexico. Furthermore, in addition to withdrawing tariff protection, government has been signalling, in the clearest way, that the days when the state would step in with subsidies to prop up a major manufacturing employer (as the Nova Scotia government did when Sydney Steel was threatened with closure in 1967) are over.

The manufacturing sector must, therefore, face the threat of international competition shorn of its traditional protections. In a world where many millions work at much lower wages than Canadian workers receive and in which technological innovation is continuous, Canadian consumers may benefit from the availability of low-cost foreign manufactured imports — but they also need jobs if they are to buy these goods. In order for Canada to import low-cost manufactured goods, it must export something. What sort of manufacturing sector can survive in Canada? How many jobs will it provide? What sort of jobs will these be? Our case studies provided some fascinating glimpses of the survival strategies of manufacturers.

"Major Forest Products" — The Disappearing "Good Job"

Rocky soil and a cold climate mean that in most of Nova Scotia (as in most of Canada), the land can only grow trees. It is therefore not surprising that forestry-based manufacturing has long been a prominent feature of Canadian economic life. Small companies geared to the production of lumber and related products predominated in the 1800s and early 1900s, supplying the building materials for residence and business construction, the wood for boats and wharves, crates and other containers for vegetable and fruit crops, pit props for the mines, fuel, and a host of other uses.

More recently, the big employers have been pulp and paper plants owned by large, multinational companies. These companies are capital intensive operations, geared to producing wood pulp and paper products for the international market. "Major Forest Products" provides a clear example of the kinds of stable, well-paid blue collar jobs that are now remarkable by virtue of their scarcity. At the time of our interviews, the company directly employed some 1,000 persons working in and around the main processing site, as well as an additional 1,300 persons engaged in wood cutting and hauling operations (many on a contract basis). Plant workers are members of the Canadian Paperworkers' Union, earning wages ranging from $15.00 to $29.00 per hour, and an extensive array of fringe benefits. Wage increases from year to year have kept up with, and generally exceeded, the rate of inflation.

Historically, these jobs were secure, well-paying and structured so that workers moved up a job ladder of increasing pay, responsibility and security as their seniority increased — the sort of job that labour economists have described by the term "the primary labour market" or the "central work world" of a modern industrial economy. In the 1960s and 1970s, many such stable, well-paid blue collar jobs in the manufacturing and resource sector were available to high school graduates and to many dropouts. Although such jobs were typically not available to women, the pay, security and progression-by-seniority that they entailed meant that many blue collar workers' families could afford a "middle class" lifestyle.

Primary labour market jobs did not come without any downside. Standards of employment often developed over time only after protracted labour-management conflicts for better wages and working conditions. The work itself was often physically demanding and subject to health and safety risks. Environmental degradation has also been a part of the story. Still, it is a measure of the desirability of these jobs, especially if located in an area with high rates of unemployment, that there is virtually no turnover at Major Forest Products, and the waiting list of those who have sent in their applications for possible future employment at the mill is in the order of 10,000 persons.

Major Forest Products set up operations in the 1960s as a relatively small, bleached sulphate pulp mill. The timing and scale of operation, however, were not well chosen. An economic downturn was affecting the industry, and the size of the operation was initially too small to achieve economies of scale. The pulp operation had to be substantially expanded and a newsprint operation added in the 1970s. Further modernization took place in the mid-1980s.

The company produces market pulp for sale in its basic form, and also processes the pulp to produce a range of value-added products including fine paper products and gift wrappings. Newsprint is, however, the major product for the company. In market pulp, the company has a substantial share of Canadian production (50 per cent) and Canada provides a third of world production of this material. Since market pulp in its unprocessed state is duty free, the FTA did not affect the plant much. From the Nova Scotia plant some 25 to 30 per cent of production is sold in other parts of Canada, a similar percentage in the United States, and the remainder outside of North America. The company's newsprint is sold to newspapers in Canada and the United States, but its share of the market is much smaller than is the case with market pulp.

The plant produces over 150,000 tons per year of newsprint, and the same amount of market pulp, in a very capital-intensive process. In the pulp and paper industry, capital equipment is extremely expensive — a single paper line can easily cost several hundred million dollars. Profitability can only be achieved if it is utilized to capacity, without long or frequent periods of "down time." In fact, it was remarked to us by a management consultant that he could always tell a productive paper mill, because the workers did not seem to be doing much, but the machines were running full tilt, without interruption. By contrast, in an unproductive mill the workers have a lot to do, trying to fix problems.

In pulp and paper, the key to productivity and profits is to keep the machinery humming, by careful monitoring and meticulous preventive maintenance. The role of labour is to anticipate and prevent production problems and to organize the flow of materials — i.e. to enable the machine to make the paper. Thus, although the labour force is large and well paid, labour costs as a percentage of total costs are quite small. Unions have played a role in improving wage and working conditions over time, but the key issue for the firm is the productivity of capital equipment, and it is worth paying good wages if doing so helps to improve capital productivity.

Pulp and paper has always been fully exposed to international competitive pressures, and to periods of boom and bust. At the time of our interviews, the company was facing a downturn in its markets

and was being considerably challenged to maintain profitability —
in newsprint, for example, price discounts of 15 to 20 per cent to
prime customers were being made in order to maintain market share.
That situation has certainly changed in the past year, a testament to
the volatility of the international market.

Competition comes from other pulp and paper producers in Canada, the United States and abroad. A particularly important dimension of international competition is the cost and availability of raw
material; some competitors have lower raw material costs simply
because they are located in areas where trees grow faster and larger
than in Canada. Other forms of pulp production, notably the kraft
process, are also becoming more popular, but if the company were
to build a new kraft type pulp mill, it would come at a projected cost
of $1.25 billion. As well, increased environmental consciousness is
shifting market demand for newsprint to recycled paper, but producing newsprint from recycled paper would require a de-inking plant
and a new paper machine at a combined estimated cost of $450
million. When staying in business may require investment of this
magnitude, and government environmental regulations on the transportation of dangerous goods, the storing of PCBs, air emissions, and
the removal of toxicity from discharged waters require very expensive modifications in technology and procedures, it is not surprising
that the plant's continued viability may be in question.

The company has responded to competitive pressures in a variety
of ways — acquiring new technology, increasing volume of operations so that further economies of scale can be achieved, and reducing
the time required to turn out a given unit of output. At the time of
our interviews, it took more than four man hours of operation to
produce one ton of newsprint, but the technology and equipment is
available in modern plants to reduce this number to two man hours,
and indeed the general manager thought that this figure would soon
be cut in half again.

Improving product quality is also crucial. Newsprint publishers,
for example, look for newsprint that is sturdy enough not to break as
newspapers are printed, and that meets their standards of cleanliness,
whiteness, smoothness, and so on. To keep on top of quality concerns, the mill employs a full-time representative to visit newsprint
customers and to discuss any quality problems that arise or that could
be prevented. Each roll of newsprint is identified by number, so that
if a break occurs in a newsroom, it is possible to trace the problem
back to the producer, the plant, and the particular shift responsible,

and the individuals involved can then meet together as a crew to analyze and remedy the problem.

In the pulp and paper industry there may be rapid change in prices, but the pace of change in product characteristics is not nearly so rapid as in industries driven by consumer fashions (such as textiles or apparel) or rapid technical change (such as computers or aerospace). Environmental concerns, for example, may lead to demand for products that are not made with a chlorine bleaching process, or for recycled newsprint, but these changes typically take years to come about. And while there is constant technological change, big shifts in technology are "generational" and take place at well dispersed intervals. In between, there is a steady effort to make modest improvements in the available machines and their controls. It is not unusual for a company to buy new equipment for which the original technology is a couple of decades old, but which has been continuously refined along the way.

It is perhaps partly because of this greater stability that a company such as Major Forest Products gives few indications that it is making radical changes in the "soft technology" of its workplace organization and motivation. The organization of work and employment follows traditional lines. The work force is highly unionized; jobs are defined in the collective agreement; there is a high degree of rigidity in hiring, work allocation, lay-off and recall procedures; the management of the company is quite centralized; and there is little evidence of innovation in the organization of work and employee involvement, such as quality circles or team production.

The situation is not entirely static, since as technology becomes more sophisticated and expensive, the company has responded with extensive training programs for the labour force, both in-house, in community colleges, and by sending staff to other plants around the world. In fact, the general manager indicated that in the $5\frac{1}{2}$ years that he has held his position at the plant, he has not refused one request for additional training. While management is confident that it can, for the most part, work with the existing labour force through retraining rather than importing more skilled labour from outside (electrical technology is the major exception to this rule), the challenge that continues to face the company is summed up by the following comment: "How do you go from a man throwing wood into a machine to putting him in a control room, alone, where he operates a one-million-dollar-a-minute process?" Given the importance of appropriate training, managers were quite critical of the quality of training made available by the nearby community college, although they were more positive about some other colleges in the province. They described it as out-of-date, and criticized appointments made to the college in which political affiliations have played an important role. High school education is also found to be wanting, especially in the teaching of literacy, math, and communication skills.

Indeed, the lack of workplace literacy is described as a significant problem for the company, one which really stems from the problems of the school system of the 1960s in retaining students. Most of the mill's current labour force left school in the 1960s and are now middle-aged; continuous increases in labour productivity have meant that there have been very few new hires in recent years. The jobs in the plant require the ability to read and to understand the symbols and warnings on many of the pipes and tanks that are labelled. They also require the ability to communicate ideas clearly. Despite the fact that high school graduation is now a requirement for entry level jobs (high school equivalency is accepted), older employees do not always have the basic general skills that are now necessary.

The company is also responding to competitive and recessionary pressures by reducing the work force through early retirements and lay-offs. While production levels have continued to expand, the work force was reduced by 8 per cent in the year of our interviews and by even more subsequently.

The bottom line is that this pulp mill is an example of some of the traditional "good jobs" that used to be generally available for blue collar workers, but now are notable by their scarcity. The long-run future of the mill is in doubt, so even job security for those presently employed is at risk, not to mention the lack of opportunity for new generations of workers, still oriented to seeking employment in these traditional industries. Within the plant, job security is now the major issue for the union in contract negotiations, while the management side seeks to achieve greater flexibility in order to meet the technological and competitive pressures it faces. But the bigger social issue is that there are fewer and fewer jobs like those at Major Forest Products available anywhere.

"Quality Threads" and "Comfort Textiles" — Contrasts in Soft Technology

In the pulp and paper industry, workplace change has been gradual, and the impact of free trade has been minimal, because most output was always exported. To observe more rapid changes, and more diversity in strategies in coping with the shock of the loss of protected domestic markets, the textile industry is a useful example.

The Industrial Revolution began over 200 years ago in textile mills, and for decades these were large, labour-intensive operations, usually producing many yards of standard fabrics. In recent years, however, production of standardized commodity textiles has tended to shift overseas, to locations with lower labour costs. The industry that remained in Canada primarily comprised smaller plants, sheltered behind protective tariffs and specializing in particular niches of the market. With the passage of the Canada-U.S. Free Trade Agreement (FTA) in 1988, Canadian producers began to lose their tariff protection from larger American mills, forcing fundamental changes on remaining firms. The interesting thing to observe is how those strategies for change differ. One can find companies that use the same type of technology, have essentially the same marketing strategy, are about the same size and hire labour from the same labour market, yet which have adopted quite different strategies of motivation and organization, i.e. use different "soft" technologies. The question is: Do these differences in how firms respond matter?

The textile industry in Nova Scotia dates back to the early industrial period preceding Confederation, and there are still some forty active companies.[1] More so than other sectors represented in this study, textiles face new competitive pressures from the FTA and the North American Free Trade Agreement (NAFTA). Because of the FTA, tariff barriers are expected to be totally eliminated by 1998. As tariffs come down, there is increasing concern that large-volume U.S. mills will flood the Canadian market, especially during times when a high exchange rate for the Canadian dollar favours the importation of American product and penalizes the exports of Canadian mills.

In the textile industry, fabric forming can be classified into four major processes: weaving, knitting, tufting and non-woven production. Our first case study was "Quality Threads," a firm primarily involved in the weaving and knitting of fabrics for both the general apparel and fashion clothing industries. Sales are almost entirely in Canada, where the firm captures close to 100 per cent of the provincial market and 30 to 40 per cent of the national market. However, the long-term strategy is to concentrate on specific fabric types and sell to the U.S. market. Managers anticipate that in ten years time, as much as 90 per cent of their output could be sold in the United States.

Our second case study was "Comfort Textiles," which makes both woven and tufted products. Like Quality Threads, it is located in a small town in a rural area of the province. Although it is somewhat larger in size, both firms employ several hundred workers, and are significant local employers, but very small relative to industry giants. Both firms have two main lines of products, one of which is a generic product for low price markets and a second higher quality line that is more specialized, and more expensive. Comfort Textiles has about twenty per cent of the provincial market but less than five per cent of the Canadian market in its particular market segment.

While both companies still gear some of their production to turning out standard products for the general market, neither see much of a future for "commodity" textiles under the onslaught of competition produced by the free trade agreements. Both companies see their long-term future pursuing a "high end" production strategy for niche markets, emphasizing quality of product, a substantial design component in their textiles, and on-time, short turn-around delivery. The objective of both firms is to survive by being high-quality niche producers — small, nimble and smart.

Both companies recognize the importance of investing in "hard technology" as part of their effort to become or remain competitive. Thus, Comfort Textiles spent in the order of $5 million on capital investments in the three to four years preceding our interviews, and at Quality Threads, there have been substantial investments in "state of the art" technology, especially since 1980. Like other firms in the manufacturing and resource sectors, both companies have become more capital intensive through the introduction of increasingly sophisticated, computer controlled technology.

The adoption of new, more productive technology has had a major impact on the number of jobs available. At Comfort Textiles, for example, a loom which might have had two operators working on it in earlier years now only has one. As the equipment becomes more sophisticated, workers at both firms are increasingly monitoring machinery, rather than physically changing bobbins, tying in thread, and so on. Employment is reduced with each recessionary cycle, but in the recovery period the number of employees never comes back up to the previous level even if production levels are as high or higher. The impact of technology has added to the effect of free trade agreements and the recession and has resulted in both companies laying off a substantial proportion of their work force.

Both firms rely on a rural, low-wage labour force which has few employment alternatives and relatively little education. At Comfort Textiles, for example, all the people they hired 10 or 15 years ago would have had no more than Grade 8 or 9 education, and since few of the workers hired more recently have escaped lay-off during down-sizing, their present labour force is still characterized by a very low education profile. The situation is similar at Quality Threads, with the distinction that the emphasis in recruitment has not been so much on finding highly educated recruits but rather on selecting carefully from the pool that is available.

Since these two firms make different types of textiles, for different market segments, their machinery is not quite the same, but the basic technology of weaving, knitting and tufting is common to the whole industry. Different market segments use different adaptations of the same underlying technology, but there is no fundamental difference in capital intensity or sophistication. Hence, these two firms have fundamental similarities — in the type of labour they hire, in the capital equipment and production process they use, and in the market strategies they have adopted. However, despite these similarities, they differ in important respects in terms of what we call the "soft technology" of production — the way in which work is organized and the strategies used to motivate and involve the work force in order to achieve company objectives.

At Quality Threads, the strategy of attempting to produce quality products for niche markets, with rapid turn-around on orders, has had important implications for the firm's organization of work and for its work force. Management has taken deliberate steps to reshape its approach to the work force and how it is organized for production, as evidenced by the two occupations that make up the bulk of the work force at Quality Threads: skilled maintenance employees (primarily tradesmen), and operators (loom workers, knitters, crochet operators, and finishers).

The main responsibility of the maintenance group, to keep the mill running, involves machining, heavy repairs, electrical work, boiler room maintenance, and loom and knitting machine specialists. As technology has become more complicated, the tasks of the maintenance group have become more demanding, and this will continue to be the case for the foreseeable future, as the machinery continues to move toward greater electronic (as opposed to mechanical) control, further computerization, and higher speed operation as electronic devices control patterns of weaving and knitting. Maintenance workers now deal with equipment that is more technologically advanced, but mechanically simpler because of fewer moving parts, i.e. both the level and type of skills needed have changed.

The implementation of the firm's production and market strategy has pushed the company to have maintenance done by teams, with each team given increased responsibility, while individuals within teams are being asked to master the repair of several technologies in the plant — in contrast with the earlier pattern of one person being skilled in the repair and maintenance of one particular kind of knitting and weaving machine.

Self-training or team training is expected, with the eventual result that all maintenance workers will have the ability to move throughout the plant — an important kind of flexibility, since production must meet rapidly changing specifications and tight production time lines, and a source of variety in work that helps to maintain employee interest and commitment. While there remains a hierarchy of authority and skill among maintenance personnel, this is breaking down as increased responsibility is pushed downwards.

Operators are the largest occupational group in the plant, doing everything from material handling at the raw material stage to producing and packing the finished product. Their main job, however, is to set up machines, thread yarns, redraw ends if they break, and adjust the tension of machines. Here, too, there is now a new emphasis on cross-training and job rotation, in contrast to the pattern a few years ago when each worker was dedicated to a specific task in the process (such as threading), and the loss of one person with a certain skill could shut down an entire shift and put production schedules behind.

The technical content of the operator's work has also changed as styles have become more intricate. This translates into a higher number of "ends per product," but machines must keep going just as fast or faster than before due to the competitive pressures of the market. Complicating the process further is the fact that instead of twisted yarns, lower quality "air blown" yarns are purchased, which have a greater propensity to snag, pull and break, which puts pressure on operators to watch machines more closely. Workers often find themselves in conflict between being encouraged to take greater responsibility for quality control, with the right to shut down machines and rip out deficient product, while at the same time being pressured to get the product out on time.

Rather than trying to import a new, more highly educated labour force (a strategy that would perhaps not succeed given the company's location and modest wages and benefits), Quality Threads has concentrated on more careful selection of its entry-level work force, extensive provision of on-the-job and off-site training in computing and other skills, and on reducing the high rates of employee turnover typical in earlier years.

With respect to the operators, for example, there are no fixed educational requirements for entry into operator positions, though the company no longer hires "off the street, if someone shows signs of life," as it did in the past. Applicants are screened with a battery of aptitude tests, which include such components as mathematics, motor skills, coordination, colour differentiation, mechanical aptitude, and general interest. Dexterity is an important qualification, and here women have an advantage due to their smaller hand size (on average). The company has informed the employee committee that they are looking for persons who can think and perform at a Grade 9 level, and who resemble the profile of the longer term labour force at the plant. No certificate of Grade 9 graduation is necessary. To help design the procedures for employee selection, the company imported an occupational psychologist from Texas who tested one third of the longer-term employees in order to develop a profile of job retainers, which is now applied to all job applicants. As a result, turnover has fallen markedly. The recruitment strategy is to concentrate on job applicants who may not have many employment alternatives elsewhere (due to low educational levels), select carefully from among this pool and subsequently invest fairly substantially in job-related training.

Maintenance workers are hired with trades training in the form of journeymen's tickets already in hand, or promising existing employees are encouraged to undertake the necessary training with company financial support. Currently, about half of the maintenance workers have their journeymen papers, and the remainder are all working towards this goal. The emphasis in training is on quality. In earlier years, maintenance workers knew how to get things running, but not necessarily running properly, efficiently, or for a long duration, with the result that machine breakdowns were frequent. Off-site training has improved theoretical knowledge and understanding of the running of equipment, its maintenance and repair.

At Comfort Textiles, the situation is somewhat different. Management also stresses the importance of quality production, and the company's state of the art weaving technology is able to turn out a quality product. There is also a complete quality assurance program that involves some fifty quality checks being performed for each product run. But this is the standard "check and reject" quality control department, separate from the shop floor work force. The way in which the two firms have attempted to improve quality is fundamentally different.

At Quality Threads, workers are encouraged to monitor quality themselves and individuals can, and do, bring the production process to a halt if they perceive a quality problem. Comfort Textile employees are not encouraged to take personal responsibility for product quality and production improvements. As one interviewee put it, "We don't have a problem with our production unless management tells us we have a problem." It is these sorts of differences in the workplace organization that are crucial.

While both companies work with a similar labour force, at Comfort Textiles there is not the same amount of attention paid to the careful selection of employees through testing, nor to their training once hired. Except for maintenance employees, who for the most part come to the firm with journeymen's papers and who may be sent for off-the-job training on subjects such as instrumentation, other shop floor personnel at Comfort Textiles make do with on-the-job training. (Off-the-job training is rejected by management because it is either deemed to be not appropriate because of the company-specific skills that are required, or too expensive.) For machine operators, management claims that the period of on-the-job training is of the order of three weeks, but we heard from workers about new employees on occasion being given responsibility for the operation and tending of very expensive and complex equipment after only a few hours on the job. Indeed, we were told that the time available for training was now more compressed than it had been in earlier years.

In contrast to Quality Threads, there is little evidence at Comfort Textiles of the formation of work teams or of the delegation of responsibility to workers on the shop floor. Managers are not much in evidence on the shop floor, and their offices are physically separate from the work site, which discourages interaction with employees.

Comfort Textiles management is very concerned about achieving greater flexibility in its work force with respect to work allocation within the plant, and wants more discretion as to who gets laid off or recalled. The union's concerns about job security and the seniority rule are, in practice, not much of an impediment. Since the threat of closure of the plant is highly credible, and workers have few alternatives in a high unemployment region, the union is weak. Management faces few barriers achieving greater flexibility, through multi-skilling and job rotation.

At Comfort Textiles, there is little evidence of measures that would solicit employee involvement in meeting quality and other objectives (for example, no quality circles or similar strategies). Despite the rhetoric of "quality," there is some question about the extent to which quality objectives are, in fact, being met. Management may profess commitment to quality, but we were told by employees that in fact everything goes out the door. Even though the marketing strategy may be based on high quality, workers told us of using magic marker to fill in for the failings of the dye pattern.

These two firms therefore illustrate important differences in the "soft technology" of work organization, employee involvement, relationships with management and the decentralization of responsibility to the shop floor. At Quality Threads, the company has a clear strategy in terms of what is required from the work force, and has made major changes to the internal social organization of the plant in order to achieve company objectives. The company recognizes that it must gear internal organization to its product/market strategy, and the deliberateness of its strategy is reflected in the fact that its approach to the labour force is actually quite different depending on whether the product to be produced is destined for the low end or the high end of the market.

As already noted, Quality Threads produces both a high quality line and a more standard product for the commodity market. It has physically separated the production of both lines of business, and in fact the "commodity" textile aspect of the firm's business has been spun off into a separate division, which employs its own labour force. The "commodity" textile labour force is engaged on terms that are quite different from that which is applied to the high-quality, niche market business — wages are lower, vacation provisions more restricted, different arrangements for overtime have been put in place, and so on.

Comfort Textiles follows the same marketing strategy of selling both a high priced "niche" product and a low end "commodity" product, but production in the two parts of the business is much more intertwined, both physically in terms of the layout of the work site and in terms of switching the work force from one type of production to the other.

Our two case studies in the textile industry therefore provide us with a study in contrasts within a technology and market context that is fairly similar. One firm has a clear recognition of the interdependence between quality production and workplace organization and has deliberately reorganized its operations; the other has stuck with a more traditional manufacturing philosophy. Both firms have shed labour in recent years, but the jobs that remain at Quality Threads seem to have a greater probability of survival in the long run.

As well, we have to look to the social organization of the industry as a whole. For a region to be prosperous, it is not enough to be able to find isolated examples of innovative and well organized firms. General prosperity requires prosperous *industries*, but in the textile industry, there is little evidence that firms are working effectively with each other — or with governments — through the establishment of a sectoral (textile industry) association or other means.

This gap is especially noticeable when it comes to the training of the work force. Individual companies such as Quality Threads have in the past approached community colleges for assistance in training, and have had some success with nearby colleges in obtaining access to training in existing courses. The colleges do not provide, however, general training for the industry as a whole that could be used not only by Quality Threads but also by other firms in the textile industry. A textile-oriented program could serve the training needs of both the maintenance workers (who can at present obtain general mill-wright training, for example, but little that is more specific to the technologies of their industry) as well as the operators. Apart from the knowledge and skills that would be imparted, such a program could permit both students and companies to evaluate interest in, and suitability for, textile occupations. The lack of more effective cooperation among textile firms is one of the reasons why such training programs, directed to meeting the common interests of the companies, have not developed.

Textile mills are among the few remaining manufacturing industries that continue to provide employment for a low-educated, small-town/rural work force. However, the number of such jobs has declined substantially, and the future is clouded because of the competitive uncertainties created by recent free trade agreements. To survive at all, textile firms need not only to select an appropriate product and market strategy, and invest in new machinery and training, they also need to invest in the soft technology of production. In the more unforgiving international market place of the 1990s, firms cannot afford to waste the skills and energy of their work force. New modes of workplace organization and motivation are needed if firms are to deliver the goods that will satisfy a high-quality, rapid turn-around niche marketing strategy. On this dimension, our two case study firms have gone in somewhat different directions. For now, both firms remain in business, but time will eventually tell which strategy works — our bet is on Quality Threads.

"Aerospace Manufacturing" — High Technology, Hard and Soft

The textile industry has been an important employer since the advent of the Industrial Revolution, but has shrunk in size in recent decades. Aerospace, on the other hand, is a new industrial sector whose rising employment illustrates an important historical feature of capitalism as a system — as old industries have replaced human labour with machinery, new industries have historically expanded their employment. The problem for Canada in the 1990s is that there is no guarantee that these new industries will locate here. Furthermore, these new employers may need a new type of labour force. What type of workers do new industries need? What sort of jobs do new industrial sectors create?

"Aerospace Manufacturing" makes aircraft parts at its Nova Scotia plant, but this is a very different operation from conventional manufacturing. The traditional assembly line made hundreds of thousands of identical parts for a mass market. It was based on a careful time/motion study of the steps involved in manufacturing. Industrial engineers analyzed the most efficient way to produce a particular component and specified, in precise detail, how each step in the manufacturing process was to be performed. Once the assembly line had been laid out, there was a rigid system of job specialization, which performed these operations in a fixed sequence. The jobs of production workers were almost totally defined for them by the industrial engineers — their role was to do their assigned tasks, as specified by management, as motivated by piece rate bonuses, and as policed by the quality control department.

However, modern aircraft are very expensive to make and to operate, and since they have to operate in a wide variety of roles and environments, it is cost-effective to customize manufacture somewhat for each new customer. This, plus the speed of technical change in aerospace, means that "standard" aerospace spare parts are relatively rare. Short production runs are, therefore, the norm, implying that the production process is always being adjusted. Given the catastrophic cost of failure of aircraft, it is essential that production be certifiably defect free. The continual need for change in production arrangements, plus the absolute necessity for quality, underlie the emphasis of Aerospace Manufacturing on flexibility, teamwork and internal worker commitment to company goals.

The aerospace industry, as a whole, may be somewhat extreme. Other manufacturing industries may not have quite the same speed of technical change, shortness of production runs and absolute insistence on certifiable quality. However, the same general themes of rapid technical change, niche marketing and the importance of quality do recur throughout many manufacturing industries. In some ways, therefore, our case study of Aerospace Manufacturing offers us an intriguing glimpse of the future of manufacturing.

Technically, the Nova Scotia operation is a marvel of modern computer-integrated manufacturing. Organizationally, it is an extremely flat operation, with only six managers and relatively few support staff, for over 230 production workers at the time of our interview (another 240 have since been hired). Socially, the production unit is the work team, to which "co-ordinators" have just been appointed, but among whom, by conscious effort, few distinctions are made. Although it is the robots and computers one notices on entering the plant, the invisible technology of organization and social relations are equally essential to success.

Approaching the plant, one is struck by the manicured lawns and futuristic architecture. The first thing to be seen at the entrance is a semi-circular receptionist console, with eight separate computer screens, from which a single security guard can monitor the unmanned operation of the entire plant on the evening shift. There is strict security, so all visitors present identification and are signed in before being guided down a long hall to the plant area. In the plant, rows of computer-driven machining stations are on the left, while on the right is the employee cafeteria area, completely open to the machining area, but quite spotless (with only a small hint of the smell of machine oil in the air). To anyone familiar with metal-working plants, it is remarkable how a machine shop can be this clean. The open space plan is evidence of both a high technology manufacturing process and the plant's social engineering. It is not accidental that when the cafeteria has no walls, everyone in the work group can see who is having coffee, and for how long.

Since the production manager has no personal secretary to make his coffee, he buys it in the cafeteria and carries it to his windowless office upstairs. Everything about the architecture and layout bespeaks the underlying manufacturing philosophy — high-quality technology and flat, egalitarian team management. As one might expect, they have a "mission statement": "We aim to be a competitive flexible manufacturer of the highest quality aircraft components, supplying our customer requirements on time, in a cost-effective manner, by minimizing lead time and inventories, while constantly striving to attain the best fit between the needs of each employee and the application of advanced technology."

Clearly, the production manager has caught the religion of quality and believes the doctrine of employee involvement. He is extremely conscious of the social relations surrounding production and especially of the importance of workplace equity to morale and team effort. His whole emphasis, and the guiding philosophy of the plant, is on "getting it right the first time" — the belief that organizing production for zero defects produces cost savings that cascade through the organization in reduced materials wastage, abolition of separate quality control departments, elimination of levels of supervisory middle management, and so on.

It is also remarkable that there is no effort made to figure out exactly the labour cost of individual operations performed. Although the plant's computer maintains, and constantly updates, a record of the machining time and wear rate of each of 4,000 individual drill bits used in the plant, there is no similar attempt to specify precisely the labour cost of processing each individual part, or the cost of particular operations. Clearly, a management decision has been made, based on the implications detailed cost accounting would have had for the morale and teamwork essential to the plant's overall productivity. If employees knew that the company computer was keeping track of every minute that they spent in the production of each individual part, they would be that much less likely to take the time to help each other out with production problems. Since the whole basis of the social design of shop floor work is to encourage team work and multi-tasking, accounting procedures for labour time that were too detailed would be dysfunctional.

The Halifax plant produces precision-machined parts in a computer-integrated manufacturing mode. Design of parts is done by computer-aided design (CAD) elsewhere, and down-loaded by telecommunications to the plant's computer and then down-loaded again to the numerically controlled machine tools. No paper at all is involved in the specification or design of products. Indeed, the initial aim was to have no paper at all anywhere in the plant. However, some paper has crept in, notably in the certification sheet that accompanies each tray of parts, is signed off by a worker and cross-checked by another worker.

Since the plant has been in operation for some years, the manufacturing process is now fairly smooth. In principle, it is totally automated. An automated warehouse (no human entry allowed) feeds automated guided vehicles that pick up and deliver castings to machining stations, where robot arms load, probe and locate, adjust the machining and machine parts to specification. Software is developed in-house to locate and machine parts. It is at this stage that human intervention is essential, since precisions to one ten-thousandths of an inch are essential, and at that range of tolerance small things (such as torquing under machining, "chattering" of drill bits, or temperature variations within the plant) can produce defects in manufacturing.

Workers must be both machinists and computer programmers in order to "tool proof" the machining of each part. Since there is a continuous flow of new parts to produce, there is always work to be done in writing the program to machine each part. But once the computer program has been successfully written to control the machining station, the operation becomes automatic — one only needs to push a button to start the process and "a monkey could do it." However, on the day we visited the plant, a hundred different parts were being produced and the continual stream of new parts to machine implies a continual demand for the set up operation.

Since the warehouse is automated and parts are transferred between machining stations by guided vehicles (loaded and unloaded by robot arms), once the program has been written to machine each part, the whole plant can run unmanned. During the graveyard shift the receptionist/security guard is often the only person present.

The eventual goal is to have four shifts of workers with four teams per shift in production and with all personnel completely multi-skilled (everyone will have rotated through all areas). Multi-skilling is seen as developing not by job type but by functional use for each shift (shift or team multi-skilling). Though there are no managers on the shop floor, there is a minimum requirement for a team leader/shift coordinator. Management sets some clear parameters — the machinery must keep running — but within that framework, decision making is devolved to the work teams. For example, the shift teams decide their own shift change times, as long as they meet the mandate of continuous operation. Outside of this mandate, the team can decide how much flexibility it wants around work scheduling or job rotation. Formal team meetings are held every week and a general plant assembly once per month per shift.

The next five years will see manufacture of fewer new parts, and more modifications to existing parts. This will increase the skill requirements for machinists, but all training will need to be on-site. There will be more emphasis on meeting specifications, checking tolerances, and testing. The role of the support group will change dramatically, reinforcing the need for multi-skilling, rotation, and having the skilled support as part of every work team as they deal with the one-off product runs to exact customer specifications.

Product quality is of paramount importance. Quality control and assurance is gradually being built into the shop-floor machinists' job. In addition to machine loading, monitoring, finishing, gauging, measuring and shipping, workers participate in a certification program for operators to ensure team-based quality assurance. Presently, twenty per cent of the operatives are moving through a training rotation, and the goal is one hundred per cent. Aerospace Manufacturing has a system of internal quality audits based on customer specifications or corporate procedures, which are integrated with external audit specifications imposed by government regulation.

In the past five years, customer service demands and input have increased quite dramatically. Uncertainty in the business environment, increased speed of change, and increased need for flexibility and adaptability mean that the length of production runs has experienced a big decline. The time taken to move from new product idea through design and production has decreased dramatically with the adoption of concurrent engineering and the joint involvement of personnel from manufacturing, marketing and repair in the design process.

In order to do all this, employee participation and involvement is essential. In this plant, management does not believe there is a trade-off between quality and cost of production — higher quality and lower costs are seen as two sides of the same coin. Cost savings from getting it right the first time come partly from the elimination of middle management. When we were there, there was one production manager, and six other managers, with 230 employees in work teams (shortly thereafter employment doubled with the addition of two new production lines). Work teams are intended to report directly to top management.

Aerospace Manufacturing also employs thirty "process planners" to support the manufacturing function, ten of whom are formally trained engineers, and twenty with equivalent credentials to shop-floor machinists. Since so much of the manufacturing process is driven from a central engineering design office 1,500 kilometres away, these process planners have specific responsibility for troubleshooting at the plant, making changes in process design where necessary, and modifying technical blueprints and equipment to suit specific needs. The planners are on a two- to three-year rotation through manufacturing, with a goal of eventually integrating them onto the shop floor and then allowing every manufacturing worker to rotate through the process planning function. A job rotation committee, now in place and made up of worker representatives, decides on the rotation process and implementation, including what percentage of team members will be moved. The goal of Aerospace Manufacturing is eventually to have all team members rotating, on a two- to three-year basis, through process planning, human resources, finance, and systems analysis, with sixty per cent of the workers' time spent in manufacturing and the remaining 40 per cent in the other four areas.

Job rotation is one way of getting everyone in the plant to appreciate the relationship between their individual jobs. A network of committees also helps to ensure the same result. A "steering and design committee" comprising management and worker representatives chosen by co-workers has the job of developing structures and guidelines because, according to the management team, "Sociotechnical systems need rules and flexibility, not just trust." Though the system is based on "fairness, consistency, and honesty" the company is insistent about two basic premises: "The machines must run," and "Benefits are not negotiable." The committee's role is to monitor the just-in-time production system to guarantee stability of supply, and ensure that the company, with its enormous spare parts business, stays well positioned for the cycles of demand. According to management representatives, workers get involved in management decisions as much as any manager, and "sometimes know more." As a result, an appreciable amount of technical change in the firm comes from the bottom, from the trouble-shooters and the machinists.

Although economists typically assume that pay is the main motivator of worker performance, this is not the operative philosophy at

Aerospace Manufacturing. The plant is not unionized and the company wants to keep it that way, but paying top wages is not the method adopted. Management surveys the local labour market and sets a wage that is consciously not the highest in the local area, but respectably above average. It recognizes that too low a wage structure will create discontent, hence average wages must be relatively decent. Otherwise, pay policy is a minor part of the motivation strategy; there is, for example, no system of bonuses, no merit pay, no "payment by results" and no piece work. Within the plant there are three pay curves, for manufacturing, support personnel and technical/clerical. Everyone is on salary, and pay curves are determined by skill attained and time employed, (plus a small premium for work team coordinators). As multi-skilling becomes pervasive, management hopes to revamp the payment system to closely link it to skills acquisition, but not to modify the basic principle of payment by annual salary.

In making its socio-technical system work, Aerospace Manufacturing has had the advantages of youth. Since the plant is new, workers are still on the segment of the pay curve where salaries increase each year, but in a few years many will begin to reach the maximum of their pay scales. Since new production lines are being installed, the plant has not yet had to adjust to a situation of declining orders. As a result, although local unionists report receiving a few inquiries from workers about the possibility of unionization, there has been no real attempt at organization. Management's response to the possibility of future business downturn has been to organize workers into committees to plan how to allocate work if a downturn should occur. The plant employs a number of workers through a temporary help agency, in relatively low skill jobs, at about half the pay rate of regular workers — they would be the first to go in a downturn. However, if a future downturn is severe, this buffer would not suffice, and since the social dynamics of an interdependent team are so crucial to productivity, the firm is planning now so that any future reduction in work hours is done in a way that workers feel is equitable.

In this environment, management has the delicate balancing act of setting standards, but devolving responsibility to the lowest feasible level. The problem is how to maintain, and increase, production standards over time. "Leadership" and "motivation" are the operative principles; simply advocating employee involvement does not necessarily produce desirable results, because work teams do not, of themselves, necessarily know how to solve problems, even if they want to. At Aerospace Manufacturing, managers continually use the metaphor of a "coach" rather than "boss." There is a clear recognition that simply telling people to do things does not work very well and that it is the more subtle skill of the coach in motivating, team-building and strategizing that is required.

In developing an environment of teamwork and employee involvement, the two key issues are equity in administration by top management and the social skills/attitudes of workers. Each team schedules its own work to meet business needs and operates in a flex-time environment, hence workers must be able to work together, dependably. The importance of team work is indicated by the fact that after pre-screening by management, it is other workers who conduct the job interviews, and these interviews focus on team issues. The company, and existing work teams, are looking for new workers who are "team players, responsive, have a sense of urgency and a work ethic — people who are a 'fit'." At Aerospace Manufacturing, the possession of technical skills is taken for granted, and there is impatience with educational institutions that have not kept up in teaching the technology the workplace needs (such as three-dimensional tolerancing). However, the company's concerns have really moved to a different level, since they take it as a given that when a technical skill is needed, training is provided.

The problem is that although technical skills can be taught, social skills are much more difficult to impart. As the production manager put it to us, "It is not that difficult to teach someone to program a computer, if they want to learn, but it is next to impossible to teach someone not to be a jerk." The effective participation of workers in work teams depends on their possession of social skills, but it is not obvious how to teach adults self-confidence or dependability or co-operativeness.

The bottom line is that at a time when traditional high-paying blue collar jobs are becoming increasingly scarce and low-wage manufacturing has to struggle for survival, Aerospace Manufacturing is prospering. The pulp mill and both the textile mills we interviewed have laid off a significant fraction of their work force. Despite the recession and despite a high exchange rate, Aerospace Manufacturing has, in recent years, doubled its employment; and, although the plant's initial establishment came with government grants and subsidized training, no government subsidies or grants were involved in the expansion. In part, Aerospace Manufacturing is expanding its production in Nova Scotia because its parent firm is transferring to Nova Scotia work that was previously done at another site, where work organization is more traditional and there is a history of bad labour relations. The success of the Nova Scotia plant in the competition for product lines within the company is due to its ability to combine hard and soft technology — computerized machining stations and "flat team" workplace organization and employee motivation.

"Joe's Machine Shop" — Old-Style Metal Bending

If Aerospace Manufacturing is the wave of the future in the metal shaping sector, one can also easily find examples from the past. It is easy to see, as one drives up to Joe's Machine Shop, that one is approaching a very different sort of employer. The yard is muddy and potholed, littered with pieces of equipment and stacks of rusting iron of various types. A lot of work is, in fact, going on out of doors. On the day we arrived, two workers were measuring sheets of iron with a tape measure, marking them with chalk and cutting them to size with an oxyacetylene torch, free-hand. Using an ancient set of heavy rollers, the iron sheets were then bent into a ring collar, with one worker communicating the appropriate width to the machine operator using hand gestures.

Clearly, this is not a place where precision work is done and it is equally clear that modern management techniques have not penetrated: as one enters the cramped office, one notices that the personal computer in the corner is underneath a very dusty dust-jacket and a pile of ledger cards. The owner inherited the firm from his father thirty years ago, and he inherited the accounting system as well. The sole bookkeeper/secretary/receptionist posts journal entries by hand in a large accounting book and tallies the pay packets with a hand-written voucher.

Most of the work at Joe's Machine Shop comes from local orders for repairs to agricultural equipment, custom fabrication jobs and structural steel work for local building projects. It is not a certified welding shop, has noticed no real technical change in the last twenty years and expects none for the next decade — but it has more business than it knows what to do with. Sales depend heavily on the level of construction activity, but since structural steel work is always needed in the construction of schools, shopping malls, commercial buildings, and so on, the firm is extremely busy. It is the largest welding shop in the area, in part because it possesses heavy equipment which can handle larger metal fabrication jobs. Fifteen shop floor workers are supervised by one foreman and the owner, who attends to all details of marketing, tendering, and administration.

Profit margins are, however, much lower today than they were a few years ago. With the recent decline in building activity, some competitors are bidding at close to cost, just to stay busy. It is clear that Joe's Machine Shop does not engage in high level accounting techniques to allocate costs, but their estimate of profit margins was $5\frac{1}{2}$-6 per cent, a considerable decline from the 15-20 per cent margin normal a few years ago. Both foreman and owner agree that Joe's Machine Shop competes mainly on price.

Basically, Joe's Machine Shop is in the "rough carpentry" end of the metal working industry. Its continued prosperity is a reminder that although the leading edge of the metal working industry may work to tolerances of one ten-thousandth of an inch, there will always be a sector of the industry that sells low precision product to a local market.

To its workers, Joe's Machine Shop offers a very traditional bargain. It makes a sincere effort to provide steady work by taking on small repair jobs to fill in slack times between major contracts. At an average hourly rate of $13.50, plus a medical plan and a small Christmas bonus, the pay rate is fairly good, for the local area. Educational credentials are not demanded — workers need to be able to read blue-prints and do the basic mathematics required to cut angles, or calculate circumferences (or get someone else to do it for them). However, the key thing is to be "job smart " — as long as someone can do the job, they can stay.

In return, Joe's Machine Shop asks for hard work and loyalty. It is a low skill, low overhead, high volume operation. Although four additional workers could be used at the current time of our interview, the firm likes to try new employees out. New workers are hired for three or four months to see if they can work at the intensity the job demands, and they are laid off at the first opportunity if they prove unsatisfactory. In general, labour relations are not particularly sophisticated, amounting basically to how well each worker gets along with the foreman and the owner.

Joe's Machine Shop is a family business that has not changed much in organization since the current owner inherited it from his father. Both foreman and owner reported to us that the only major innovation in welding they could cite was automatic wire feeding for arc welding, an innovation which dates from World War II. In fact, welding technology is changing very rapidly and quality assurance programs are essential for any welding firm that wants to bid on high-tech contracts in, for example, the off-shore oil drilling industry. Joe's Machine Shop is not in that sort of market. Indeed it is completely out of touch with technical change. For example, they informed us (erroneously) that welding is not a certified trade — despite the existence (since 1947) of CSA-approved welding certification standards for welding engineers, welding procedures, welding supervisors and welders.

Both Aerospace Manufacturing and Joe's Machine Shop cut and shape metal, but there the technical similarities end. At Joe's Machine Shop workers drill holes in metal with manually controlled drill presses. At Aerospace Manufacturing, robot arms select computer-coded cutting tools which are mounted on a numerically controlled machining station, programmed to probe, rotate and align a dye-cast blank to within one ten-thousandth of an inch. These differences in the "hard technology" of production are easy to observe, but the differences in the "soft technology" of work organization and personnel strategies are equally essential.

Both Aerospace Manufacturing and Joe's Machine Shop are non-union, but this is their only organizational similarity. At Joe's Machine Shop, technical and educational credentials are not demanded; indeed illiteracy is entirely tolerable, if another worker will read the job order. The owner is on the premises, and he can tell if someone is working hard and is "job smart." It is a small scale, low overhead operation that sells on the basis of its low prices to an undemanding local market, and hence sees no need for advanced principles of socio-technical design.

Aerospace Manufacturing, on the other hand, must meet the unyielding quality standards of an international market place in which technical change is extremely rapid. By its nature, it is part of a large firm, which is part of a larger network of suppliers and sub-contractors, each of which demand a certifiably zero-defect product and a competitive price. Aerospace workers must not only have strong technical skills in computer programming and machining, they must also be motivated to use them, and it is simply too expensive to supervise closely their complex and ever-changing tasks, and try to catch all their mistakes after they have been made. Getting it right the first time requires both the hard technology of computer-integrated machining stations and the soft technology of sophisticated coaching and employee empowerment.

Both employers have a coherent set of expectations which fit the technology they use and the market place they supply. Both are prospering — indeed both are in a position to hire new workers. However, despite the fact that they are nominally in the same broad industrial classification, it is hard to conceive that they could hire the same workers or that either firm could adopt the personnel policies and labour force strategies of the other.

The contrast between Aerospace Manufacturing and Joe's Machine Shop illustrates the interdependencies between production strategies and market strategies. Firms have a four-cornered choice of a market strategy based on price and quality, and a production strategy based on the hard technology of production machinery and the soft technology of workplace organization. Only some combinations are feasible. Joe's Machine Shop could not compete in the high-quality segment of the metal shaping industry, without undertaking a complete reorganization of its capital equipment, skills training and internal workplace organization. Similarly, if Aerospace Manufacturing were to try to follow a low-wage strategy, it could not hope to attract the type of labour force it now has, or maintain the type of workplace organization and the level of quality assurance it now depends on.

In a very real sense, employers have to choose between "packages" of labour force and product market strategies. Since the market place continues to demand a mix of high quality and low quality goods, both types of employer continue to survive — but from a national point of view, there is a crucial difference. Joe's Machine Shop sells primarily to the local construction trade, with new orders depending on expansion in the local population base, and such trends as the level of local retail sales. None of Joe's production is exported, even outside the province, to help pay for the things local people import from the rest of the world. Aerospace Manufacturing, by contrast, sells over ninety per cent of its output internationally. The U.S. and Canada eliminated customs duties on aircraft parts long before the Free Trade Agreement in 1988, so Aerospace Manufacturing has never had tariff protection, and was unaffected by passage of the FTA. Its success in export markets helps to generate the foreign exchange Canadians need in order to purchase foreign goods. In a very real sense, employment at Joe's Machine Shop depends on the level of local prosperity, but it is the exports of firms like Aerospace Manufacturing that create prosperity.

Conclusion

In many ways, Major Forest Products exemplifies the old-style "good job," but the shrinking number of such jobs is a major social problem for Canada. Aerospace Manufacturing represents the future Canadians would like to see in manufacturing: it is technologically dynamic, it exports most of its production (thereby earning the foreign exchange Canada needs in order to import goods from abroad), but, most important, it offers relatively secure jobs with good pay and working conditions. It has also been increasing its work force at a time when such jobs are rare.

Some of the other firms we interviewed (e.g. Quality Textiles) were also following the same strategy of devolving responsibility for quality control and eliminating layers of middle management, but the socio-technical systems design of Aerospace Manufacturing contrasts sharply with the traditionalism of Major Forest Products and the low-price/low quality/local sales strategy of Joe's Machine Shop. Its ability to follow through on its quality promises differs, as well, from the partial implementation of organizational change at Comfort Textiles.

Aerospace Manufacturing is able to deliver a high value-added, certifiably defect-free product to its international customers because it is good at both hard and soft technology. The firm has consciously integrated the social design of the workplace with state-of-the-art capital equipment and computer technology — but its success is not just due to what happens within the four walls of the plant. In order to operate effectively, the plant needs a dependable infrastructure of public services, transportation and telecommunications links. And since the plant needs workers with a high level of social and technical skills, it has to be sited in a region where the educational system, and the broader society, produces such workers. If Canadians want more of this sort of manufacturing, Canadians need to recognize that it is the *combination* of technical and social inputs that make it possible.

3

The Low-Wage Service Sector

If most firms in the goods sector are reducing employment, where will people get jobs? What options are there for someone who is laid off from the resource or manufacturing sector?

In Canada more than seven out of every ten workers are now employed in a service sector job. Although some service sector jobs are well-paid and secure, the shift to services has been disproportionately in sectors paying below average wages. The popular expression "McJobs" has become a metaphor for the transition from manufacturing to services. The example of a factory worker, laid off from his $20 per hour job, accepting a minimum wage job flipping hamburgers in order to support his family is undoubtedly dismal, in terms of both underutilized human potential and lost income. However, the view that service jobs are uniformly low-wage and manufacturing jobs pay well is over-simplistic.

Chapter 4 will describe some of the high-wage jobs in the "knowledge" or "information-based" service sector, and the hope for the service sector is in the type of services which are knowledge- or information-based. However, while workers with general skills are in high demand across industries and can move easily from one sector to another, others have poorer options. High-paying service jobs often require higher levels of basic education, and good mathematics or writing skills. The skills that goods sector workers have, on the other hand, are often firm-specific, learned through on-the-job training. Although manufacturing jobs often require a great amount of expertise, training has usually been provided by the firm, on the job, and its portability to a new employer is very limited. Entry-level educational credentials needed for the high-wage service sector tend to be higher than those required for jobs with similar pay in the manufacturing sector. As a result, those unable to make the transition can easily find themselves in the low-wage service or "dump" sector, or begin a history of multiple interactions with social assistance and unemployment insurance, or both. Particularly when jobs of any kind are scarce, many workers find themselves depending on short-term jobs — contract employment or temporary help agencies.

In our current labour market, when the only options available are jobs that are low wage and highly insecure, people are often forced into reliance on transfer payments, and employers are becoming increasingly dependent on this. The firms we examined in the low-wage service sector (a fast food restaurant, a temporary help agency, a domestic cleaning firm, a large retailer of fashion and household goods, and an international hotel) were all sophisticated multimillion-dollar companies, but their entire business strategy was based on the continued presence of a readily available low-wage work force.

Twenty years ago, low-wage service employers were often informal, low-technology small businesses. Today they are more likely to be the franchised operation of a sophisticated multinational corporation. Increasingly, these firms now rely on a "just-in-time" labour strategy of hiring workers only as and when they are needed for production. Although this may be profitable for the firm, the success of this corporate strategy depends on the ready availability of a queue of qualified workers. This queue has been created and maintained by the macroeconomic policies of government, which have emphasized the control of inflation over the attainment of full employment. But the deficit problem of government is also worsened by the fact that these people often need a social welfare system to enable them to survive while not employed.

"Multiburger Inc." — Mass Production Food

Undoubtedly, the archetypical exponent of low-wage services is "Multiburger Inc.," the franchiser, par excellence, of hamburger restaurants. Although it is now a multibillion-dollar multinational company, its beginnings lie in the small, and traditionally "Ma and Pa," business of selling hamburgers and fries.

In the old days, independent restaurants were a mainstay in the growth and expansion of the American Way, along with the hardware store, tavern, blacksmith, dry goods store and several others so characteristic of "main street." They were places linked to the community, a source of contact and social relationships. Value was less important than meals that were "home cooked" to replicate what was being missed at home. Speed of service was not essential, nor necessarily was cleanliness.

In owner-operated restaurants, the range of home-cooked meals was large, and a domestic atmosphere was created with plates, cutlery, glass, and a large choice of condiments. In different regions, characteristic regional cuisines gave a focus to the menus and restaurant workers cooked a range of meals from start to finish, all custom ordered and prepared. Table service and customized "table talk" by friendly, familiar, variously uniformed waitresses were the essential links between the kitchen and the customer. The entire industry was characterized by the fact that each restaurant, and each meal, was different. In this sort of individualized production, restaurant cooking was like home cooking — quality was inevitably variable and portion control was unheard of.

By the 1990s, the restaurant provision of meals had developed into a sophisticated system in which the unpredictability of home cooking was replaced by the dependability of franchised food — in much the same way that mass production factories have replaced the uneven quality of individual artisans in the manufacturing sector. The formula was straight-forward: simple food, quick service, stiff franchise fees, cheap labour, ownership of real estate lying under the units, and a string of faithful suppliers. Though there continue to be many places to eat, Multiburger dominates in the low-price end of the market by providing an absolutely consistent product, quality assured and predictable in every way.

Multiburger Inc. has a simple product that moves from start to finish in a streamlined path. Hamburger patties are machine-cut to exact size and weight specifications. Everything is calculated, down to the exact fat content of meat (19 per cent), the size of the bun ($3\frac{1}{2}$ inches), and the weight of garnishes ($\frac{1}{4}$ ounce). Buns are made with extra sugar so they brown faster. All food items have specified shelf lives: french fries are thrown away after seven minutes, hamburgers after ten, and coffee after one half-hour. Nothing is left to chance — Multiburger headquarters even specifies the amount of food they expect a restaurant to throw away (3 per cent).

No customization is tolerated since individual variations are too expensive to allow. Since the cost of the raw material would stay the same, Multiburger could have followed a strategy of customizing each product to the tastes of individual customers (as some fast-food franchises have), but speed of service and food preparation are measured in seconds, and labour costs could easily double or triple. Multiburger, and businesses like it, have effectively transformed the low-wage food service sector from informal "ma and pa" operations to highly specialized operations employing sophisticated production and employment strategies. Overall management control is driven by top-down central strategy and tight franchise control.

Multiburger has led the way in bringing the benefits of technology and efficiency planning to the food industry. The most important technological and organizational changes introduced in the past five years are the "clamshell" hamburger grill, speedier bun warmers, and wireless headphones for drive-through order-takers who can now relay orders without the need for loudspeakers. While all three were introduced to speed response time to customer orders, the clamshell grill also had the intended effect of removing the "flat grill" cook from the critical skilled position in the restaurant.

Prior to the introduction of the clamshell grill, the flat grill was the technology for preparing hamburger patties, which are the mainstay product of the franchise chain. The entire production process was dependent on the ability of the flat grill operator not only to judge the quality of the cooked product, but also to gauge required grilling quantities based on the number of customers entering the restaurant. Average cooking time on the flat grill was three minutes per burger, and the patties had to be individually handled. This dependence, and the potential for bottlenecks to develop, led the company to introduce the clamshell grill. Clamshell operators place hamburger patties on the grill surface, pull down the lid, and the product is cooked on both sides simultaneously in under one minute. Cooking duration is monitored automatically by the technology, which notes when the lid is closed and unlocks it when the product is ready. Total preparation time of a hamburger, start to finish, is now under 3 minutes for regular hamburgers, and 4.5 minutes for premium products. All aspects of all operations are measured and analyzed and there is a constant search for small improvements in efficiency.

Multiburger's labs and a small group of dedicated equipment makers supply the company with an endless stream of labour- and time-saving gadgets designed to automate the cooking and serving of food: computer-run fryers and grills, pre-measured scoops, infrared warning lights, cameras for monitoring interior and exterior customer flows, instruments for testing the solidity of raw potatoes and the fluffiness of milk shakes. Rigid standardization has improved the profit picture on otherwise low-margin items. Multiburger's famed wide-mouth scoop allows an unskilled teenage worker to funnel and stack bags of french fries identical in content with almost no wastage. The premeasured scoop is symbolic of the whole merchandising scheme — it not only avoids costly spillage but gives the impression of abundance by making each bag look slightly over-filled.

For all of Multiburger's franchised operations, delivery time is enhanced through new technology, and product quality is monitored through corporate head office, which is also responsible for supplier selection and standards. Head office centrally selects suppliers to service a large area, rather than having individual franchisees seeking out local sources or develop in-house expertise through their employees. For example, bread products are sourced regionally, and lettuce is trucked in to Nova Scotia from Montreal already shredded, arriving within thirty-six hours of preparation. Product design considerations are handled at the U.S. headquarters. Physical layout and work flows are centrally designed, and then cloned across the franchise chain. Training in customer service is the only corporate function done at the individual restaurant.

Standardization is the method, but the fuel that has powered Multiburger Inc. is available low-cost labour, and a conscious and sophisticated managerial strategy for channelling the morale and motivation of large numbers of young, largely unskilled workers. It is clear that at Multiburger nobody can be indispensable. Both product and employees are standardized: creativity and customization are not valued or rewarded. Operating policies are formulated centrally and are applied consistently throughout the world. The business and the labour market it draws from is premised on a low-wage/low-skill labour force. Technology is designed for a low-skill work force; indeed, as the example of the clamshell grill indicates, the objective is to deskill the production process as much as possible. Overseeing all this are information systems providing constant feedback on a host of indicators to employees and management on operational performance.

The main occupational groupings at Multiburger are classified either by position in the organizational hierarchy, or by primary task in the production process. For the latter, the two main groupings are customer service and food preparation. Customer service personnel deal directly with the public, either at inside service areas, or through the drive-through window. They are traditional "front-of-house" personnel — taking orders, operating cash registers, filling orders (including monitoring product levels), operating the french fryer, preparing drinks, cleaning, and providing overall restaurant care. Food preparation employees are "back-of-house," involved in all aspects of kitchen based food service. No one is dedicated to a particular line of work; all crews rotate through both areas of the restaurant, with the only exception being special aptitudes and the specific wishes of an employee.

The drive for speed and efficiency has put increased pressure on workers in recent years, though constant deskilling through standardization of production processes has made food preparation easier to learn. The clamshell grill and bun warmer have increased the pressure for speed, as has the conveyor system running from front to back of the kitchen for servicing the take-out window. Judging grill quantities has been enhanced by placing video monitors in front of grill operators to allow them to spot traffic building in the parking lots and to adjust cooking quantities accordingly. The substitutability of labour allows crews to be rotated easily and quickly in response to shortages in another area of the operation.

Although at the front of the house the number of products on the menu (124 items) has increased the complexity of cash register operation, the problem is not one of numeracy, since the registers automatically look up prices for the employee and enter them, but one of visual and motor skills — actually finding the right key on the board, quickly. In some U.S. locations, even the need for basic literacy is absent — all the keys on the cash register have pictures of the product, and training in food preparation is done by video and behaviour modelling (watching someone else) rather than using manuals. Multiburger's goal of using new systems to free up more crew time to interact with customers hits hard up against the contradiction that in the fast food industry the more quickly the customers are served, the more quickly they leave. The Multiburger operation is a finely tuned instrument producing a high-quality and magnificently packaged product with largely unskilled players. But regardless of the machine's reputed efficiency, the kitchen still employs between fifty and eighty workers in part-time shifts.

Multiburger's primary labour pool has always been and remains high school students. Indeed, the company's busiest times coincide with students' availability — after school and weekends. All of the skills required in the operation are available in young workers, particularly speed. Historically, the motor-skills-based work has not been difficult to recruit and train for, but personal skills have proved much more troublesome. With an increased emphasis on customer relations and suggestive selling, training requirements in these areas have been increased and enhanced.

The fundamental problem for Multiburger, as for any service organization driven by cost, consistency, and speed, is that the intensive standardized training required to keep a consistent quality work force results in standardized outcomes. The commonly heard "Have a nice day" becomes a depersonalized friendliness that substitutes for personal contact. In a business where the profit generated depends crucially on wages that are as low as possible and an assembly line production that moves so quickly that it allows very little room for individual discretion, how does the organization control the quality of those characteristics involving human behaviour such as warmth, friendliness, quality assurance, judgement — the output of emotional labour?

A separate quality-of-behaviour system is needed to parallel the service system, taking in such functions as interpersonal skills, performance, and organizational climate, as well as support systems such as recruitment and training. Multiburger's assembly line approach to service focuses employee interest on outcomes rather than process (a characteristic of organizations interested in speed and efficiency and moving product through the service delivery process). Motivation and morale revolve around the workings of teams and the interaction of team members. Indeed, the owner of the Multiburger franchise we interviewed maintained that working for the company can teach young workers the discipline and skills they need for a productive future, that they were fortunate to get a full-time training program in the basics of how to work.

Here too, Multiburger leaves nothing to chance. Franchise owners maintain that training is meant to "convince the employee (team member) of the necessity of being taught, guided and controlled not only during the initial training period but throughout their entire work experience with [Multiburger]." Training is therefore particularly important, with its dependence on a set of standardized operations as well as a carefully indoctrinated attitude of service and loyalty.

The success of Multiburger depends on inculcating the widest spread of skills and attitudes in a work force that, for the most part, has never worked before, and needs to acquire expertise in a series of simple, elementary tasks quickly and thoroughly. Each Multiburger restaurant has a training area, typically in the basement, where new employees are given six days of instruction in such things as "Buns," "Fries/Shortening," "Beverage Electives," "Shakes," and so on. They study "Basic Refrigeration" and "Frozen Product Care," and "Cooking Methods" before they are allowed to work in the upstairs production area or deal directly with the public. The training room boasts a full video library and large viewing screen on which new students watch such titles as "A Lot of People Sell Hamburgers" (about teamwork), "What's the Matter with you People" (crew morale), "How to Conduct a Tour," and "If You Want to Work Hard" (motivation). The students cling to prescribed steps to take them through the myriad of subjects that have grown over the years.

Multiburger's sophisticated psychological methods for managing their work force of largely teenage and part-time employees include "rap" sessions, competition, recognition, and praise. Competition takes the normally dull and exhausting work of window people, grill workers, and others and makes it into a game. The idea is not to create a program, but to instill an attitude and transform the feelings of workers toward their jobs. Employees, in teams, vie to outflip and outfry one another, and the Multiburger kitchens accelerate. The idea is to turn working for low wages into a sport to see who can be the fastest and most efficient — and it has been immensely successful. As young workers compete to see who can outfry and outflip each other, the pace of work has accelerated, and the best workers vie for a place on Multiburger's All-American Team. Beginning in 1972, the company has held a yearly "First National Hamburger Olympics"; Multiburger workers from around the world fly in to match their skills against other teams in such areas as stuffing bags of french fries, most hamburgers perfectly prepared in an hour, and tidiest cash drawers. The final ceremony rewards the best contestants with "Oscars" for their performance, and the celebration indeed resembles the glitter and excitement of the Academy Awards, complete with television cameras and extravagant gifts.

Competition, combined with recognition and "ego stroking," exerts strong motivational force. Indeed, Multiburger's success owes a great deal to the sophisticated methods it uses to encourage and motivate its army of temporary, part-time young workers, a work force with very little prior experience of the working world. Nothing is left to chance — the training manual for supervisors has, for example, a section entitled, quite openly: "Manipulative Flattery — How and When to Use It." The fact that workers are young is critical to the strategy — adolescents are searching for an identity, and are used to play and team competition, not work. Multiburger provides just that.

Significant group-based training, teamwork and team competition, and a supportive work environment maintain the level of enthusiasm necessary for the production line to maintain its dynamic. Achievements, however small, are recognized through such management techniques as praise, manipulative flattery and ego "stroking." The "rap" session is a characteristic method, adapted from Transactional Analysis, used to channel energy which might otherwise find its way into complaints and work-directed unhappiness, and to show workers that the company "cares." Managers of every Multiburger stand receive detailed instructions on how to conduct rap sessions, what topics to cover, and how to use the results.

In rap sessions, workers can air grievances and let off steam in an atmosphere that is ostensibly informal but in reality is carefully controlled by the organization. In an organization that has for many years been intensely fearful of union infiltration, the rap is at once a monitoring method and motivational tool, allowing the company to gauge worker dissatisfaction and dissent, substituting talk for action, and rewarding the best "rappers" with the opportunity to attend regional and national rap sessions with senior executives of the organization.

Clearly, Multiburger's strength and distinctiveness is the sophistication of its labour force strategy. The company selects and trains new workers, uses a multilevel motivational strategy, and leaves nothing to chance. Selection, training and socialization, teamwork and team play, competition and "fitting in" are all part of a sophisticated approach that is far easier to achieve with teenagers than with adults. Food preparation is a very old business, but it has been revolutionized by the methods of such organizations as Multiburger Inc.

Multiburger is another organizational example of the four-cornered interdependence of price and quality, and the use of both hard and soft technology. In this case, the operational definition of "quality" is cleanliness and absolute consistency in product — one can buy a Multiburger hamburger in many different countries around the world, but it is always the same. The firm's objective (consistent quality at a low price) is achieved primarily through hiring of young, quick workers at low wages. New technology in capital equipment and process design is used to speed up the production process and eliminate the necessity for increased skill. Multiburger is the new routinized food factory and it is here to stay, a multibillion-dollar, multinational operation that uses sophisticated socio-psychological tools to achieve its objectives — and which needs a continual supply of low-skill, low-wage labour.

"Sally Servant" — Sanitized Service for the Middle Classes

In the 1890s, middle-class Canadians often employed servants to cook and clean. The live-in maid and the faithful cleaning lady were relatively common in Canada, as they still are in many countries. Affluent merchants often had a retinue of servants, while school-teachers and ministers made do with a "girl," who essentially lived with the family, often in an attic room. In both affluent and middle-class households, however, the employer/servant relationship was an intimate mixture of personal familiarity and power.

In the 1990s, middle-class Canadians usually do their own cooking and cleaning, but when they do not, they often eat out at Multiburger and hire in-house cleaning services from franchised operations like "Sally Servant." The relationship that used to be personalized and informal has become a clearly specified market transaction. Even though providing a clean house or a cooked meal is performing the same function now as it was a hundred years ago, today the buyer of that service contracts not with an individual but with a multinational franchise, and the service itself has become substantially more standardized.

Sally Servant is a prime example, a franchise operation that fills a very specific market niche — residential light house cleaning. In Halifax, ninety-five per cent of total revenue comes from residential cleaning, with an additional five per cent from office cleaning. In its own market niche, Sally Servant has been quite successful and is now the largest domestic cleaning franchise in Canada, by far. The local franchise is among the biggest in Canada (during the recession, the sales of the perennial rival franchise in Ontario slumped considerably more than elsewhere), but the franchise had grown continuously up until the time of our study. Clearly, this is a prosperous and expanding franchise in an expanding business.

Firm estimates of "market share" are difficult to make, in part because the aggregate size of the market is hard to estimate with any precision. Sally Servant is likely the largest firm in the local area, but it is hard to be precise about how many people still employ the traditional "cleaning lady" directly.

Why do people pay Sally Servant to do what they could do themselves? Why do people not hire directly, at half the hourly rate of pay? Sally Servant is not cheap, averaging a charge of $55 or $60 for the average house, cleaned every second week. The major selling point is product quality and reliability of service. Though a significant number of lost clients might quote price as the reason for discontinuing service, there is typically not much variation among cleaning service firms and it appears that people are willing to pay to get the image of professionalism, the assurance of a reasonably good cleaning job and reliability, and to avoid the hassles of direct hiring.

Sally Servant works by setting up two-person teams (a "head maid" and a "helper") who are assigned a route. Space in their schedules is left vacant on Mondays and Tuesdays for "one-shot" cleaning jobs, which are charged on an hourly basis. However, a major feature of the marketing strategy is the direct quotation by the owner, who personally visits every client wishing regular cleaning and quotes a fixed charge, which varies with the size of the house, number of residents and style of living. The owner attempts to build up a route for each team corresponding to full-time work and, together with her supervisor, would like to spot check at least one house on each route each week in order to maintain assurance of quality (but in practice does not have the time to check this thoroughly).

Two of the maids (Wendy and Suzanne) confidently explained to us that maid service is specification work, and although every contract reflects basic similarities, each client may specify particular tasks or methods pertaining to their situation or home. Since maid service is a direct replacement of work done by the clients themselves, often clients are very demanding and particular about both the methodology and the results.

Wendy and Suzanne cited work efficiency as one of the most important aspects of the job. They viewed themselves as "professionals," and indeed the idea of professionalism is the very heart of the Sally Servant philosophy. From the uniforms to the type of material in the training videos, workers are told that they can clean a home better and faster than the average homemaker. Suzanne said, "I used to think my own home was clean. Now when other people call something clean, I often disagree."

There are specific methods followed to increase efficiency and help ensure that there are no tasks left undone before the maids leave the home. The work is always done left to right and top to bottom. The "art" of cleaning thoroughly and efficiently is a skill increased by practice. Since the maids work on straight commission, they usually try to add as much to their results as possible within the time frame they must adhere to, since any extras or "treats" for the client that can be done quickly can add to repeat business.

The maids have a large part to play in building up clientele for the company. Several clients ask for specific maids, and will only book the house cleaning when they are available. Since part of the regular clientele is made up of older seniors as well as two-parent or single-parent working families, some of the clients are at home when the work is being done. In those cases, a rapport is built up between the clients and the maids and additional work may be brought in through neighbours and friends of clients. However, this old-style personal contact is more the exception than the rule; it is more common for no one to be at home while the maids work.

Since the maids are paid a percentage of the customer's fee, they operate as "subcontractors" and there is an inherent incentive for efficiency. Substantial business can be brought in for your team by doing a good job. Though there is minimal on-the-job supervision, the common occurrence of customers' complaints (and the desire to avoid them) acts as an incentive for thoroughness. The head maid is responsible for the job being carried out as specified in the contract. Before leaving the house she will go over the checklist to ensure that the job has been completed. In the event of a complaint, we were told that the owner typically sides with the maids, based on track record, before she goes to the home to follow up, but knowing the head maid will be held responsible for any mistakes or errors made on the job reduces incentives to "shirk" for both partners.

Wendy suggested the problem of high turnover in the maid business stemmed from the fact that there is a definite stigma attached to domestic labour jobs. Many people who start with Sally Servant and leave after a brief period are those that have preconceived notions of the type of job they would like. Often people just don't want to work as a maid. Those who do leave Sally Servant tend to be younger individuals who have not had a lot of experience in the job market. They usually try "the circuit" — work in the fast-food business, as a waitress or as a salesperson.

Wendy and Suzanne stressed that they had "been out there" working in several restaurants (fast-food and otherwise), and as housekeepers (in hotels and privately), and both emphasized that working at Sally Servant had definite advantages: guaranteed work hours five days a week, weekends off, minimal supervision, not having to stay indoors in one place all day long, and often the avoidance of contact with the client. Even though there may not be any set lunch hour or break periods, depending on schedules and travelling time, it is often possible to do errands on some days between clients.

Workers get paid on a commission basis, starting at eighteen per cent for a helper and twenty-five per cent for a head maid and increasing by one per cent each three months for the first year to a maximum of twenty-two per cent for the helper and twenty-eight per cent for the head maid. Thereafter, increases come only with the yearly increase in contract price, which in recent years has averaged slightly better than inflation. Helpers make, after three months, about $210 per week and head maids between $250 and $280 for between 32 and 35 hours of work a week. Note, however, that at twenty-two per cent for the helper and twenty-eight per cent for the head maid, clients are paying twice the hourly rate actually received by the workers.

The head maids are clearly the stable core of the business and although there is a very high rate of turnover in the industry, several have been with Sally Servant for some years. Head maids get to drive the car and take it home with them, a significant fringe benefit for this income level of workers since the charge made for repairs, insurance, and so on is substantially below cost at $15 per week.

The owner clearly identifies staffing as her major ongoing business problem and the major reason why new entrants to the industry go under. Almost without exception, the company's identifiable labour pool is the marginal work world of near minimum wage employment. Over the years, the work force has tended to become a little older and is now in the thirty-five-year age bracket, compared to ten years ago when twenty-five was a more typical age.

Of the current work force of twenty-six full-time employees (thirteen teams) eleven have early school age, or younger, children. Since there is no specific educational requirement, and most employees have Grade 9 or 10 education, these are women with limited employment alternatives elsewhere, for whom child care is typically a major issue. In a context where many other low-wage employers demand a shift work schedule, or (like the retail stores) have shifted to part-time employment, the fact that Sally Servant offers relatively full-time hours, Monday to Friday, during the day, represents a significant employment advantage, since it is feasible for employees to make stable daycare arrangements for their children. In a very real sense, Sally Servant fills a niche between the household economy and the paid economy — both in the sense that the major market for Sally Servant is two-income households and in the sense that its employment strategy is aimed at women who must work outside the home, and who often have child care responsibilities.

Nevertheless, turnover is still a problem and training a major expense. The owner has a core of approximately half her work force who are fairly steady, while the other half turn over fairly frequently. With twenty-six full-time cleaners, one supervisor in the office, and two part-time fill-in workers (who work part-time from personal preference), she will prepare between 130 and 140 T4 employment forms at income tax time. Although there is a great deal of stress in company literature on "The Sally Servant System" (a typical strategy of franchise systems), training consists of two twenty-minute videos, a manual, a training day, or perhaps two (for which new employees are paid $30) and then three days training with an existing work crew.

The major feature of the "Sally Servant System" appears to be organization, in the sense that training emphasizes a systematic approach to cleaning (room by room, systematically left to right within each room, and so on). The claim is that they can clean better and faster because of this organized approach.

Nevertheless, a lot of new employees work only one day, or a week. A significant number of employees also work for a while, leave, and then return. There is some seasonality to labour supply, and some of the employees are "rolling stones" with unstable job histories. In addition, many (quite understandably) would like to make more money, and a few would like simply to qualify for unemployment insurance, although it is worth noting that the owner did not claim that unemployment insurance or social assistance were responsible for an important part of the company's staffing problems.

The owner and her supervisor joked that the "minimum qualifications for an entry-level job in this occupational group" are "a pulse." There is no minimum education standard — anyone who can meet the pace and quality of work demanded, and shows up regularly for work, can enter the firm. The company has experimented with "work experience students" who have the equivalent of a Grade 5 or 6 education, and as long as they can keep up the pace, they are retained. The only capital equipment in use is a standard household vacuum cleaner, so adaptation to technology is simply not an issue. The head maid must be able to keep a worksheet, and to drive, but there are no other literacy requirements.

To keep up morale, the franchisees use positive reinforcement "human relations" strategies to motivate and support their work force. Prizes are awarded to high performers, and compliments from customers received at head office are rewarded with gift certificates at local retailers. Customers are asked to fill out rating cards on each team.

Employees must share in the risks of the business, since they are on commission. There is some decline in the business in the summer months but apparently not a lot, and it is somewhat balanced by a surge of one-shot cleaning requirements for the Christmas season in December and for moving day, June 30. (One-shot cleaning accounts for about six per cent of total revenue.) Days off are taken without pay, and there is some flexibility in the company regarding such requests.

Altogether, it is not hard to see why people might want to try for something better, and the owner expects to train five new employees for every one who stays. Nevertheless, two of her workers have been with her seven years and about half her employees have over three years seniority (mostly head maids). In this region, very few of the work force are immigrants (presumably the situation is different elsewhere in Canada) and relatively few are recent migrants to the region (although some have worked for Sally Servant in other cities). Most of the work force consists of local people who are usually referred by word of mouth from friends or relatives. The firm prefers referrals, but newspaper ads are also used to locate workers. Though it is somewhat more difficult to get a job now than five years ago, it is also harder to get applicants, and continual hiring is necessary to fill vacancies. (Men typically do not apply to Sally Servant, since they have better alternatives in "heavy cleaning" in the industrial/office sector.)

Some of the broader trends in the changing world of work are not particularly relevant to Sally Servant. International competition is clearly not a factor, and there is essentially no technical change. The Sally Servant head office, is (apparently) continually passing on hints about advertising, training and motivation of staff, accounting, and so on, but this is marginal change within an established "loose" franchise and does not reflect the "tight" central control found at Multiburger Inc. High-level skills are not demanded, and there is no change in the need for flexibility/adaptability on the part of the labour force, since both workers do essentially the same job. With essentially no capital equipment, no technical change and minimal training, literacy and educational qualifications are simply not a factor.

The major factor driving Sally Servant is demographic change. The local market (roughly 200 house cleanings per week) breaks down as sixty-five per cent two-income households, twenty per cent affluent one-income households and fifteen per cent singles and seniors (who will often want only once-a-month cleaning, compared to every second week for the others). Two-income households and affluent seniors are growing segments of the population.

Demographic change is also an important factor in creating the labour force for Sally Servant. Growing numbers of single parents and the increased need for second incomes in two-parent households, plus the relative lack of attractive employment alternatives for poorly educated women and the constraints of arranging child care, all combine to create a labour force. Given the pay and working conditions, it is not surprising that there is substantial employment instability, but there is also a stable core of long-term employees.

When people eat out, or hire someone to clean the house, instead of dining at home and cleaning their own home, they are transferring activities which would have been done by family members within the household to the market sector. The increase in jobs observed in the labour market is balanced by a decrease in household production, and the time people spend in paid employment is no longer available for home production, or for other aspects of family life. Therefore, only part of the increasing employment in the fast-food industry or in home cleaning can be seen as contributing to a net increase in goods and services available for consumption.

Part of what is going on in the Sally Servant phenomenon is surely also sociological in nature. Sally Servants are performing for the affluent the same sort of services that traditional maids used to perform, a century ago. Part of the Sally Servant marketing strategy is to trade on this image of the traditional maid, by insisting its employees wear maid uniforms, and thereby cultivate an "upstairs/downstairs" image of the competent English maid. However, while trading on the form of past servant relationships, Sally Servant dramatically alters the content. The relationship of the traditional maid to the household is extremely intimate and personal. On the one hand, the traditional master/servant relationship was characterized by great familiarity and intimate knowledge. Since nobody knows you better than the person who picks up your laundry, a maid knows virtually everything about her employers, while they may know very little about her. On the other hand, in the traditional relationship, the employer supervises, determines the terms and conditions of employment, must make allowance for illness and unforeseen contingencies, decides the rate of pay — in short, the employer has power and a long-term multifaceted relationship with the person who is dependent.

Sally Servant sanitizes this relationship and reduces it to its pure commodity dimension. In some cases, a long-term customer and a stable employee may get to know one another, but it is more common for the client not to see the maid, since work is done while the client is at work, and the Sally Servants let themselves in with their own keys. The personal contact that does exist is between the franchise owner/manager and the client, i.e. a commercial relationship between members of the same class. The Sally Servant operation assumes all responsibility and all knowledge for the pay and working conditions of the maids, so that the relationship of personal dependence and power which is characteristic of the traditional maid/employer relationship is replaced by the tidiness of a market transaction. Since middle-class Canadians do not really know what to do with "servants," they are willing to pay a hefty premium (about $6 per hour) for this sanitization.

"Retail Clone Inc." — Deskilling Sales

Retail trade is Canada's second largest employment sector, employing 12.9 per cent of the labour force in 1991 — a 14 per cent increase from 1986. However, statistics on trends in the number of retail jobs can be very misleading, because there has been, over the past decade, a major shift in the nature of those jobs. As our interviews at "Retail Clone Inc." made clear, deskilling and the fragmentation of full-time jobs into part-time and casual employment is the dominant trend.

With over a billion dollars in sales, and hundreds of stores across all ten provinces, Retail Clone Inc. is one of the largest retailers in Canada. A market leader in the retail industry for decades, the 1980s found the company lagging as the result of a squeeze from the discounters and the fashion-oriented retailers, with an employment structure increasingly out of step with a fast changing business environment. The result was a fundamental retargeting of the company and dramatic changes in Retail Clone's employment strategy, shifting as much as possible to a deskilled, low-wage, part-time labour force.

Like many other department stores, Retail Clone was organized prior to the mid-1980s as a decentralized group of departments with buyers or sales managers running departments as independent profit centres. Department heads were responsible for purchasing, merchandising, marketing, sales, the staffing of their particular department and day-to-day personnel management. However, computerization has enabled centralized control, and many of the independent functions of the departments on a store-by-store basis have now disappeared. Centralization was also driven by the sheer numbers of branches and the increasingly difficult job of managing independent departments in the stores. The growing importance of the media and advertising made it harder for departments and buyers within those departments to handle marketing functions, especially in view of the perceived need to promote an overall corporate image across departments and market areas.

As well, personnel management became increasingly difficult as the retail industry began to develop longer business hours. Departments were also less able to deal with merchandising functions as merchandising increased in complexity, options multiplied and product runs shortened. The management reaction has been one of centralization and standardization — all the company's stores from coast to coast are today essentially run directly from Toronto. Retail Clone has eliminated sales managers for each division in all their department stores, replacing them with supervisors in each division with little control over product selection and ordering.

The last vestige of the department organized system that can be seen in many retail department stores, including Retail Clone, is in consumer durables, otherwise known as the "washing machine" trade. This is the remaining area where one often finds a small core of full-time, commission-paid employees, usually men, with long service to the company and very specific knowledge of the product line they are selling.

In the rest of the store, the occupational structure has been split to create a very small group of full-time centralized managerial staff, and a large pool of auxiliary personnel primarily handling sales functions. The full-time managerial staff is organized along clearly defined functional lines, including merchandising, store management, sales promotion, personnel, financial audit and operations and control, each with its own line of command and responsibilities. Where at one time there were many specialists in every commodity area in the store, and a large number of supervisory and department head staff, they have been replaced by auxiliary workers. Inevitably, according to management, these employees are less knowledgeable about product lines, in-stock and out-of-stock items, and assume less responsibility.

The reorganization of Retail Clone was aimed at unbundling the two key functions in the retail trade, merchandising and sales, in order to make them more manageable and controllable than under the old system. This unbundling of functions seems to have had the unintended consequence of unbundling a skills package, which in the past had typically been found among the full-time sales personnel. As well, the new organizational structure centralized managerial operations, particularly merchandising, and decentralized the sales function while ensuring the company was less reliant on it. Advertising now does the selling, while clerks ring in the sales.

From coast to coast, each of the stores of Retail Clone is a carbon copy of other stores, and all report directly to Toronto; indeed the sales rung in at each cash register are automatically downloaded to the central computer by high speed data line on a continuous basis. As at Multiburger, standardization is the name of the game. Standardization is not the operating philosophy of expensive gourmet restaurants or high fashion boutiques, which depend on the personalized selling and individualized attention of their staff, but they sell to a much smaller target market than Retail Clone or Multiburger.

An aggressive approach to labour cost-cutting has produced a rapid shift to part-time employment. Until the mid-1980s, roughly seventy per cent of the retail staff was full-time, thirty per cent part-time. By 1992 these figures had been more than reversed, leaving only twelve per cent in full-time position, the remaining eighty-eight per cent part-time. The changing character of Retail Clone's labour force is directly related to the wages offered and the technology adopted and employed by the firm. In retail trade, technological advances have decreased skill requirements and therefore shaped the labour force and wage patterns.

The policy of Retail Clone's head office is not to permit the hiring of full-time workers, quite deliberately because they "don't have to pay benefits or do training." There are three categories of sales people. Approximately 240 auxiliary sales personnel, with an additional 150 at Christmas, work flexible hours (i.e. 4 hours some weeks, 15 hours in others). Workers are called in on an as-needed, when-needed basis. Shifts vary but resemble 3½-hour days. According to management the "very, very good ones might work 12 hours a week." (Since workers with less than 15 hours of work per week are not eligible for coverage under unemployment insurance or Canada Pension Plan, the company saves the cost of paying employer premiums.) Virtually all of the auxiliary staff are women, and many are university students or graduates. Turnover is extremely high with a thirty-five per cent turnover in the spring at the end of the university year. The average length of employment is expected to be about one year.

All auxiliary sales people are hired in the same manner: people walk in off the street and make an application. After an initial scrutiny for customer relations aptitude ("whether or not the applicant is smiling"), work experience and education level are assessed. With high unemployment producing many applications, and severe cutbacks in training time, Retail Clone finds it impractical to hire workers with less than a Grade 12 education, and most workers typically have some university. After the pre-screen selection, the final screen is a 2 to $2\frac{1}{2}$-day training package, consisting mostly of familiarity with point-of-sale terminal operation. This is followed by a two-week pairing with another sales clerk on the selling floor. There workers learn terminal operation, product variation, customer relations, loss control, vertical signage, visual identification and presentation.

Retail Clone is a clear example of deskilling within the service sector. Emphasis on training has weakened substantially, seriously cut back at all levels because of cost and turnover of staff. The training which, some years back, might have been learned from professional trainers over a lengthy period is now acquired on the job through the buddy system. Almost no training is undertaken to deal with technological change, and indeed the local management of a Retail Clone store noted (with some exasperation) that they themselves will not be aware of any minor system changes until they actually happen over a weekend. With larger changes, for example the introduction of a new point-of-sale system, more lead time is given, but minimal training is provided.

A second category of worker, newly created in the early 1990s, is the regular part-time employee. This type of worker is typically guaranteed a minimum of 18 hours per week and averages 22.5 hours. This group comprises five per cent of the sales force. Although small by comparison with auxiliary sales personnel, it was created largely because it became clear that Retail Clone could not operate without some core group of regular workers who would understand the operation and take responsibility on the sales floor. Turnover is extremely low among this group; once workers get regular jobs they hang onto them. Competition is fierce when hiring is done for positions through in-house postings for positions as they come open.

Regular part-time staff have more responsibility within the departments, including authority to accept cheques, to do voids, to give direction to auxiliary staff, and to call in replacement staff when other employees call in sick. Recently, they have also been encouraged to become involved in "item exploitation," focusing on one high-selling product, tracking sales, marketing the item, and seeking approval from the sales manager to order more product through the company purchasing system.

The third category of workers are full-time division heads and specialists. Although the survivors have full-time work, the number of such workers had been cut in half during the five years preceding our interview. In a Retail Clone store there are typically twelve division heads with as many as ten departments within their division. An earlier era would have seen a full-time department head for each separate sales or product unit. Each division head answers to one of nine supervisors. Division heads are responsible for doing the weekly schedule, in-store marketing, and are the first level of authority to speak to the auxiliary and part-time staff about their performance.

The supervisory staff are responsible for staff, product knowledge, getting vendors to provide demonstrations or information about their product lines, implement changes in procedure through on-the-floor training, control the floor budget (labour costs), and maintain contact and accountability with the store manager for costs. They are also accountable for weekly sales performance and loss prevention, item exploitation and display. The supervisors work directly on the floor, a noticeable departure from past practice, but they have little role to play in business decisions about what is sold. Supervisors have only a limited say in ordering of goods, since there is a chain of approval through the store manager to the head-office-based regional sales manager who makes the final decision. Local store management is basically responsible for keeping the shelves stocked and the aisles clear and making sure the store is clean and open on time — head office takes care of the brain work of deciding what to sell, at what price.

Most manual functions have been computerized and the latest technology is utilized for controlling the operations of the stores. For example, sales are automated through the point-of-sale terminals, tied directly to inventory control and purchasing. Management in Toronto can account daily for items that sold well the day or week before, what items are arriving and when, where product lines are located in the system and in what quantity, and how long it would take to get them — for every store in Canada. The technology can manage price changes, coordinate with other stores for buying, and track workers' hours.

Additionally, management can trace worker errors and obtain daily reports on sales activity at any given cash terminal during the shift of individual staff members. Because of this technologically driven monitoring of work, increased scrutiny by supervisory staff, and more intensive pace of work resulting from fewer staff, one of our worker respondents commented, "You don't stand around and get caught. It's no longer a social job."

Management admits that its commitment to training has declined. As a result, the computerized inventory control system does not work properly because of errors made by the staff in keying in inventory sales. The level of service and quality of service has dropped and the store is now operated almost entirely with a very unstable, uncommitted, female and student part-time labour force. Wages are low and have not kept pace with inflation, nor are they expected to in the foreseeable future. Staff turnover is extremely high. Although the average level of education of the work force has increased from approximately Grade 8 to Grade 12 or university, in a broader sense the quality of the labour force has declined.

Those workers who get more than fifteen hours work in a week can qualify for unemployment insurance and draw UI during the summer, while a few also get some form of welfare, such as family benefits. With fewer regular employees there are also seemingly fewer regular customers, the revolving door of clients paralleling that of the work force. Local management observed that with part-time employment, you get part-time commitment and part-time motivation. Auxiliary workers are characterized as "having a slack attitude and no loyalty." They are more likely to question authority, and ignore directions, and they are reluctant to arrive fifteen minutes before the shift to find out what's been done and what needs doing. Management sees most sales personnel as "simply putting in the time to pick up a pay cheque," while at the same time the job clearly now requires more than simply smiling at the customers, being helpful, and operating a cash register or terminal.

Clearly there is some tension between management expectations and their practices. On the one hand management wants commitment and professionalism, while on the other hand admitting that "if we want creativity, we contract the work out." Although the emphasis is still first and foremost on customer service, the company has introduced the "Ten point selling standards program," comprising ten phrases about customer relations and sales on a small card. Apparently, the only motivational program Retail Clone has for auxiliary staff is when a worker is approached and asked to list the ten points, they are rewarded with a free cup of coffee if they list all the points correctly!

Wages are uniformly low, averaging ten to twenty per cent above minimum wage, with little negotiation. However, even wages this close to the minimum put Retail Clone second in the wage ranks of major retailers. The only employees who actually bargain are the specialized sales staff, and they do so in the traditional way — based on their sales performance. For example, a high- performing cosmetics salesperson, with a competitive offer from elsewhere, was offered more pay for her position linked to sales, but as management noted, "we don't make deals very often."

Changes in the workplace at Retail Clone are exemplified in the experience of "Bob," a loading dock worker who started with the company in 1952. Bob's first jobs were as stock boy and elevator operator, and in 1954 he was hired as a full-time hardware salesman. He had a brief experience with the vocational school system in its early years, but decided it was not appropriate or necessary for him in his new career. In the 1960s Bob was section head of hardware sales for the store, but by the latter part of the decade the department was discontinued and he was moved to a driving and delivery job for several stores and later to the distribution warehouse.

With the construction of a large automated warehouse intended to service a multi-store area, Bob was taken on first as a driver and later appointed supervisor. In 1986, the central warehouse was closed, sixty-five of its seventy full-time employees were laid off, and Bob was offered lay-off or demotion. In choosing the latter option, he moved once again, back to the main store loading area, and is now one of three full-time dock workers.

After more than forty years with the company, Bob's hourly wage is $10.50, and has been frozen at that level for the last five years, ostensibly to allow the other dock workers to "catch up." In real terms, Bob's wages have shrunk with each move and demotion, as the firm has pursued its strategy of work-force casualization.

From the regional distribution centre approach of the 1970s, Retail Clone has moved to national distribution, with each store receiving tractor trailers from Toronto or Montreal. Dock workers are responsible only for unloading and confirming that the stock has arrived. Most merchandise now arrives already "ticketed" (priced) and ready to go to the floors, or comes in arranged on racks that are rolled off the trucks and sent directly to the floors. While the amount of manual work has been significantly reduced for dock workers, so has the responsibility. Floor sales people now receive goods in the departments in bulk and do all floor arrangements. Bob is apprehensive about the next five years with the company. "The top people, not this store management mind you, but the head office people dump people so fast I'm scared to think about what might happen. People in this business are expendable."

Firm-level economies of scale have produced a shift of managerial emphasis from the establishment to the firm level and a substantial transformation in retail and consumer service delivery. Retail Clone has been able to shift the functions of inventory control, purchasing, advertising, promotion of brand names and trade mark, and long-term financing to the level of head offices, while restricting the functions of the regional establishment to the delivery of the main line service itself.

Retail Clone is far from unique — the model of centralization of brain work and cloning of the service delivery outlet has also been applied in recent times to numerous lines of services: hotels, restaurants (especially fast-food), car repair, movie theatres, car rental, residential real estate brokers, personal (home) services, temporary labour agencies, and others. In all these cases, scale economies for the firm come from the standardization of services that were previously highly personalized, standardization of the service delivery/production process, and the introduction of computer technology to monitor performance and link the local operation tightly to head office.

New technology, particularly computerization, has allowed head office to tie large numbers of small units into a single organization. The legal status of the sub-units may vary — they may be franchises or they may be legally all part of the same firm. At Retail Clone, all the stores of the firm are company owned, but some of its competitors in retail trade sublet some of their floor space to franchised sales operations of other companies — one may be shopping at XX Co., but the shoe department is really run by Company Y and the drugstore is a franchise of Company Z. Indeed, one of Retail Clone's competitors in men's and women's clothing follows the practice of selling under different brand names and different store fronts within the same malls. Some companies (such as Multiburger) run both company-owned stores and franchises. Although these differences illustrate how flexible modern capitalism is as a system of ownership, the operational pattern of centralized control of standardized outlets is common across a variety of ownership structures.

The older pattern of many-layered organizations was developed in an era of slower communications technology, and less developed "soft technology" in organizational structures and managerial expertise, and it has now disappeared. With the disappearance of that structure, the middle-level managerial jobs that used to be spread around the country have also vanished, replaced by centralized head office jobs. In many industries, particularly service-based industries like hospitality, fast-food, or financial services, economies of scale previously thought impossible in labour-intensive sectors have been realized. The result has been less reliance on human resources in general, and mid-level skills in particular.

Within Retail Clone it is easy to observe the trends to increased inequality of income, casualization of employment and decreased job security that have been such a worrisome feature of the labour market as a whole. Head office staff in Toronto are well paid, but there are few of them. Where the retail sector used to provide middle-class jobs as division or store manager (with real responsibility) and full-time sales positions, all across the country, the jobs that could support a middle-class lifestyle have largely disappeared from the regions. The chance of upward mobility for Retail Clone's casualized, low-wage labour force has also become almost non-existent.

"Temporary Help Ltd." — The "Waiting Room"

Casualization of employment — a switch from full-time jobs to employment only for peak hours of operation — is a general theme of the low-wage service sector. Indeed, a growing part of the service sector is based directly on the idea of hiring workers only "when needed, as needed" — a "just-in-time" employment strategy. No firm exemplifies this trend more than "Temporary Help Ltd."

While their operations in Nova Scotia are only a small part of the billion-dollar, 980-branch international parent company, Temporary

Help Ltd. is the ultimate service sector firm — the service it provides is providing the services of others. Basically, it is a labour market intermediary. Temporary Help Ltd. employs workers of a variety of skills, assuming the full legal responsibilities of employer, and then sells the services of those employees to other employers at a markup sufficient to cover all labour and operating costs plus a profit. Where the skills of the employee are not employer specific, THL can perform the training, screening, and hiring the employer would ordinarily have to do, and charge a markup for its services. Firms are willing to pay this markup because of two fundamental trends — segmentation of the labour force into secure and insecure sectors and the shift to a "just-in-time" personnel strategy.

Many firms now maintain a core work force, carefully selected, in which the firm makes substantial investments. The benefits usually associated with workers in the primary labour market are provided: good wages, career progression and comprehensive benefits packages. In addition to this group, the same firms develop a fluid, flexible staff of temporary workers, operating in a secondary labour market. Characteristically these employees get intermittent or part-time work, and limited access to the range of fringe benefits, including higher wages, the core group of employees receives.

The temporary help agency is for some employers a device that acts as a buffer against business fluctuations, and allows for the retention of a stable, committed labour force to whom some form of implicit or explicit employment guarantee is made. The morale of the primary labour force, and their commitment to company goals, is easier to maintain when it is "temporary" employees who bear the cost of any lay-offs. When workers are employed under a different legal regime — either as short-term "contract" workers or indirectly, through a temporary help agency — no promise of future employment is being made, and everyone knows that it is very easy for the firm to not renew any temporary employee who is deemed to be unsatisfactory.

We were told by the management of Temporary Services Ltd. that larger and more unstable firms are the ones that use temporary workers. The sophisticated human resource management systems of large firms apparently allow them to easily and effectively predict and plan their need for temporary workers. Firms on the margins, experiencing either product demand growth or decline, are also more likely to use temporary workers since they can be added and dropped quickly without threatening the core labour force.

Our conversations with four employees of Temporary Help Ltd. — two light industrial workers and two office employees — illustrated the characteristics of the temporary labour market. The office workers were women, one a homemaker who was returning to the labour market and the other a recent immigrant to Canada. The light industrial workers were both twenty-year-old high school dropouts. All of them liked Temporary Help Ltd. as an employer primarily because they felt the agency treated them well, in a personal sense. THL motivates its "employees" by treating them as critical resources of the firm. A great emphasis is put on personal relations with the temporaries, and a link with the always cheerful and enthusiastic office staff is maintained by temps coming in every week to pick up their pay cheque and a friendly daily check-in. Temps socialize with the office staff when they come in — an up-beat and open atmosphere prevails. Temporary employees are treated both as clients and employees. They are led to believe that the THL is calling regular customers when the firm knows that a temporary's skills will satisfy their needs, either now or in the near future.

The "culture" which THL has created internally is one of interested and committed staff for whom finding work for temps "is their life." When the office manager told us that the company was "the love of her life," her eyes moistened — she clearly meant every word. Personal touches cement the relationship — regular temps receive birthday cards from the firm, and also participate in an "employee of the month" program. But although the company tries consciously to create a workplace environment in which temps feel appreciated, the objective disadvantages of insecure, relatively low-wage work remain. Employees were in fact quite explicit that their goal was full-time work and THL was the mechanism to achieving it. Indeed, for some employees, one of the main attractions of Temporary Help Ltd. is its potential to create an orderly path to permanent employment.

The two male high school dropouts were representative of the population of unskilled, low-paid, insecure workers most exposed to the probability of a lifetime of working poverty. Indeed, although both clearly had the "work ethic" and reported taking most of the jobs offered them via Temporary Help Ltd., both estimated that a full year's work would produce a net income of the order of $6,000 to $8,000.

Although these workers are poor and insecure, one of the functions of Temporary Help Ltd. is to "sanitize" the relationship of hirer and hireling, removing the spectre of the depression scene of scores of unemployed workers arriving at the plant gate in vans and trucks, to be picked over for the day's work by the "boss" for the "best" of the lot and the others sent on their way. Today a distant personnel department receives the day's labour requirement and places the call to Temporary Help Ltd. which sends an appropriately screened and willing worker at the exact time and to the proper location.

"Dave" thought of himself as a technician, since he had left school at the age of fourteen and was on the road for four years with rock bands, setting up sound systems and stage shows. His expertise in sound systems was acquired entirely through on-the-job training but, as he noted, there are no credentials required to work in, or for, rock bands. Growing tired of the constant moving required of life as a "roadie," he returned to town recently and divides his time between doing occasional gigs in clubs in the local area (invariably paid in cash, under the table) and working for THL. Since he likes to work as a "technician," seeing this as his major career focus (success in which depends entirely on personal reputation) he finds the idea of temporary jobs with THL attractive. He reported to us that he makes much more money when working as a sound technician. Although there may be some bravado in such self-statements, he definitely did not intend to be working for THL when he was thirty years old and expressed a very conventional desire to move up in life.

In this case, the short-term nature of employment assignments at Temporary Help Ltd., and the possibility of declining a work assignment if a "gig" comes up, is a real advantage. Dave also wants to work, stating that he "would go buggy" if he had nothing to do, and likes the variety of job assignments. Nevertheless, working at $5.80 an hour is definitely not a financial sideline, and one does wonder whether Dave really would turn down a decent full-time job if he had the option.

While some workers may be voluntary members of a temporary labour pool (for now), and may be with THL only for weeks at a time, others work there for many years. "Ron" had been with THL for a year and a half. He "almost" has Grade 12 and lives with his girlfriend in Halifax. He had worked a number of jobs with THL, for some months as a labourer at a local manufacturing and distribution plant, and setting up and taking down trade displays for a local firm, and similar work at the convention centre, for $6 an hour at the manufacturing plant (since heavy lifting was involved), and for $5.80

an hour in the other jobs. His major aim in life is to acquire a full-time job, but he can't get one.

At both the manufacturing plant and the convention centre, Ron was employed alongside permanent unionized workers who were making over twice his hourly wage rate. He noted that some such workers had been hired on permanently, after initially working for these employers as THL temporaries. In the manufacturing plant, Ron was hired to satisfy temporary surges in labour demand in conjunction with shipments, but his hiring could also be seen as a case of the firm trying to evade the high hourly wage rates of permanent employees. The work in setting up and taking down exhibitions is inherently more subject to surges. Indeed, the week before the interview, Ron worked sixty-three hours, receiving time-and-a-half overtime pay for hours in excess of forty-eight (the first time this had occurred since he had started working for THL).

Ron's main objective is to get hired on full time. He figures that if he can establish a good work reputation, employers will ask for him by name from THL and when a permanent vacancy becomes available he may have some chance at a primary labour market job. He also realizes that he needs some sort of trade, and needs to finish Grade 12 so that he can gain access to vocational training, but he is vague as to why he has not done so. For the time being, he continues to hope that he is working his way up the queue of marginal workers, by taking work whenever it is offered and establishing a reputation with a few employers as a "good worker."

Although articulate and personable, the industrial workers wore jeans and T-shirts — not exactly "dress for success." For a person who dropped out of school at age fourteen, Dave demonstrated a remarkable concern for the long-run future, talking about his retirement years and claiming to have investments in RRSPs. But Ron had no extra income from any other source and was clearly not exaggerating when he said he had nothing in the bank, ever. Indeed, he made a remarkable effort to get to work, since he had no car, and often had to hitchhike to remote job sites, like the exhibition grounds, getting up very early in order to be there at 7 A.M. His goal in life, simply put, is to get a full-time job at a decent wage.

Ron is also typical of an interesting aspect of the unemployment insurance system. As soon as he has established eligibility, he opens a claim with the UIC and then declares any days of work for THL. Although his earnings while on claim are implicitly taxed at an extremely high rate (earnings in excess of twenty-five per cent of benefits per week are deducted, dollar for dollar, from his UI cheque), these earnings are also building up entitlement to his next UI claim. For example, he was on UI claim most of the year before our interview while working at THL, which established his qualifying weeks for the claim that had just opened. In addition to building up claim entitlement for the future, he needs money now. At his level of income, he cannot afford to wait the two weeks required if he were to file a new claim for UI, and he does not know from one week to the next whether he will get work — being on UI claim means that he will at least get a minimum level of income in a week. He is clearly hoping that one of his temporary jobs will turn into something permanent. In the meantime, the UI system is really doing what it was intended to do (tiding a low-income worker over periods when no work is available), although it is not doing it in quite the way the program was originally designed (since there were few temporary help services in existence at that time).

Why do these workers not use the Canada Employment Centres to locate temporary jobs? Although the CEC system does not charge for its services, that does not mean that it minimizes search costs. Both men stated that THL is fast in responding when they phone up and say they are available for work, and there is none of the hassle involved in visiting the CEC centre and going through the interviewing process of a number of employers.

The two office-overload, clerical temporary help employees we interviewed also exemplified identifiable "types." One had been a secretary and worked full time ten years, before staying home for fifteen years and only working part time in a variety of jobs (art education, for example). Now that her kids are older, she wants to return to the labour force but does not want to work full time, full year, since family responsibilities plus full-time work totally exhausts the week. She also feels the need to renew her skills, given the revolution in word processing technology that has occurred in the past fifteen years. To this end, she has been taking night courses in things like WordPerfect, through continuing education, and wants to work a number of part-time jobs in order to build up her typing speed, acquire recent work experience for employment purposes, and become familiar with new technology. Her real objective is a permanent part-time (i.e. full days for part of the week) position, but lots of women want such jobs, and she finds them difficult to locate.

In the meantime, working with Temporary Help Ltd. enables her to sample a large number of full-time, but short-lived, employment situations. In a two-week assignment, she gets quite tired the second week, and afterwards has time to get caught up with the house, with the children and with her husband. At the time of the interview she was averaging two weeks work per month, largely meeting the peaks of work at banks as they prepare their monthly statements. Since she comes to work with her husband by car, she is geographically restricted to the central city area, but THL is apparently quite adept at finding assignments within her working range.

For some workers, the constraints of family responsibilities mean that they prefer flexibility in job duration or hours, or have particular conditions of employment. Temporary Help is then in the position of matching the preferences of the worker with an employer. Temporary Help eliminates the costs to a worker of job search, and the employee maintains the flexibility to work as and when desired, and can even refuse job assignments (once in a while).

All the workers were a bit ambivalent about the constantly changing nature of temporary assignments — on the one hand liking the variety, but also being a bit anxious of the prospect of the first day of a new job. However, in most cases employers are habitual users of temporary employment services, and workers in those situations usually know how to integrate temporary help into the work process. All of the respondents reported that THL was very pleasant to deal with, mentioning in particular the cheerfulness of the local office manager, at all hours of the day or night. They reported there was some flexibility if they turned down a particular work assignment — for example, one of them said he'd like to have his weekends off in the summer to visit his family, while another said she would not accept an assignment over March break, since her children would be home from school. There are some ways in which temporary work fits in with the needs and desires of workers.

However, the more general function of Temporary Help Ltd. is as a "waiting room" for the primary labour market. Most workers passing through the firm want a regular full-time job, and work as a temporary performs the function of "double screening." THL screens and selects temporary workers from the general pool of applicants, and those who will work at the wages offered must, of necessity, have a strong work ethic. Employing firms have an opportunity to look over workers at length, with no fuss about terminating an individual worker and no presumption that employment rights are being established. Conversely, young workers who are unsure as to what they want to do, or re-entrants to the labour market, also get some chance to sample employment situations. One of the functions which Temporary Help Ltd. performs in the labour market is to enable both workers and firms to acquire worker- and job-specific information, but the underlying reason for its existence is occupational segmentation within the firm, and the adoption of a "just-in-time" approach to personnel needs.

"International Hotel" — Top Dollar for a Classy Product?

No examination of the low-wage service sector would be complete without a case study from the hospitality industry. The firm we chose, an international hotel, is particularly interesting because it made the transition from one business era to another, and because it so clearly illustrates the limits on what good management can hope to achieve in the face of adverse business conditions.

The original hotel property was secured by its location adjacent to the rail terminus. Travellers, including many new immigrants to Canada, would complete their ship-board portion of the journey from Europe, the Middle East and Africa and board the train for points west. During the Second World War the adjacent docks became the shipping-out point for troops bound for war-ridden Europe. Anyone stepping off the train would be awed by the immenseness of the hotel — a brick monolith rising ten stories above the station, whose grand foyer and polished walnut front desk bespoke elegance. For many years the hotel was home to royalty, the wealthy, and political leaders. It had the only ballroom in the city and every social event of worth took place there. Until the 1970s, before the restaurant trade exploded, it boasted one of the few "Four Star" dining rooms in the area.

However, tied as closely as it was to the railway, the grand old hotel faded in step with the decline of rail travel, as air and automobile travel overtook the train. Poor performance gave way to a succession of owners, all seemingly less interested in or capable of renewing the property than the previous. In the 1980s, new owners, by acquiring the hotel at a distress price, focused on revitalization from renovation, links to a major international hotel chain through management agreements, marketing to the new class of business traveller, and careful training and re-training of its employees. As with many hotel renovations in the last decade, California style prevailed — brass, greenery, pastel colours and chintz — an attempt to internationalize the decor and recreate the large hotel ambience, while retaining and restoring the tone of an era gone by. In all facets of the hotel's operation, there was a conscious effort to combine the best of the old with the success of the new, using a technology/service quality mix that adeptly repositioned the hotel and changed the way its employees operated within it.

Information is key to success in the hotel business, and franchising provides both access to industry-specific technology and name recognition. In a market of national travellers, the identity of an individual property has little meaning except to a local market. On the other hand, a brand name conveys meaning to travellers from any area, and suggests the kind, degree, and probable cost of the services available. The link to an international hotel chain, with its array of services — referral and reservations systems, design expertise, operating procedures, and cost control — was achieved by way of a management contract. In exchange for a fixed percentage of gross sales, a percentage of net income, some defined portion of the improved financial results, and agreement to renovate and operate to an external standard, the national chain provided management expertise and access to the brand name and associated services.

One of the most significant changes for International Hotel was labour shedding. Employment dropped from 450 two decades ago and 350 as recently as 10 years back, to a stable work force of 135, and a peak of 215 when occupancy was running at 100 per cent. It has become normal in the hotel business for temporary chamber maids to be called in, in order of their seniority, to clean and prepare rooms as and when rooms are occupied. Any instability in hotel occupancy rates is, therefore, immediately passed along to the earnings of workers. Maids want to work their way up the seniority ladder and get more hours of work, but for those with low seniority who are continually subject to lost days of work, reliance on a running unemployment insurance claim can (as at Temporary Help) put a floor to weekly income. However, even with substantial casualization of the work force, the hotel was exposed to cost pressures since a stable (minimum) work force was required whether occupancy was sixty per cent or twenty per cent, and occupancy rates in the industry spiralled downwards throughout the recession.

Elimination of specialization, cross-classification, and re-training of staff allowed International to shed workers. In the past, room service was a specialized and separately staffed area, but work was reorganized so that the room service attendant served breakfasts, staffed the restaurants of the hotel, and spent "downtime" periods stocking mini-bars and refrigerators in the guest rooms. Similar rotations occurred in other areas: telephone operators, front desk personnel and parking office attendants were all interchangeable; the general cashier maintained payroll records; data processing clerks assisted in front office accounting; maintenance was no longer staffed by the ticketed (specialized) trades but by multi-skilled "property management engineers." In past years the hotel operated three kitchens with specialized cooks to prepare food for the various service units (breakfast, gourmet dining, banquets); this was replaced by one central kitchen, linked to a sophisticated information system for ordering, supplying the entire hotel.

Venturing into the "back of the house," one was immediately struck by the amount and sophistication of computer technology driving the operation. Management maintained that computer technology in the hotel improved efficiency and cost effectiveness of operations by doing jobs better, faster, and with fewer errors. The major improvement in operations attributable to technology was computerized "total property management," a sophisticated system linking together point-of-sale units, call accounting, room management, telephone systems, payroll, and energy management. The drive to a high-tech environment improved guest service through accurate, faster dissemination of information (including room status reports, mini-bar stocks, and specific guest requirements), improved internal operational controls by adding a level of standardization that is difficult to establish and maintain in a manual system, and generally improved operational efficiency, reduced payroll, and eliminated outside service costs.

With a modern management information system, food costing can be done daily (as opposed to the old monthly, and often inaccurate, traditional system) by tracking sales in the food service units against kitchen inventory use monitored by scanning devices. Labour costs can also be assessed daily, since the work hours of each employee are input by way of cash register or time recording device linked to a central computer.

Standardization and computer technology may be the route to lower costs in the back of the house, but personal service and individualized attention is the route to higher prices. International Hotel wanted to be able to charge a premium price for a "quality" product, but "quality" in the hotel business is much more than simply a clean room and a bed with a firm mattress. The contradiction at work at International Hotel was the interplay between the drive for efficiency and a resulting standardization of operations, and the provision of quality, personal customer service.

Throughout our case studies, in both the goods and the service sectors, we often heard firms saying they wanted to improve "quality," but what exactly is "quality"? The Multiburger case study was an example of industrialization of service for consistency and reduced costs. When all procedures are rigorously standardized, the result is "quality" in the sense of cleanliness and total consistency. Low customization and low interaction with the customer mean low production costs, which are crucial when competition is based on low prices. Standardization also allows the services to be cloned. As we saw with Retail Clone Inc., standardization is the principal strategy for many chain operations. However, in the hotel business the effects can be unanticipated and undesirable.

Hotel services can become so standardized that they lose the ability to interact with the customer. In hotels, especially expensive ones, a guest expects some sort of interaction and personalization of service, but training is often scripted, with staff told to respond in certain ways to given situations. For example, one evening a guest, upon arriving at International Hotel, noticed a band setting up in the lobby, and asked the desk clerk what was happening. The clerk replied that he did not know. The guest asked who would know, and the clerk replied that the assistant manager would likely know, and he proceeded to complete the check-in routine for the guest. The clerk then handed the guest his key and stated that "if there was anything he could do to make the guest's stay more enjoyable, please let him know." The guest stared him in the eye and retorted that the one thing the clerk could do to make his stay more enjoyable would be to answer his earlier request: find out what the band was doing setting up in the lobby. Shocked out of his scripted routine, the clerk went to find someone who might answer the guest's question.

Management contended that the ability of International's staff to respond in a personalized service-oriented manner was met through continual training and retraining. A training-needs assessment was done locally every year, and apparent needs were addressed through professional development programs provided by the international chain head office. Although some of this training may have produced a superficial "have a nice day" style of interaction, the emphasis on learned skills must be contrasted with a time in the industry when virtually no training was done on a continuing basis and most skills were learned on the job.

Employees at International Hotel were particularly ambiguous about the role of the union at International. The union monitored wage rates in the industry and bargained the monetary side of the contract, but had little impact on work practices otherwise. The many changes in the number and character of the work force in the past ten years were not delayed by the union's opposition. Wage rates were high for the industry but management had no qualms in paying them, since they trained for quality and service.

Again, as at Sally Servant, we found many employees who regarded their jobs as "professions" and themselves as professionals. "Joe the Bartender" was illustrative. Joe had been with International Hotel for forty-one years, his entire "career." He glided effortlessly through the bar providing exceptional service, similar to that in the most exclusive of urban private clubs. This was his private venue, and customers were remembered by what they drank and when. Joe provided the complete service, from order to preparation, to service. Even when unknown, the customer was made to feel part of the place, drawn in by Joe's individualized greetings and manners. Quality of service was reflected in uniform, grooming, sound, and professionalism. Clearly, the aim for management is to have all employees "buy into" the hotel business in this way, which, it is argued, takes intelligence and consistent goal-setting, attitude rather than aptitude.

Although International Hotel did succeed in offering a high standard of personalized service, it was also operating a large hotel during a major recession. When we interviewed at the hotel in 1992, business travel was down substantially due to the recession and tourism had not recovered from the high exchange rates of 1989–1991. Vacancy rates in the city as a whole were high, and each hotel in town was competing furiously for market share. But when there are not enough travellers to fill the available rooms, all that an individual hotel can do is take business away from its competitors. International Hotel kept going for another year, but closed in late 1993, laying off all but a handful of maintenance workers.

Conclusion

As the diversity of our case studies illustrates, there is a wide variety of jobs in the low-wage service sector, but instability is a common dimension. Short-run fluctuations in demand are passed along in casual or part-time work that is neither guaranteed nor well paid. As a result, outside of a core staff, the insecurity of employment is very high.

In Temporary Help Ltd., Sally Servant, and Retail Clone Inc., most of the new jobs are held by female, part-time and young employees, within highly segmented occupational structures. A significant proportion of jobs do not have career ladders, because they involve either casual or highly repetitive work. In all these industries — retailing, hotels and catering, temporary help, personal services — pay levels are, in general, low.

In the low-wage service sector, the capability of the computer to collect and analyze work-flow information has enabled employers to expand their use of part-time employees. For example, at Retail Clone Inc., modern point-of-sale computers enable management to estimate with considerable accuracy daily, weekly, and monthly variations in requirements for sales people, which makes it easier to make more extensive use of part-time personnel. These workers can be scheduled for minimum (or maximum) blocks of four hours work around peak periods in the day, week, or month. In addition, the record-keeping and scheduling necessitated by an employment strategy of having large numbers of part-time staff has been facilitated through the use of computers.

The rise of the service sector has increased the importance of part-time workers and the growth of part-time employment. Manufacturing work is typically driven by capital equipment which must be used in a coordinated sequence to create the product, hence the work force is typically organized by full-time shifts. By contrast, service industry work can be effectively, and often desirably, organized on a part-time basis. Because limited training means firms have little invested in workers, job security in the service sector is extremely low by comparison with the traditional job security provided in manufacturing and resources. There are typically few unions, no licensing requirements, and few work rules. The large number of small firms, the absence of unionization, and the large proportion of part-time work mean that employment in this sector is virtually unsheltered.

Some of the employment growth in the service sector, especially in the low-wage sector, may reflect simply the shifting of existing service functions, such as the sub-contracting of professional services or janitorial and clerical activities from one industry to another. This "unbundling" helps to explain some of the increase in employment for the lower-wage consumer and producer service industries. Organizations switch from in-house staff to outside suppliers because specialized service firms can often offer lower costs or higher quality through specialization or economies of scale. Companies also unbundle to cope with fluctuating work force requirements. Rather than staffing their operations with enough permanent employees for peak demands, many companies now staff with just enough permanent employees to handle the average load and hire temporary workers at peak production or sales periods. Just as many companies in recent years have adopted just-in-time inventory practices, many seem also willing to adopt just-in-time personnel practices to meet any surges in demand.

The social implication is that access to jobs that carry the chance of moving upward into attractive career paths has been significantly diminished. New technology has brought about an increased gulf between a homogenous group of low-skill, low-wage, part-time workers and a core group of permanent full-time career employers. Many jobs once performed by workers as they moved up an occupational hierarchy, starting at the bottom of the career ladder, have now disappeared. Job ladders within a firm or industry have often been lost, and many workers now enter a firm at specific levels based on the skills and training they bring with them, and stay there.

People hired into upper level jobs may have career potential, but the remainder do not. The people who are forced to rely on low-paid, insecure and part-time work are also often forced to rely on transfer payments through unemployment insurance or social assistance; indeed, whole industries are becoming dependent on the idea that transfer payments are there to finance their work force during the times when they are not needed by firms. The problems this situation creates are not limited to those who lack the marketable skills now critical for employability and success. The working poor are the people who must live with the consequences of firms' just-in-time labour strategies. They bear the biggest share of the burden of insecurity that dominates the low-wage service sector, but all taxpayers share in the costs, through UI and social assistance.

One cannot really expect these trends to greater insecurity and increased transfer dependence to be reversed, unless macroeconomic policy — especially monetary policy — starts to emphasize more rapid growth in aggregate output and employment.

4

Information Services

In the 1991 Census, 71.57 per cent of the experienced Canadian labour force reported that they worked in one of the service industries; in 1986, 68.9 per cent worked in the service industries, while in 1946 only 40 per cent of the labour force did.[1] The trend to increased employment in the service industries is very clear, but service industries are very diverse, including fast food production and consulting, engineering and legal advice. As conventionally defined, the service sector includes both the computer programmer and the waitress. Service sector jobs may have the tenured security of university professors or the day-to-day insecurity of the temporary help agency work force. Pay may be as high as that of a plastic surgeon or as low as the minimum wage received at "maid for a day" housecleaning firms.

Chapter 3 looked at the low-wage service firms; this chapter will examine the glamorous part of the service sector — relatively high-wage firms that specialize in the production of information. However, we need to start with a caution. Since this book examines a series of case studies of firms, it is natural to organize the discussion by broad industrial category of firm, but the shift to an "information economy" is largely embedded *within* industries, and *within* firms.[2] In most industries, the occupational structure of employment is shifting, and an increasing percentage of the labour force is employed in the managerial/professional/technical group of occupations. In only five years, these occupations increased their share of all jobs from 26.9 per cent in 1986 to 30.0 per cent in 1991. Not only are firms employing more people in the occupations that process information; job duties are also changing within occupations, as, for example, when secretaries shift from routine copy typing to increasingly complex wordprocessing and desktop publishing.

Our case studies have already noted the increasing importance of information in many industries. For example, although there is no older occupation than that of "farmer," our case study of "Modern Farms" demonstrated how important up-to-date knowledge of international trends in marketing and crop technology are for the survival of niche agricultural producers. Within the manufacturing sector, computerized machinery is a prominent feature of the new technology in use at pulp and paper mills and at textile mills, as well as at aerospace manufacturing plants.

We stress this point because although this chapter will focus on the firms that specialize in information production, we do not want to create the impression that the "information economy" is a distinct sector; rather, we think that the transition to an information-based economy is a general phenomenon which permeates all industries. Furthermore, even within the firms that specialize in information production, there is a distinct difference between what is happening to people whose job has been to transfer or store information in routine ways (keypunch operators in computer centres, for example) and people whose job it is to solve nonroutine problems (for instance, computer programmers). Increasingly, computerization and information technology are replacing the routine jobs of the information sector — bank clerks are being replaced by automatic teller machines and voice mail is substituting for receptionists. Much of what is going on in the information economy represents a shift in the occupational structure of employment within firms as much as between firms.

In Chapters 1 and 2 we pointed to the loss of jobs in resource industries in rural Canada and to the disappearance, in both manufacturing and resource industries, of jobs that require heavy physical labour. Historically, these were mainly male jobs that did not demand advanced educational credentials. Expanding employment in the information services sector has not replaced these jobs, in part because knowledge services usually require advanced educational credentials and in part because the new jobs of the information economy are in the wrong place.

Overwhelmingly, the new jobs created in the information services sector have been city jobs. Improvements in telecommunications have made it easier for firms to centralize white collar employment. Banks, for example, have created centralized data processing facilities to replace the thousands of bookkeeping jobs that used to exist in bank branches all over the country, when bank branches employed clerks to manually type accounting entries into the financial records.

In the early days of the telecommunications/computer revolution, there was a degree of technological optimism about the possibility that telecommunications could also work to encourage a diffusion of jobs from the city to the country. However, although futurists used to paint a rosy picture of lawyers living on the farm and submitting court documents by fax, it has become increasingly clear that only a limited number of major urban centres in Canada have been able to attract the better paid jobs of the information services sector. National metropolitan areas (Toronto, Montreal and Vancouver) and regional centres (Edmonton, Calgary, Winnipeg, Quebec City and Halifax) have benefitted disproportionately from the structural shift in total employment towards knowledge and information services production.

With good telecommunications and rapid air travel, jobs in the information services sector have become fairly footloose. But although these jobs could often be in any of the major urban centres, they cannot easily transfer to rural areas. Big cities have many advantages. Face-to-face contact remains important for specialized professionals and, in many professions, a "critical mass" of people is only available in larger centres. Advertising agencies, for example, use a network of sub-contractors to help produce their product (graphic artists for print work, camera crews for TV ads). Unless there is a certain volume of business, these specialized sub-trades cannot survive, and if they are not available when needed, the ad agency cannot survive either. Larger centres also have cultural amenities and the greater opportunities of a larger labour market for the employment of both husband and wife. Transportation links make it far easier to service national and international markets from a metropolitan hub. For all these reasons, it is hard to move the information service sector to rural areas.

These macro trends in occupational and industrial shifts and the greater urbanization of employment can all be observed in aggregate statistics.[3] Aggregate data can also reveal an increasing number of firms that specialize in the production of information services, and the rising importance of information services in international trade. Since jobs in managerial/professional/technical occupations and in firms that specialize in information production tend to be relatively well paid, Canadians would like to have more of them. Since jobs are being lost in goods production and jobs in the personal service sector tend to be low-wage and insecure, Canadians would like employment in the information sector to expand relatively rapidly, in order to absorb the unemployed and underemployed of other sectors. However, the limitation of aggregate statistics on macro change is that such statistics cannot reveal *why* it is that some information sector firms are successful, and it is for this reason that we turn to our case studies.

In the information service sector, we observed many of the same managerial themes as in the manufacturing and resources sector. Managers in both sectors used the same jargon, and for much the same reasons. The same sort of paradigm shift is in evidence, as senior management attempts to eliminate layers of middle management, by devolving responsibility to "empowered" workers. There is the same emphasis on "quality," but there is also often an even greater difficulty in the service sector in defining exactly what "high quality" actually is.

Many writers (such as the Economic Council of Canada, 1991) have pointed to a "convergence" between goods and services. The classic definition of a "good," as opposed to a "service," is that goods are tangible, storable and can be produced without direct interaction between producer and consumer, while services are defined as the opposite (i.e. intangible, perishable, requiring direct contact). However, to an increasing degree goods are sold along with a bundle of services (for example, automobiles are sold with a new car warranty and roadside service). New types of production (computer software stored on a disk, for instance) may be difficult to classify as a good or as a service. Services and goods are often sold together because sophisticated capital equipment (such as the coal shearer we saw in action at Coal Mine Co. or the computer-controlled machining stations we observed at Aerospace Manufacturing) depends on the computer software that guides its operation, and the maintenance and service contract that ensures its dependable functioning.

Since goods and services are increasingly being bundled together, it is not surprising to observe in services the same emphasis on organizational change and quality improvement we observed in the goods sector. However, given the potential for ambiguity in the definition of quality in services production, it becomes especially important to ensure that service workers are highly motivated. As a result, movements like "total quality management" can acquire an intensity which is almost religious. (One of the offices we visited was clearly in the middle of a campaign with banners flying above every desk, and lapel buttons on every jacket, all proclaiming the desire to serve the customer effectively.) Along with the total quality movement, there is a new emphasis on "delayering" organizations by cutting out levels of supervision.

In large organizations, this new managerial paradigm of a flat-team structure can lead to the elimination of scores, sometimes hundreds, of middle-management positions. Top corporate decision-makers may refer to this as the empowerment of production workers, but empowerment only works if production workers come to think of themselves as "professionals," who derive job satisfaction from independently deciding to do what the company wants them to do.

In the old system of hierarchical supervision, each manager might only supervise five or six subordinates. When the span of control is five or six people, fairly detailed supervision of subordinates is possible, but a limited span of control may also require many layers of supervision in the hierarchy. When organizations cut out layers of middle managers, the channels of communication from top to bottom become much more direct, but the managers that remain have many more people reporting to them.

In order to be successful, therefore, the new managerial philosophy requires workers who can work independently, and who can be depended on to do so. This means that the motivation of workers is now the crucial issue. In order to be sure of this, sophisticated firms are practising an unprecedented degree of intervention in the formation of worker attitudes. In some respects the process can be most clearly observed in small firms — and our interviews with "Quality Architects" provided a classic example.

"Quality Architects" — Quality Assurance in a Custom Product

In Canada, there are about 3,200 architectural firms, with a total of approximately 11,500 employees. The vast majority of architects work in one- or two-person partnerships; there are only a handful of large (fifty plus) firms. Although "Quality Architects" is one of the larger architectural firms in the local area, with thirteen employees (eight architects, three technicians, a comptroller and a secretary/receptionist), it is a small firm by most other standards.

Architectural firms are small because they provide a very customized service, and because very few clients have an ongoing need for repeat business. Historically, architects specialized in the conceptual design of buildings, with the details left to others. The president and founder of Quality Architects caustically refers to this period as the era of the pinstripe architect with the silver cane. In the old days, firms employed a whole retinue of draftspeople to turn design ideas into specifications (and laid most of them off when the job was done). The architect conceived the grand design, but he left all the detail of actual construction to others, and although much of the firm's work was repetitive, there was no formal mechanism for ensuring quality control.

As long as buildings were fairly simple and as long as clients were not terribly sophisticated, architects could continue to function in this manner. However, modern buildings contain a whole set of sophisticated systems. Some, like electronic fibre optic networks, are entirely new types of systems, while others, like fire control or heating and cooling systems, have become computer monitored and operated. In addition, there are the traditional mechanical systems, such as the elevators, the plumbing, and so on. Some people have referred to the meshing of sensor systems, computer controls and service systems as defining a new era of "smart buildings" that can automatically regulate heating, lighting and other functions. In building design, as in all the other industries we studied, modern technology has created new potential for optimizing functions and minimizing costs. For most people, however, these advances are largely invisible. Since the various systems of a modern building are usually hidden behind the plaster, the users of buildings really only notice them when they malfunction. But building owners increasingly demand assurances that their multimillion-dollar investments will function as specified, and architects are increasingly being held legally liable for the expenses if they do not.

The market place has, therefore, become much more demanding, and architectural technology has changed dramatically. A dozen years ago, Quality Architects had between thirty and thirty-three persons in the firm handling ten to twelve projects at a time. In 1980 they made a major investment in computer work stations, which paid off in increased credibility and reliability for clients, and in the ability to handle the same volume of work with half the number of employees.

Before computerization, each project had a lead architect, a back-up architect, a senior technician and two or three draftspeople. There was a hierarchical organization of work, in which the client verbally communicated his requirements to the lead architect, who passed designs to support staff for the manual production of drawings. However, since the repetitive detail of drawings can now be stored in computer memory and specifications can be directly converted into images, there are far fewer jobs today for support personnel.

If computerized drafting were the only change, architectural firms would simply have laid off workers. But buyers now also demand higher standards in such things as energy conservation, maintenance costs, wheel chair accessibility, etc. Older buildings were "fault tolerant" — since the design was much less carefully optimized, waste was built in, in all these functions, and this had the saving grace that a small error in one function did not interfere much with other functions. However, if heating costs are to be minimized, all air leaks must be sealed, which means the ventilation system must now be much more carefully designed to vent dangerous fumes and recirculate clean air, and the amount of heat generated in the building has to be very carefully calculated. Since modern buildings have become much more complex, the potential cost of misunderstandings in the design process has increased. The meshing of specialized systems therefore increases the need for teams (a partner, a project architect and a technician) to work together to provide the assortment of skills the modern building demands.

One of the innovations of Quality Architects is the development of an explicit, CSA-approved quality assurance program. The objective is to document every single step of the process of design and construction of buildings and to certify that each step has been performed exactly to specification. Historically, builders tended to leave some details to be filled in as they went along, and to make adjustments as necessary. This method of operation more or less made sense, as a way of economizing on design time, when the various systems of a building were not finely intermeshed. However, filling in the details later can also mean that the cost of construction can easily go over budget. Most new buildings have also needed a period of "debugging" before they operate correctly. The quality assurance program in architecture aims at providing for building construction the same certifiably zero-defect product and assured cost that the aerospace industry has long demanded. Quality Architects is pioneering this field, with the expectation that large corporate and government landlords cannot afford the uncertainty involved in current construction methods. Although they do not expect that they will be able to prevent imitation, they do think that their experience in quality control will give them a four- to five-year lead on potential competitors.

At Quality Architects, the president (and principal shareholder) asserts that the prime asset of the firm is its people. Since architects have always had the option of splitting off and forming their own firms, it has always been necessary to maintain the individual morale of professional colleagues. The growing interdependence of specialists in project teams has, however, greatly increased the importance of maintaining a team commitment to corporate goals, on the part of both architects and technicians. (Since the repetitive aspects of drafting have been computerized, the technician's role is now considerably more skilled.) In part, a commitment to company goals is encouraged by employee participation in ownership. With one exception, all the current employees are shareholders who participate in the gains when the company does well.

When the recession hit, however, new commercial construction almost ceased, and with it much of the demand for architectural services. In order to maintain team morale, and prevent the departure of key employees, Quality Architects followed a policy of equal sharing of the pain of the downturn in business. All employees, including the founder, participated in work-sharing — initially with a twenty per cent, and subsequently with a forty per cent, reduction in salary, partly offset by UI benefits, through the Unemployment Insurance "Work-Sharing" program.

It is clear that the firm's founder could have coped with the recession in the traditional way — by laying off some workers and keeping the remainder on (including himself) at full salary. We do not think he chose to share the pain because he is some sort of altruistic angel. Rather, we think that he recognized the new reality of team production. Since the productivity of the team depends in large measure on the quality of interaction among its members, productivity depends on group cohesiveness and high morale; these cannot be maintained if some people are exposed to the risks of the market place while others remain protected.

For the most part, equal sharing of the losses of the recession was successful in maintaining a team of valued employees. However, Quality Architects is not really an egalitarian operation. It is clear that the founder, and principal shareholder, still retains substantial authority within the firm. It is also clear that when hiring he selects employees who will fit into a team environment; he prefers players of team sports, like soccer or hockey, rather than prima donna individualists (he used the example of tennis players). Team building at Quality Architects involves a new level of conscious intervention in the goal-setting of individual employees. At Quality Architects the pressures from the market place for greater quality and the changing hard technology of computer workstations are combined with a whole new soft technology of motivational and organizational strategies.

The firm's founder sees himself as the coach of the team, the conductor, the person responsible for communicating the firm's vision by strategic planning and the development of each person's commitment and understanding. However, "coach" is a very active role. The firm has a corporate mission statement, as well as more specific goals and objectives for each of its constituent parts. Each individual has a personal development plan, mostly work related, which specifies results to be achieved. The plan is re-visited monthly and there is also an annual assessment. Staff score themselves in relation to the plan, and review it with others, and with the firm's founder. All this material is written up and kept in a loose leaf binder in the employee coffee area, so that everybody is aware of the goals and achievements of everybody else. Today's workplace clearly demands much more involvement than was typical ten years ago — it is not just a place where one is expected to show up from 9 to 5.

From the firm's point of view, investment in computerization, the organization of work in project teams, and conscious involvement in worker motivation has paid off — the company survived a recession that bankrupted many other architectural firms, and its order book is now recovering. For employees, the firm offers interesting, relatively well-paid work, with some assurance that the cost of any future downturns in business will be shared among all employees through short-time working, rather than concentrated on a few laid-off individuals.

The only disquieting trend that some might discern is the loss of worker autonomy. In the old system, the lack of conscious design in the soft technology of the workplace did at least mean that the workplace had some space for the tennis-player type individualists, as well as for the team players. The new sophistication of soft technology has benefits for the firm, but costs for those who are not selected.

"Telecom Company" — Delayering at a "Good Employer"

At "Telecom Company" the new religion of total quality commitment was also much in evidence. There was the same emphasis on a team approach to identifying and satisfying customer needs and there was the same formalized goal-setting procedure for individual "empowered" employees. But Telecom Company is a large employer, with several hundred employees, which has long had a deserved reputation as a "good employer." The interesting thing about the telecommunications industry is the way technological change and the pressures of competition have interacted to produce very significant changes in what a "good employer" now does and how it operates.

The telecommunications industry in Canada was historically organized as a collection of provincial monopolies, which were regulated as separate public utilities. Cooperation between provincial companies was made easier by the fact that they did not compete directly for customers and they had to cooperate technically to provide long distance service. They also depended on a common dominant supplier of hardware. Diffusion of new technology was, therefore, fairly rapid. Telecommunications is a new industry, characterized by very rapid technological change, and by the necessity to plan ahead of demand in order to have infrastructure in place when new customers demand phone service. Rapid technical change, the need for common standards, for cooperation and for advance planning, plus a protected local monopoly position — all this tended to produce an "engineering culture," in which the general expectation is that there is "one right way" to do things. If there is one right way to do things, but technical change is continuous and rapid, there is a continuous need for training to ensure that workers are always being brought up to date. Training has, therefore, long played a major role at Telecom Company. All craft and clerical workers get at least two weeks classroom training per year in addition to the two months training new employees initially receive. Some training programs are designed internally, and some are bought in from outside suppliers (the actual amount depending on the pace and type of new product and technology development). However, one gets an idea of the extensiveness of training from the fact that service representatives have an initial course of five weeks and that one training facility (at which trainee linesman are instructed in the correct way to climb a utility pole) has thirty permanently employed trainers.

The old news about Telecom Company is that it has long been a good employer with a strongly established training culture. Along with continuous training, the company historically provided good pay, employment security and a full range of employee fringe benefits (such as an early retirement option with full pension after thirty years, and an employee stock purchase plan with twenty-five per cent matching company contribution). Employee loyalty was maintained through such traditional mechanisms as an annual honourary dinner for employees with twenty-five years service and the informal promise of summer jobs for the children of employees. In addition, the company was alert to wider social demands — for twenty years it has been working actively with the Human Rights Commission and the local black community on outreach programs to encourage qualified applications for employment.

Telecom Company clearly wants to continue to be a good employer, but being a good employer in the 1990s requires significant organizational change. To a very large extent, telecommunications companies are, today, managers of large, sophisticated computer software systems. In the past, wires had to be added or removed in order to add or delete circuits or to connect individual subscribers. Now, a dedicated cable goes to each household and the telephone connection is activated and deactivated by computer. Administrative and operational systems are being integrated so that a subscriber's order will be automatically transferred both through the switching department and to the billing system and repair systems. This central, computerized assignment of cables eliminates an entire occupational category (assignment clerks) and totally alters the skills needed by repair personnel.

In the past, technicians had to have electromechanical skills to connect and repair switching gear. Today, repairs involve either software or electronic problems. New software enables analogue signals to be converted into digital format, and to be compressed so that one line can simultaneously handle several transmissions. This new technology saves both capital and labour, while the labour that remains requires a whole new set of skills.

The job of a telephone operator provides a particularly clear example of technical change in telecommunications — and, in general, of the interdependent four-cornered problem of modern managers of balancing hard and soft technology and of maintaining both low cost and high quality. As in manufacturing, some of the change is highly visible. In the lobby of the Telecom building there are black and white pictures of the rooms of operators who used to connect calls by manually plugging connections into a "cord board." In those days, in a very real sense the local telephone operator sat at the "hub of the community" and knew exactly who was calling whom, for how long and why.

Over the years, however, new technology has drastically changed the content of the telephone operator's job, as well as significantly increasing its stress level. Initially, electromechanical switching systems only replaced the need for operators to manually connect local calls. The number of operator positions shrank with the introduction of long distance direct dialling. Jobs also disappeared when a computerized voice began to answer information requests and deal with reversing the charges on long distance calls. Today, a small anonymous box houses a computer that can do most of the jobs that rooms of operators used to do.

There still are telephone operators at Telecom Co., but they handle a lot more calls, with a lot more stress, than they used to. In the days of manual switchboards, operators handled approximately 150 calls per day, compared to 700 to 1,000 calls per day now. With manual switchboards, the time taken to deal with an average call was approximately sixty seconds, compared to twenty-three seconds today. The capability of computer systems to route calls to unoccupied operators has minimized the amount of down time (now about five per cent). In addition to increasing the pace of work, automatic feeding of calls to operators has led to a loss of control of the worker over the work process; in the old days the operator used to control 100 per cent of the call, but now the caller does most of the work and the operator only intervenes to obtain specific information. This loss of control over time and discretion means that the operator is really "automated" in a machine-driven work process. As well, more and more of the routine aspects of operator services are assumed by computer technology.

Because routine calls are now handled by computer, the mix of calls operators encounter is now dominated by those with more critical operator interventions — for example, crisis events such as fires. Consequently, the introduction of computer technology implies both a decrease in the amount of contact customers have with employees of Telecom Company, and an increase in the stress level of the average call. Because of this, the quality of the remaining customer contact has become much more crucial to customer satisfaction, as well as being much more difficult to maintain. Increased labour productivity (in the purely technical sense of number of calls handled per day) therefore runs the risk of decreasing the perceived quality (in terms of customer satisfaction) of the remaining functions provided by operators.

If customers had no options, it would not matter much to the profits of Telecom Company if stressed-out operators provided brusque and abrupt service. However, the long distance telecommunications market is being opened up to competition. Since long distance calls provide fifty per cent of total revenue and the profits necessary to subsidize the low revenues obtained on local service to household subscribers, telecommunications companies across Canada are scrambling to re-orient themselves.

Telecom Company does not aspire to compete solely on the basis of low prices in the new competitive environment for telecommunications services. The objective is, rather, to be a high-quality service provider and to benefit from the premium in prices that high quality will enable. However, this marketing strategy forces the company to examine carefully what exactly "high quality" is and what labour strategy is consistent with "high quality."

The same new switching technology is available to all firms and, because of its technical advantages, it is being used by everyone. However, a high-quality telecommunications service is more than simply a static-free phone call. The objective at Telecom Company is customer satisfaction with the totality of the customer's relationship with the firm (i.e. customer satisfaction with the courtesy and helpfulness of staff, with the speed and effectiveness of repairs required, with anticipation of customer needs for new types of service, as well as with price).

In part, the labour strategy at Telecom Co. involves an attempt to create interdepartmental quality improvement teams and involve the union more directly in adaptation to change. In part, the company is also backing away from the full utilization of technical change, in recognition of its human impact.

Computer technology creates the potential for much closer monitoring of the average wait time of operator response, but the company claims to have backed away from detailed monitoring of response time of individual operators, based on the perception that such monitoring hurts the quality of service. Operators are urged to "take the time to deal with the customer's problem," since the automation of much of the operator's historic role means that a far higher proportion of calls nowadays represent serious problems and the operator (plus the telephone installer) represent the major human contact customers have with the company. The company does state that it will intervene if response time is "way out of whack" but it is recognized that too close a focus on the technical efficiency of production (average wait time) will produce lower "quality," i.e. brusque operators and bad customer relations.

As well, the company's engineering mindset has produced a "scientific" response to the problem of increased job stress. Consultants have been hired to analyze the ergonomics of the operator's job; a six-day training course (in ten modules) has been designed to teach operators to recognize body stresses and provide exercises to relieve muscular and psychological stress induced on the job. Operators are limited to two hours at a time at the board, are increasingly being used for sales functions, and are being trained in inter-personal skills and stress management. The changing hard technology of computers and software has therefore produced changes in work roles and definitions, as job design is altered to balance both cost and "quality" considerations.

It is the combination of competitive pressures on both costs and quality of service that drives a fundamental rethinking of the labour strategy at Telecom Company. The "internal labour market" with a rigid hierarchy of positions was characteristic of good employers in the 1960s and 1970s, but this sort of job ladder does not seem able to cope adequately with the demands placed on the firm in the 1990s. The emphasis on training remains, as does an attempt to maintain employment security. Given that telecommunications is a very capital-intensive industry, wages and salaries are a relatively small item in total costs, and there is not much to be gained by following a low-wage strategy. Telecom Company expects to continue to be a relatively high-wage employer in the local labour market. Although there is a long queue of applicants for jobs (the personnel manager reported receiving eight thousand formal job applications in 1992 — actual hires were zero), there is no intention of cutting wages. The company expects to keep up with inflation, and then some, over the next five years. The same is true of Telecom Company's competitors, who pay about the same (plus, in some instances, a premium to attract trained employees away from Telecom Co.)

The route to profitability in telecommunications is not cutting wages but increasing productivity and improving quality. In order to achieve this, Telecom Company emphasizes flexibility in job assignment, team production, continuous quality improvement, the empowerment and multi-tasking of lower level workers, and the elimination of intermediate levels of middle management. But none of this will work if employees are not highly motivated at all levels of the company. In the old days, senior executives were expected to be motivated to go the extra mile for the company, but among blue collar workers there was a more relaxed attitude. The job of supervisors and middle managers was to ensure things didn't get too relaxed. Now that those layers of middle management are being eliminated, there is much more conscious and greater emphasis on all employees internalizing the firm's goals compared to the traditional internal labour markets of the 1970s.

An important part of the new regime is an attempt to restructure the collective bargaining relationship. There has only been one strike at the company (in 1975). Management and the union have generally accepted the pattern bargains struck at other public communications companies, and industrial relations have been generally peaceful. However, two years before our interviews, 120 workers were laid off in a corporate down-sizing. Since mass lay-offs had never occurred before, the union felt shocked and betrayed. Management claims that lay-offs were necessary because not enough workers (170) took early retirement. But since the lay-offs management has also begun a very conscious attempt to improve channels of communication with the union.

There are now consultation committees at the unit and district levels and the union hierarchy meets regularly with senior management. The company tries to provide advance notice of changes and to involve the union in a problem-solving approach to minimize the impact of technological change. There is a technological change clause in the collective agreement with a mandatory 120 days notice in writing of the nature, location and number of employees affected. Adaptation to technological change follows a sequence specified in the collective agreement (which also bans lay-offs that are the result of contracting out and restricts management's ability to replace regular employees by temporary workers).

The corporate strategy of Telecom Company involves new technology in switching gear and the training of installers in its repairs — as an emphasis on "hard technology" would predict. However, the strategy also involves two rounds of training courses in customer relations for installers and new methods of work organization for repair personnel. Since so much of the delivery of telecommunication services is now computerized, the phone installer (like the operator) is now seen as an important part of the human face of the company in customer relations. Phone installers are now being trained in customer skills, including how to accept criticism and deal with complaints, as well as how to sell customers on new services. Social skills are now a necessary part of the job.

Since basic residential telephone service is a money loser for the company, it is the new services to subscribers (such as call waiting or call forwarding) that are crucial for profitability. Once the computer code is written, in many cases the cost of providing the service to an additional customer is just the cost of changing the list of telephone numbers that activate the computer program — the revenue the service provides is almost entirely profit. However, the pace of technical change in telecommunications, from the computerization of standard telephone services to the introduction of digital cellular telephones and the growing list of functions the telephone line performs, mean that the sales function is more technically complex. One can, for example, program the phone company's computer to put two telephone numbers with different rings on the same line, but will it all still work if the subscriber installs a fax machine or an answering device or a voice mail box? Installers are now expected to know all this technical detail and have the social skills to sell and to handle complaints. Clearly, a temporary, low-paid work force cannot be expected to have the skills or the motivation the new design of jobs requires.

In addition, it is anticipated that installers and repair personnel will shortly be shifted to home dispatch. Significant savings in time can be realized if workers go directly to their job sites from home, and take the truck home with them in the evening. The company also benefits by the elimination of large work centres and the deletion of the expense of supervisory middle management. Workers benefit because less commuting time is involved, and they may be able to save the expense of an additional vehicle to get to work. Technically, home dispatch becomes feasible because computers and cellular telecommunications enable job assignments to be centrally organized and directly transmitted (blue prints can be sent directly to a mobile truck by cellular fax phone). The savings involved are particularly great in rural areas with widely dispersed service requirements. But this mode of operation may involve repair personnel working without direct supervision for weeks at a time; it will only work if employees internalize the company's goals and are willing to be flexible in their work roles.

One lesson from Telecom Company is that it is not good enough in the 1990s just to have the latest hard technology of fibre optics or computer switching gear. Realizing the full potential of new technology and new market opportunities also requires a new level of soft technology — substantial organizational change and a whole new motivational strategy — if the new "delayered" company is to deliver a quality product at premium prices.

Telecom Company continues to provide secure, well-paid jobs, but there are substantially fewer of them now than there were ten years ago. The company has always hired people with above-average educational qualifications, but the standard has gone up. In addition, there is a new emphasis on selecting more carefully for motivation and social skills — even in jobs like installing, which previously had little need for worker involvement or customer relations ability. In a variety of ways, therefore, Telecom jobs are now more demanding and more difficult to get than they used to be.

"Megabank" — Struggling to Change

Sometimes, a company's building (like a person's clothes) provides a clue to the firm's identity. Telecom Company has its offices in a bland and efficient downtown office tower, while Quality Architects (like the boutique, high-tech firm it is) finds its home in a converted Victorian mansion close to the university. The head office of "Megabank" leaves no doubt as to the impression it desires to convey. The venerable marble and granite walls and floors, the high-ceilinged and chandeliered customer service area, the hand-rubbed and polished brass fittings, and the massive door to the vault — all these things are designed to create an impression of power, security and stability.

In fact, of course, real power is elsewhere — in the office towers overhead where major financial decisions are made. The more lucrative profits are also elsewhere, in marketing new types of financial services. The major operational problem for Megabank is that its image of solidity, so carefully cultivated over the years, and the labour market strategy it implied, is admirably suited to the low-profit business of "cash custodian," but is less appropriate for the higher profit business of "financial service provider," Megabank wants to become.

Canada's major financial institutions have long had an image of being conservative institutions in which an army of poorly paid women are commanded by a few WASP male generals. To a very large degree, this stereotype retains validity; at Megabank, there are only seven female vice-presidents, out of a total of over forty, while counter-level staff remain overwhelmingly female. Furthermore, since Megabank, like many large financial institutions, has followed a policy of promoting from within, the sixty-year-olds at the top of the pyramid are drawn from the cohort of twenty-year-olds who entered banking forty years ago, in the early 1950s. At that time, the bank hired primarily white Anglo-Saxon Protestant males for managerial positions, and a high school education (then a relatively rare educational credential) was all one needed for a career in banking. (For example, one of the senior vice-presidents we interviewed mentioned that when he was hired [like the chairmen of the bank] after Grade 12, his rural high school had twelve graduates, and the two banks in town each had a tradition of taking one a year.)

In the years since then, there has been dramatic change in all aspects of the business, from the technology of record keeping to the nature of financial markets. But the organizational culture of the industry was formed in the days when deposit-taking institutions were primarily guardians of the cash deposits of the public. A primary organizational requirement in those days was that institutions should never make mistakes in their manual accounting systems, and that individual employees should never misappropriate cash. These requirements created a highly centralized, hierarchical structure with an obsessive concern for detail.

A top-down, "tight" organization may do well at delivering low-cost transaction banking services (such as processing cheques); for highly standardized banking services (such as providing a chequing account) it is standardized procedures, attention to detail and low-wage costs that are crucial to profitability. If the aim is to provide low-cost "commodity banking," there is little need for employee involvement or complex training, and few costs to high turnover. A centralized, military-style organizational structure can be an efficient way of catching mistakes and controlling costs. As one vice-president put it, "The bank is a little like the army. The prevailing attitude is that the branches are stupid." Within Megabank, power continues to be highly centralized; to this day, outside consulting contracts have to be approved personally by the president and the chairman of the board.

However, routine record keeping is something computers do very well and very cheaply. Increased computerization has vastly decreased the labour required to update customer records; nowadays when a customer keys in a withdrawal at an automatic teller machine, the customer is, effectively, supplying the labour to perform the data-entry function that bank clerks used to perform. The clerical and accounting jobs that manual record keeping used to require have disappeared from the branches of financial institutions all across the country. As automated teller machines and cash dispensers have spread into drug stores and supermarkets, bank and trust company branches have themselves disappeared. One vice-president at Megabank estimated that forty per cent of its branches could easily disappear in the next five years, resulting in a potential loss of over 3,000 jobs.

Computer programmers and technical repair people are still needed by financial institutions, but their jobs are centralized in a few urban areas. Some financial institutions are also shifting to telephone customer service centres, operating on a twenty-four-hour basis from a central long distance connection. With digital telephones and the security of personal access numbers, there is no technical reason why customers cannot perform most banking transactions via telecommunications from the privacy of their homes.

However, although computerization and telecommunications enable banking services to be delivered locally, the employment they create is located centrally. The centralization of financial services is accentuated by both social and technical factors. The social fact in Canada is that the presidents of banks and trust companies like to have the feeling that they are keeping a close tab on operations, and they therefore want their data processing centres close at hand. The physical fact is that there is still a large flow of paper associated with financial transactions. To make this paper flow work efficiently, financial institutions have to be in close proximity to one another. For example, Canada's financial institutions now provide same-day cheque clearing services across the country — and the intricacy of that operation has to be seen to be appreciated.

Every evening across Canada, all cheques deposited are collected into one of five regional cheque-processing centres. Each cheque is coded and keypunched, sorted by paying institution, and presented for payment, with settlements (and returns of cheques) occurring at 6:00 P.M., 9:00 P.M., midnight and 3:00 A.M. Every business night hundreds of thousands of documents are collected and transferred by truck or airplane over hundreds of miles. The fact that this is going on day in, day out, through winter storms and summer gales, demonstrates the importance of the dependability of the public infrastructure of airport services, highway snowplowing and road maintenance. The fact that this whole operation is mounted in order to save the cost of interest that would otherwise be payable on the "float" of cheques that have been credited to a payee's account but not yet debited from the payer's account is an indication of the pressure for performance in financial services.

The daily processing of millions of cheques is a high-volume, standardized procedure with relatively low profits. It is also suscep- tible to technological change, and could potentially become obsolete, if the electronic transfer of funds (for example, through debit cards) becomes widespread. Major pressures on revenue come from the operating cost side, via the rising expenses of labour and the main- tenance of premises. Megabank does not want to be locked into the low-profit, declining end of the financial services market.

However, the problem for Megabank is that while "commodity banking" may not be very profitable, it does provide the asset base on which its lending activities depend. The millions of customer contacts at the branches also provide an unparalleled opportunity to sell more profitable financial services. Since the Canadian population is not growing rapidly any more, keeping market share in retail banking is essential. Megabank has followed the "four corners" strat- egy of always being one of the four banks that occupy the corner lots at the major intersections in town, because locational convenience is seen as the number one factor in maintaining a retail banking base. Quality of banking services is seen as a necessary condition, and price (i.e. fees) is a secondary consideration overall (although very important in mortgage financing and for particular customer seg- ments such as senior citizens). In the financial industry, the impor- tance of traditional ties is widely emphasized, since it is considered to be much easier to sell to an existing customer than to recruit a new customer.

However, in Canada, as in the other developed countries, financial markets have been dramatically affected by deregulation and by the new competitive pressures of globalized financial markets. The term "disintermedization" has been coined to describe the increased ten- dency for companies to loan directly to consumers (for automobiles, for example) or raise financing directly (for instance, from pension funds), thereby cutting the banks out of the picture. Banks, trust companies and credit unions are all competing for the deposits of consumers, and there is even more competition, from brokerage houses and insurance companies in the provision of more sophisti- cated financial services (such as retirement savings programs). All of these competitive pressures accentuate the importance of retaining customer loyalty. Megabank, like any other financial institution, would like to be able to charge a premium fee, based on the perception that they are providing a premium quality of service. However, what exactly is the "quality" of a financial service?

If the financial service is simply that of keeping a chequing account, quality amounts to ease of access and the minimization of errors. Since computers have largely taken over the record keeping function, the imperative for tellers is to keep the line of customers moving. The quality of basic banking services, for a customer, amounts to being in a short line-up and getting a courteous teller.

The least-cost labour strategy for commodity banking is fairly simple. Not much training of labour is needed. Since there is little investment in the skills of employees, high labour turnover is quite tolerable and the bank can rely heavily on part-timers. With an extensive data base from operations, it is entirely feasible for financial institutions, such as Megabank, to predict customer usage by fifteen-minute intervals, in each of its 1,200 branches, and to hire part-timers to meet specific surges in demand (from 3:00 P.M. to 6:00 P.M. Fridays, for example). However, when part-time labour is hired to handle any peaks in customer demand, no "slack times" remain for the permanent staff; the overall intensity of work increases and it becomes more difficult to maintain friendly customer relations.

Megabank faces a conundrum. The labour market strategy consistent with a low-cost retail transaction banking network is not consistent with the needs of a high-end provider of financial services. A policy of minimizing labour costs to maintain its traditional position as a low-cost provider of basic banking services implies emphasizing the increased use of automatic teller machines and centralized telephone service centres, cutting branches and maintaining a low-wage labour force at remaining branches (with a high percentage of part-timers and relatively little expenditure on training).

As one vice-president put it, however, "An automatic teller machine can't sell." The quality of a financial service is an ambiguous thing — "quality" cannot really be defined in isolation from the specific needs of particular customers for security, income, capital gains potential, convenience, and so on. Whether or not Megabank is a high-quality financial service provider depends on whether or not its employees can figure out what each customer wants, and provide it for them. The sale of complex financial instruments to a highly diversified market requires greater knowledge and motivation on the part of workers, a different package of worker skills, and different performance indicators, as well as a different managerial style and greater decentralization. Within the bank, it is recognized that the big profits of the future will come from more sophisticated services. Megabank wants to become, essentially, a marketer of information, matching up the information they have on the financial needs of individual customers with the information they have on tax laws and the returns available in financial markets.

In principle, Megabank could provide both new services to corporate clients, such as customized payroll management, and detailed "micro marketing" of asset management services for personal clients. Financial institutions have an enormous amount of data on the characteristics of their customers. In addition to the traditional data bankers have always had on salary, mortgages, loans and deposits in chequing and savings accounts, Megabank can also use its records of credit card transactions to identify the types of expenditures each of its customers makes. It can match a customer's address by postal code to Statistics Canada data on neighbourhoods, in order to build a picture of what "keeping up with the Joneses" would actually imply for each of its customers. Megabank could, in principle, build a detailed psychological/sociological/economic picture of each of its clients, in order to target-market a customized financial service product that would have a maximum chance of acceptance.

The problem is that this strategy would require a tremendous diversity of services, and a corresponding diversity in sales approaches. In order to appeal to a diverse market place, the bank would need a decentralized organizational structure and a motivated, knowledgeable labour force. Knowledge has to be decentralized (via personal computers, for example) and decision-making has to be immediate (i.e. local). However, in order to achieve that, low employee turnover is essential. Only with a stable work force can employees be expected to build up customer contacts and product familiarity. High employee motivation is also crucial for effective selling. The conundrum for Megabank is that the labour market strategy appropriate for low-cost delivery of basic banking services is not really consistent with the high-profit business of selling complex financial services.

Megabank has inherited a centralized "top-down" management culture that is increasingly inappropriate for the change and diversity of complex, high-profit financial services. It is trying to manage the transition from being a guardian of cash to becoming a provider of financial advice. Although one of its major functions has always been keeping track of routine information on accounting balances, the future of the company's profitability lies in providing the non-routine knowledge and advice that fits the needs of a diverse clientele. The success of the bank in coping with this transition, while keeping the benefits of low-cost operations, will likely determine whether it remains a major player in the financial world, or withers away in the competition of the 1990s.

In either case, there will be fewer clerical jobs. The telecommunications/computer revolution is inexorably altering the labour requirements of financial institutions — each step in the gradual replacement of paper flow by electronic transfer of funds brings a decrease in record-keeping labour required. If Megabank is successful in altering its organizational culture, it can hope for growth in the financial services area, which would provide increased employment in the knowledge-intensive end of banking, to counterbalance future declines in clerical employment. If not, other financial institutions are willing and able to perform those functions.

"Nova University" — Unconscious Tradition, Limited Social Skills

The problems of Megabank can be usefully contrasted to the problems of "Nova U," which has inherited a completely different organizational culture from the past, but faces, in the present, enormous pressures for lower costs.

Diversity and change are central to the modern university. One way of appreciating the diversity of the modern university is to visit a large examination hall at the end of term. There may be hundreds of students, most of whom have never seen each other before (and who are not paying much attention to each other now). They find their ways to their separate sections to write examinations in MBA accounting or exercise physiology for nurses or remedial mathematics for transition-year students. Their examinations may cover questions on myths, symbols and rites in comparative religion, or on synthesis, characterization and structure of macromolecules in polymer chemistry, or on inflation, unemployment and macroeconomic policy or on twentieth century Russian prose and poetry. Some will have worked with multimillion-dollar pieces of lab equipment, while others have developed skills in dissecting nerve tissue or constructing survey questionnaires. They all write with intensity and leave with relief, but most will also leave with only the vaguest awareness of the depth and complexity of the issues their fellow students have addressed.

The production and transmission of non-routine information to a diverse clientele is the main activity of universities. How does a university meet the diversity of demands it faces in a world where knowledge is exploding at an exponential rate? At Nova U, as at other universities, faculty are central to the university's operation. Faculty members set the curriculum for their individual courses and sit in committees to decide the mix of courses to be offered and the hiring or firing of those who will teach them. Their work involves a multitude of roles, ranging from class preparation, student and thesis supervision, research, administration, consulting, and various forms of community service. Since their work is highly diversified, it is almost impossible to routinize.

The rapidity of the accumulation of new knowledge means that, for faculty, there is an ever-changing base of information that needs to be mastered for both research and teaching purposes. Furthermore, as knowledge becomes the new currency of economic development, and the university's role in regional development expands, more and more, universities are being asked to respond with suitably tailored academic and research programs to an increasingly diverse set of constituencies. At some point in the past, universities were only expected to teach Chaucer and Plato. Universities are still expected to do that, but in addition they are expected to mount courses in the management of toxic wastes and to provide in-service training for social workers specializing in child abuse, while also providing the research base upon which governments and industry depend, in areas as diverse as clinical pharmacology, fisheries biology, and social policy analysis.

It is not really possible for organizations to respond to these demands optimally if they are centralized, "top-down" organizations. In manufacturing and in other services, firms have responded to the pressures of diversity and change by adopting decentralized, responsive and participatory organizational forms. The university is no exception, and in fact the academic side of universities has always been characterized by a very significant degree of decentralization. Faculty members enjoy considerable autonomy in shaping their work and the hours that they contribute to it.

People in business and government often expect universities to act in the same way that their organizations do, deciding on policies at the top and implementing those decisions down the hierarchy. However, although there is a subtle hierarchy of influence and status among professors on the academic side, there is virtually no hierarchy of power. Academics are oriented much more to doing a good job in the eyes of their colleagues in the same department or of their peers in their academic discipline than to the organization that employs them. It never has been remotely feasible for central administrators to judge personally the content of courses or the quality of research. (How, for example, could one dean be expected to evaluate simultaneously course reading lists in molecular biology, organic chemistry and advanced topology? If one had to wait for the dean's approval, how long would it take to get a new article on the reading list?) Academic traditions such as academic freedom, the awarding of tenure, and collegial decision-making (as well as more recent provisions in collective bargaining agreements) considerably limit the powers of central administrators.

This decentralization of the university meets the needs of the 1990s in many respects, but it has been a feature of academic life for several centuries. Universities emerged out of the self-governing cloisters of academics established by religious orders in the Middle Ages. In many respects, the roots of contemporary academic disciplines and of relatively autonomous academic departments give the university an eighteenth-century form of organization — one that is sometimes appropriate to the need for decentralized, responsive operation at the end of the twentieth century.

Because faculty members must have completed their Ph.D.s, they are selected from among those who have the ability to work fairly independently, for a long time, at a large research project. Although the process of socialization and motivation of workers is a very conscious part of the labour strategy of Quality Architects or Telecom Co., in universities the socialization of professors is an unconscious byproduct of the years they spend in graduate school. When they enter graduate school, for example, most economists — like most of the world — would not understand why publishing an article in *Econometrica* is a big deal; by the time they get their Ph.D. they will consider it something clearly worth several thousand hours of effort.

When it works well, the university system can work very well indeed. Because of selection and because of their socialization, faculty are largely self-motivated. Because of their autonomy at the micro level, they are able to adapt quickly to changing conditions. From day to day, faculty members typically juggle the demands of individual students, class preparation, committee work, thesis supervision, research, consulting, the updating of curricula, demands for media interviews and community service, as well as hustling for grants and contracts to finance their research projects. However, the system does not always work well — and the downside of a system with substantial decentralization is the stagnation that can occur if horizons become limited and standards become local.

Moreover, most university employees are not professors. Professors represent the public face of the university; the academic side of the university illustrates the fact that old organizational forms need to be analyzed carefully, since some aspects of the soft technology of the past may (unconsciously) be highly appropriate for the future. However, while the academic side of the university is characterized by considerable decentralization and autonomy, such is not the case with the non-academic side (i.e. the provision of university infrastructure and services). In these areas, a more traditional, top-down form of organization prevails. Employees in these parts of the university remark on the limited autonomy they have in the performance of their work and in the decisions of their work unit.

As in hospitals (see Chapter 5) the university has a distinct social hierarchy. Beneath the veneer of democratic informality, there is a distinct caste structure. It is obvious to everyone that only professors can aspire to becoming university president or faculty dean, and that maintenance people, clerks and secretaries are never promoted to be professors. Those at the bottom of the ladder are quite conscious of their low status within the organization and of their limited prospects for career mobility out of their occupational category. The bifurcation of the university between academic and non-academic staff also entails different rules (the opportunity for flexible work hours, for instance) and benefits (such as having a dental plan) being applied to different groups within the same institution.

The university is, therefore, an illustration of how different parts of the same organization can have very different organizational cultures. The difficulties this creates, in envious comparisons and in poor morale, are a warning to other organizations. Like hospitals, universities are highly segmented by occupation and they depend heavily on the sense of "professionalism" of key employees. However, because of this strong orientation to professional success within their academic discipline, professors have very little identification with organizational goals. Employees who have a professional ethic want to do a good job because doing so earns them the respect of their peers, not particularly because they value the opinion of their boss. Such employees are conscientious self-starters, but they need to be persuaded, not told, if they are to change their way of working. Organizations that depend on a sense of individual occupational professionalism for worker motivation therefore do not find it easy to align the behaviour of workers with the goals of the organization.

Furthermore, because professionals need specialized skills, they also need long periods of training and education. This means that they are costly to replace, so the old "stick" of fear of dismissal is less effective, and somewhat dysfunctional, since the effective performance of their specialized jobs depends heavily on their morale and initiative. As well, since each profession has its own set of training requirements and credentials, it is much more difficult to motivate workers by the prospect of promotion, since organizations can no longer promote across occupations from within.

Many companies have historically depended on promotion from within. Formerly, trainee tellers were hired by Megabank out of high school, and they could (like many chairmen of the bank's board) hope to work their way to the top. There was a homogenous employee culture and decisions taken at the top would be swiftly implemented down the line. Universities have never been like that. But as organizations like banks try to create a "professional culture" of internal motivation and entrepreneurship, they will also encounter some of the downside of academic organization — blocked mobility for lower level employees, and the difficulties of persuading, rather than ordering, people to change.

As things are, academic programs emerge from, and are governed by, faculty members within each discipline and department and faculty. While some coordination and integration is achieved by higher level structures (by each faculty and by senate), the university is slow to respond to new problems in an interdisciplinary manner and finds it hard to meet the demands for cooperation and rationalization among universities. There is a dramatic contrast between the speed of individual and of organizational responsiveness. Due to the decentralized nature of decision-making, the content of teaching and research can be changed immediately — a professor can read a new article on Tuesday and, if it is a good article, it can be added to his class reading list on Wednesday. Academics who are engaged in research have to keep up with their field by going to conferences, reading the latest working papers and corresponding on the Internet. If their own articles are to have a chance of being accepted for publication by international academic journals, they have to use relevant research findings from across the world to improve their own research without delay. However the same academics who individually take pride in being "up to the minute" in the latest international research can, when assembled as a group, take months or years to re-organize departments or faculties.

Furthermore, although university researchers may be working with the hard technology of the twenty-first century, university administrators have to straddle the academic and non-academic worlds, and they often work with the mind-set of the nineteenth century. Unlike private sector firms, the university administration spends little effort in a planned way to socialize its members to common, university-wide values or to a commitment to the institution as a whole. Central academic administrators seek to set out institutional directions and have them implemented, but they devote little or no time to explaining new measures at the unit level or in building the commitment to carrying them out — steps that are essential in a decentralized organization in which local commitment is critical.

In our private sector case studies, there was a very conscious personnel policy of training, goal-setting and motivation. Planning the soft technology of motivation and organization was a major preoccupation of management. Managers recognized that making personal relationships work is an essential part of getting the whole organization moving in the same direction. But in the university, there is the unstated assumption that since ideas are what is important, persuasion and personal relations are unimportant — hence internal problems can be "solved" by the sending of an executive memo.

Central administrators may well be committed by choice or necessity, to taking steps towards employment equity, for example, or to increasing the value of teaching in decisions pertaining to tenure and promotion. They may send memos announcing new university policies. However, the will to undertake these steps and the decisions that will make them a reality depend crucially on faculty and administrators at the local level within the university. Without the cooperation and enthusiasm of the lower levels, policies and practices established at higher levels will not, in fact, be implemented. When enforceable administrative decisions are made at a central level, they lead to resentment and resistance, particularly if it is felt that a better decision, more tailored to local circumstances, could have been made if the individual department had been given the flexibility to allocate available funds. Driven by external pressures to cut funds and rationalize programs (and perhaps by traditional models of management from the private sector), central administrators consistently run into difficulty with top-down management styles.

The university also lacks a deliberate human resource training strategy, especially for academics (for teaching, for example) and for academic administration. Professors are thrown into the teaching role with minimal preparation, yet this is one of the most important functions they will perform. Similarly, the university is characterized by management largely untrained in academic administration. Academics typically select "one of their own" to assume posts as department chairs, deans, or higher level positions. Despite the fact that these are onerous and responsible positions, little or no time is spent in formal management training, and there may be little or no organized transition period when one appointment is completed and a new one begins. In many ways, universities are somewhat "nerdy" organizations — knowing a lot of facts but having a distinct lack of social skills.

These problems of management structure are particularly important when, as now, the university faces enormous external pressures. At Nova University, the administration proposed in 1993 that several departments be closed, since escalating costs and a cut in government funding meant that the university was facing the necessity of drastic budget cuts. Major controversy ensued, but when the provincial government later included universities in its rollback of public sector salaries (followed by a freeze at the new lower level), the budget deficit problem was alleviated, temporarily.

However, massive uncertainties remain. At the same time as the federal government announced in 1994 its intention to withdraw its contribution to post-secondary education financing, the provincial government was considering how to amalgamate and rationalize the province's university system. Education may be crucial for the information economy of the future, and research may be key for technological change, but it is not clear that there will be many jobs for teachers and researchers at Nova U. Despite the fact that universities face a wave of retirements as the cohort of professors hired in the 1960s begin, in the 1990s, to hit sixty-five, it is very unclear how many replacement jobs will become available.

Conclusion

Even though employment in the information sector in total is growing, the employment of less skilled labour within the information sector is declining. Quality Architects has laid off the draftsmen who used to use paper and pencil in favour of technicians who compose architectural drawings at a computer terminal. With computerized switching gear and voice response software, Telecom Company no longer needs as many telephone operators, while Megabank now hires computer programmers in place of bookkeepers and clerks. The information sector is itself an example of the increasing relative importance of knowledge-based occupations — a trend we also observed in manufacturing and resources. Jobs that involve solving non-routine problems continue to need people to do them, but computers are increasingly replacing people in the jobs that involve routine record keeping or the transferral of standard data. The hard technology of computers and telecommunications is forcing change in the types of jobs in information processing firms, and the management challenge is to find the soft technology of workplace organization and motivation to suit this new work force and its new products.

In the information service sector, change is too rapid and knowledge is too specialized to allow central administrators to supervise in detail the quality of what their organizations produce. The primary resource of those organizations is the people who work in them, but since the "quality" of information services cannot easily be defined in a routinized way, the success of the organization depends on whether or not individual workers have the ability and the desire to solve the problem of quality, as the customer defines it. Successful organizations must therefore create an organizational culture of "professionalism," in which their employees internalize organizational goals and independently decide to do what the organization wants them to do. Decentralization of organizational structure and the motivation of employees are key to success.

Modern Architects, Telecom Company, Megabank and Nova University are all wrestling, in their own ways, with the organizational pressures introduced by the modern revolution in the information services sector. Modern Architects is an example of the small-scale providers of customized, highly sophisticated services that have found that prosperity in the modern market place demands both the technical changes of computerization and the social changes of team-building, coaching and motivation. Telecom Company is much larger, and it is a company that has always been used to a rapid rate of technical change. What is new about the 1990s, however, is the competition of other service providers — if Telecom Company is to compete in the high price end of the market place, it must provide a high-quality service, and the demand for quality has spawned a wholesale rethinking of the social organization of the company.

Nova University and Megabank have inherited very different organizational cultures from their historical roots. The university tradition of decentralized decision-making stands in sharp contrast to the top-down management style of Megabank. University administrators take for granted the internal motivation and flexibility of response of faculty members and, faced with a continued squeeze on operating budgets, Deans and vice-presidents yearn for the simplicity of subordinates who take orders and the low-cost operations that they imagine exist in the private sector. Megabank executives, on the other hand, wonder how they can get entrepreneurial initiative from managers who are used to being supervised in obsessive detail. In both institutions, the hard technology of production is in place — both have plenty of computing power and lots of well-trained personnel — but neither have devised the soft technology of organizational structure and motivation to adapt optimally to the pressures for diversity and change that each face. And in both organizations, the imperatives of "professionalism" block the careers of lower paid employees, and accentuate the problems of managing change.

5

The Public Sector

If there aren't enough good jobs, what can government do? In the decades after the Second World War, the public sector could often employ people directly, providing jobs that were, on the whole, reasonably stable, full time, and well paid. In the 1960s and 1970s, many of the "baby boom" generation found employment either in government departments directly, or in the myriad of publicly funded services that are so prominent a part of the employment base of most Canadian communities.

Those days, however, are over, as our four case studies of the public sector illustrate. We examine cases drawn from the three levels of government: a local school board serving a disadvantaged rural county; a small town hospital; a provincial commission and a large federal department engaged in the provision of national security services. We picked these particular case studies because they illustrate some of the different types of pressures on the public sector. The differences in their responses illustrate how important decentralization and de facto competition can be within the public sector, but there also are some overriding similarities.

In our studies of private sector firms, the pressure of the competition they face was very clear. In the public sector the external pressures are somewhat different, but they have the same result — continuous striving to improve efficiency. The public sector is being forced to respond to three major challenges. First and foremost, there is the money squeeze. The deficit crisis has hit governments hard at all levels across the country, but the squeeze is particularly tight in Atlantic Canada.

With a relatively high debt load and a small tax base, Nova Scotia, like other poor provinces, is heavily dependent on federal transfers through equalization grants and established program financing for health and post-secondary education, making financial pressures especially severe. The federal government has been offloading its deficit problems on the provinces by cutting transfers, but the provinces can only offload part of those cuts to municipalities — the rest must come out of operations. Interest payments on the provincial debt are the third largest item of annual expenditures (more than sixteen per cent of the budget). The provincial government and the agencies, commissions and municipal governments it supports are subject to increasingly severe funding constraints, while the demand for their services is not abating. Indeed, the demand for services in such areas as health care, post-secondary education, and social assistance has been increasing. This reality of the public sector — decreased funds and increased needs — is, in many ways, the equivalent of the competitive forces in the private sector; both produce enormous pressures to cut costs and increase productivity while maintaining services.

The second major challenge for the public sector is that the money squeeze comes at a time of significant demographic transitions that are forcing government to change the mix of services it provides. The proportion of the population sixty-five years and older is eleven per cent now, but is forecast to double in the next twenty-five years. The fifteen- to twenty-four-year-old population in the Atlantic Provinces in the year 2011 is only expected to be seventy-five per cent of its size in 1986, a projected decline that is more substantial than for any other region of Canada.

The changing nature of the Canadian family also entails changes for the kinds and quantities of services that governments provide. The decline of the extended family has, for example, heightened the tendency to have seniors cared for by institutions outside the family, while continuing increases in the employment of women and the growth of single-parent families have produced new demands for child care facilities. These trends mean that government not only has to do more with less, government also has to change what it does.

A third factor influencing the public sector has been a change in the conception of the kind of role the public sector should play. Funding problems have been part, but only part, of the debate regarding the provision and regulation of services by the public sector. In Nova Scotia, as in the rest of the country, some services are being deregulated and privatized, and the threat of privatization hangs over others. Governments are both less able and less willing to respond to demands for new services or higher levels of existing services. Traditional lines of demarcation of public and private responsibility are being re-drawn and new non-governmental institutions (such as transition houses) which mingle public and private identities are emerging. As well, the increasingly competitive international environment has placed new limits on the effective powers of government. Powers of regulation and labour market standards are less often invoked when firms can move relatively freely to other jurisdictions, and free trade agreements have limited what governments can do to favour local industries at the expense of their competitors elsewhere.

These constraints on what government *can* do interact with the political debate on what government *should* do to produce an enormous amount of questioning of the role and size of the public sector. All the same, many of the needs of citizens remain familiar — children still need schools to go to, sick people still need to go to hospitals, and nation-states still require armed forces. The dilemma for the public sector is how to cope with new needs and continue to fulfil ongoing social responsibilities, with less money.

"Department of Security Affairs" — New Technology in an Old Profession

With the end of the cold war, the Canadian military faces a fundamental shift in its role and responsibilities. Clearly, a lessened external threat means there are likely to be fewer military personnel in future years, so the services cannot be expected to provide more jobs. However, the broader social role of the military is also of interest. There has often been the suggestion that time in the military can provide useful training, as well as boot camp discipline. In the U.S., for example, "joining up" has been a popular route out of poverty for some members of minority groups. Is there a potential new role for the military that could combine defense and labour market development?

Like coal mining, fishing, and forestry, the military has traditionally provided an important source of entry-level employment for young persons in the Maritimes — especially for those from rural backgrounds and with modest levels of education and training. For decades, the minimum educational entry requirement was Grade 8 and a willingness to learn; only gradually over the past twenty years has the requirement moved to a Grade 10 level. Once in the military, the new recruit could count on obtaining extensive training and often could move up the occupational and command hierarchy. Training served to impart both cognitive and attitudinal skills, with an emphasis on discipline, social control, motivation and performance. Fairly generous retirement provisions, available at an early age, meant that one could leave the military with a pension in hand and with a background in skill training and discipline that was widely valued in a second career.

Many of these features still characterize employment in the military today. In addition, the military continues to be a major employer in the Atlantic region. In Nova Scotia, it accounts for 6,000 to 7,000 military positions and a further 4,000 to 5,000 civilian jobs, as well as providing spin-off economic stimulus to other businesses in the region. Federal spending in Nova Scotia is relatively high as a percentage of economic activity, and defence spending is the major part of all federal expenditures. The local importance of defence spending arises mainly because Halifax is home port for the Atlantic-based part of the navy. As a result, military spending exercises an important stabilising influence on the Nova Scotian economy. The provincial unemployment rate is relatively high, but the impact of recessions is somewhat moderated in comparison with the sharper fluctuations found in other parts of Canada.

Our interest in the military was partly prompted by the perception that, as in the U.S., "signing up" has been a way out of poverty for disadvantaged youth. But it appears that things work somewhat differently in Canada. Because of high unemployment, the department is able to find a ready supply of recruits for entry-level positions. In fact, approximately a third of the national quota of entry-level positions is filled by persons hired from within Atlantic Canada each year, although the region's share of the national population is only ten per cent. For these people, the military continues to provide an opportunity. The military offers stable employment with considerable training opportunities and a good salary — an attractive option for people with low educational levels who have very poor prospects in other parts of the regional economy. However, while rural and francophone youth take advantage of this opportunity, the Canadian pattern differs from that in the United States in that the Canadian military has historically provided far fewer opportunities for youth from racial minority communities to achieve employment and occupational mobility. While a few limited efforts have been made to correct this imbalance, few Aboriginals and blacks have signed up.

Our respondents expressed different points of view on how the characteristics of the new recruits have changed over time. One perspective might be described as the traditional complaint that the younger generation isn't like it used to be: "These kids don't want to go to sea as much as they used to, or slug it out as infanteers. There's been a cultural, lifestyle change, and it is reflected in the educational system, a sort of liberal, free choice dynamic." In another interview, the perspective was more positive, to the effect that, "New enrollees are less naïve, less likely to tolerate arbitrary commands and hierarchies, less accepting of nonsense, and more likely to leave."

With the end of the cold war, it seems inevitable that the level of defence expenditures, and employment opportunities, will diminish. The current budget of the department in the region is on a downward trajectory and the level of direct employment is also forecast to decline. There are also strong indications that at least one of the province's military bases will close as soon as political considerations permit — a major blow to a rural region of the province that has few major employment alternatives. Troops are also being brought home from Europe, decreasing job openings as these personnel are integrated into Canadian bases.

In addition to down-sizing, it is clear that the role of the military is also changing. Technological advances are more gradual than revolutionary in nature, but they are continuous. Our interviewees listed an impressive array of new technologies adopted in recent years, from night scopes and new rifles for the infantry, to new guns and navigational systems for the navy, and sophisticated electronics for the air force. Even the entry-level occupations, such as the infantrypersons or the boatswains, are more sophisticated than they used to be, in large measure because of the new technologies. As a recruiting officer pointed out, it is no longer accurate, if it ever was, to refer to persons holding these positions in terms of the comic book idea of potato peelers or cannon fodder.

However, some members of the rank and file were less impressed with the rate of change and more impressed with doing the same job year after year. A boatswain told us, for example, that there have been some changes in equipment, such as new cranes for loading, but that "we've progressed as much as the equipment, which hasn't changed much." He went on to say that the skill levels required to do the job are different rather than more demanding: "The skill required to do this job hasn't changed, although we now teach different things. The watch system is different, the classes of ships are different, shipboard operation has changed, but tying a knot is still tying a knot."

Although technologies have advanced unevenly, the peace-time military has had to offer training on an almost continuous basis to its personnel. The extensive training is one of the remarkable features of military life — one estimate suggested that it took up seventy per cent of the time in the first five years of employment. All new non-commissioned personnel begin with a ten-week basic training course where the emphasis is on testing the physical and psychological makeup of the candidates in order to assess whether they have the potential for a military career. While some military components are included, such as military lifestyles, military history and law, this portion of the training is not occupation specific. For many of the recruits, this is their first time away from home, and a difficult transition for them, especially around the third or fourth week. However, the emphasis is on getting the recruits through this initial program, while weeding out those who are unsuitable. After basic training, the emphasis shifts to a series of more skill-based modules specific to individual occupations.

In addition to entry-level occupations, a whole host of new trades, based on more advanced technical and scientific skills, has developed to the point that more than 100 occupations are handled by the recruiting and personnel division. Some (like that of truck driver) have clear civilian counterparts, but most of the training effort necessarily goes to highly skilled and specialized occupations (sonar technician, for example) for which the military must provide the training as there is no civilian counterpart. While it used to be the case that much of the work of the military was performed by a few occupations such as infantryperson, boatswain, vehicle driver and administrative clerk, such is no longer the case; for example, it is now common to have 250 people on a ship, of which only 15 would be boatswains.

The role of military personnel is also changing because the United Nations, no longer stymied to the same degree by cold war politics, is taking a more aggressive position in international peacekeeping and famine relief operations. Canadians are invariably asked to participate, and to make a contribution at short notice and in difficult circumstances. As with police in multi-racial, multi-ethnic urban areas of North America, the military is also encountering the explosive conflicts arising from ethnic and racial strife — and as Oka illustrated in the summer of 1991, not all of these conflicts are located overseas.

Because down-sizing is likely to be handled by attrition and early retirements, existing personnel continue to be reasonably secure in their positions. The number of bodies available to do the job has decreased, and we heard complaints from all quarters about increased workload in the context of stable and declining numbers of staff. Upward occupational mobility is of particular concern to those in the entry-level occupations among whom we conducted our employee interviews — the infantrypersons, boatswains, vehicle operators and administrative clerks. Their opportunities for movement to the technical/scientific occupations involve an occupational transfer process whereby an individual prepares an application and is ultimately considered by a national board, which makes its decisions on the basis of merit, but in the context of a restrictive quota system that is based on needs in the occupation of exit as well as the occupation of entry. There is also a compulsory transfer process for persons who can no longer fulfil the requirements of their own trade. (The combat arms occupations have a special program whereby they can apply for a transfer after three years of service.)

While these opportunities for upward mobility are available, applicants often need to take academic upgrading to the Grade 12 level or higher. There are few openings in the more highly skilled trades, a problem that is exacerbated in an environment of down-sizing, where openings are likely to be filled by surplus personnel rather than through mobility from the lower ranks.

Traditionally, the great divide in the military is the distinction between officers and enlisted men, but even within each broad group there is a clear pecking order. The division between entry-level and higher occupations is reflected in the day-to-day interaction of the two levels. Onboard ships, for example, boatswains complain not only about work intensification due to declining numbers of personnel, but also about the unwillingness of the technical/scientific group to help out in meeting the work requirements faced by the boatswains. As one of our respondents put it, "The cream of the crop get all the cream-of-the-crop jobs — by this I mean the trade groups in electronics and engineering. A lot of the new recruits in the boatswain group have great ideas as well, but they don't have a place to use them."

As a result, although the military still provides some opportunities for the disadvantaged to obtain stable and reasonably well-paid employment, the number of these opportunities is decreasing because the military is down-sizing and shifting to more specialized occupations, with a higher entry standard. As well, the internal rigidities of the armed forces present significant barriers to upward mobility. The bottom line is that the military is likely to provide fewer jobs in future years and is not well suited to providing "training in uniform" for the needs of the civilian labour force.

The military, as a case study, was also interesting as an example of how organizations adapt (or do not adapt) to change, because the peace-time military has the unique characteristic that it is immune from day-to-day pressures to compete on price or quality. In terms of hard technology, the military possesses specialized equipment, like fighter aircraft and naval frigates, which are state of the art. Indeed, the sophistication of the computer systems necessary for modern anti-submarine warfare or air-to-air combat is truly amazing. Yet, military offices contain manual typewriters and other office equipment that would have been junked years ago in the private sector, and it is evident that the forces continue to employ paper pushers. The military is still the quintessential example of a top-down hierarchial organization — we heard no talk of worker "empower-ment" or whispers of "delayering" in our interviews with military officers. In fact, we were rather impressed with the large number of layers of officers in the command hierarchy in Halifax and in Ottawa.

The military is an example of how organizational change does not necessarily accompany technological change. But then again, the military is just about the only large sector where there simply is no competition. Without the pressures of competition to restrain price and improve quality, it is much easier to implement technological change, while avoiding organizational change.

"Provincial Commission" — The Threat of Privatization

The importance of competition to organizational change was brought out clearly by our interviews at "Provincial Commission." The Com-mission has a monopoly on the sale of alcohol in the province, and its origins lie in the era when Canadian governments, and Canadian society at large, basically viewed alcohol consumption as sinful. Government monopoly control was intended to regulate sin, while raising revenue. It was not part of the intention to make purchase of this sinful commodity pleasurable or convenient, and the provincial commission acquired a deserved reputation for indifferent service, poor selection and inconvenient hours and locations. However, social attitudes to alcohol have changed. In recent years, with the blurring of the traditional demarcation lines between public and private sectors, organizations that for decades have been accustomed to a placid, protected, existence now face the prospect of privatization and competition in the market place — a prospect that has jolted some into rapid and substantial changes.

The Provincial Commission we interviewed has the mandate to purchase, warehouse, distribute and sell alcohol to individual purchasers at its retail outlets and, on a wholesale basis, to licensed establishments. The Commission also provides staff for the board that carries out the licensing function in the province. Employment totals some 900 persons, of whom 600 are regular full-time, 140 regular part-time, and the remainder employed on a casual basis for tasks such as unloading trucks or managing the cash register in stores during periods of high demand. In terms of occupations, the regular staff includes about 450 store clerks, another 150 store managers or assistant managers (the latter category is slowly being eliminated via attrition), some 50 to 60 office clerical staff, 40 persons handling the warehouse function, and a number of other administrators.

The Commission has always had a monopoly, and still does. Although one might think that a monopoly faces little pressure for change, the Commission has recently undergone a substantial reorganization. The main reason is the persistent threat that the retail functions carried out by the Commission might be privatized, in the sense that grocery and other stores may be permitted to sell alcohol. Although governments of the recent past have floated this idea on several occasions, and privatization has been implemented in Alberta, governments have been careful to limit the privatization proposal to the retail sales function. There is no interest in privatizing the purchase, warehousing, distribution and wholesale functions, since it is these latter functions that permit the province to control the collection of taxes, which are currently the province's fourth-largest source of income.

A form of implicit competition is therefore being introduced into the operations of the Commission. It is implicit in that the Commission still has a monopoly on the sale of alcohol, but if the Commission is not efficient and responsive to the consuming public, private stores will be allowed to sell alcohol, or the Commission's retail outlets might be turned over to private control. The Commission therefore has to compete with public expectations about what the private sector could provide.

The possibility of privatization is not the only source of increased competition for the Commission. In a broad sense, the Commission is also competing with other public and private producers of goods and services for a share of the public's discretionary spending — a level of spending that, in real terms, has been declining in recent years. The cost of alcohol, ratcheted upwards by taxes, is becoming increasingly important to alcohol sales, especially during economic recessions.

The Commission is therefore faced with a declining market for its products. Nova Scotia already has one of the lower rates of per capita consumption in the country, and the trend is downwards for most varieties of the product, in part for demographic reasons. As the population ages, consumers pay more attention to health and lifestyle considerations in making their consumption choices, as well as to public campaigns against excessive use of alcohol. In addition, the smuggling of alcohol is a growing concern as the spread between United States and Canadian prices widens. Home brewing and the sale of 0.5 per cent beer in supermarkets also intrudes upon the Commission's monopoly position.

Faced with these kinds of competitive pressures, and a fairly high level of complaints from the consuming public, suppliers, and licensees, the Commission has undertaken a substantial reorganization over the past five years. It came to the conclusion that it could no longer operate in a bureaucratic and centralized fashion, in an environment of considerable challenge and rapid change. Recognition of the need for change was widespread within the organization, and the departure of a number of senior executives through retirement made it possible for new approaches to be implemented. The first step was simply to shift away from "regulation of sin" as a philosophy and begin to place heavy emphasis on the Commission as a service organization, and on customer service as a principal driving force for the Commission.

Management went by the book (the new book) in implementing change. They met with small groups of staff to discuss how the principles of the mission statement could best be turned into reality. All-day sessions were held at which staff could talk about anything they wished, and could vent their frustrations with the existing style of top-down, authoritarian management. Undoubtedly the tenor of these meetings was difficult because they took place at a time of militant union action (followed by a strike), and in the midst of threats of privatization and down-sizing. A comprehensive survey of staff was also employed, and indeed surveys of customers and employees are now a regular feature of the Commission's agenda.

One of the major results of this process was the conscious decision to undertake a significant decentralization of authority and to enhance the capacity of individuals in the organization to make their own decisions. This is most noticeable in the retail stores, whose managers and staff have been given more responsibility for day-to-day decisions. For example, it was finally recognized that a central bureaucratic organization could not reasonably be expected to make the decision on whether customers could take shopping carts to their cars. As the private sector has long known, these local decisions are best made at the local level, not by senior management.

With the new organizational structure, the idea is that central directives are to be considered as guidelines; if stores can meet the bottom line as far as sales and service are concerned, they are free to innovate. Central control over relations with licensees has also disappeared, with local retail stores now having the responsibility for regular visits and services. We were told that, as a result of this more flexible and decentralized approach, complaints from licensees have been sharply reduced. An internal complaint system, with mandatory response by management, has also been instituted for both employees and for customers.

New technology has played an important role in making the new organizational arrangement possible. Selling alcohol and selling groceries involve much the same sort of information systems, and the commission has upgraded its systems to the standards of the retail sector. The data base at the store level, linked to the central office, is now completely computerized. Cash registers are linked to computers which record the entire cycle of a transaction comprising an on-line, real time inventory. When a sale occurs, inventory and other store records are automatically modified, making possible daily reports on such aspects as sales, cash control, services to licensees, products on hand, and updated files used for ordering. Orders can also be transmitted directly from this system. The Commission, therefore, has much better information than it used to have on inventories, and can receive quicker and better reports from individual stores.

At the head office, the inventory system consolidates orders from stores and from licensees, makes automatic calculations of costs, and confirms the orders of the purchasers. With this system, as well as an automated process for warehouse ordering, the time required to satisfy a customer order (whether from a Commission retail outlet or a licensee) has been reduced from three or four days, to twenty-four hours. To anyone familiar with the retail trade sector, all these changes will sound quite unremarkable, but the point is that in both hard and soft technology, the Commission is doing exactly what many supermarket chains in the private sector have done.

Apart from decentralization and a measure of worker empowerment, senior management has been freed from routine, day-to-day decision making, and from paperwork, to concentrate on long-range planning. Decisions on routine matters are now made at local levels, and both levels have access to full information as a result of the computerized information system — in effect, approaching a paperless office. Managers now do much of their own typing on personal computer terminals, resulting in fewer secretarial positions than before and a revised role for those secretaries who remain. There are also somewhat fewer senior and middle-level managers (in the latter case with the gradual elimination of assistant store clerks) than there were four years ago. Staff at the store level are also freed up from paperwork and are therefore able to concentrate more on meeting the needs of customers.

The proportion of casual and regular part-time employment has increased as the Commission has moved, like other firms in the retail trade, to tailor employment more closely to the peaks and valleys of customer demand. More than half of its weekly retail business is done on Friday evenings and on Saturday. In earlier years, a store would have full-time staff standing around for much of the week, but now casual and regular part-time workers are brought in during times of extra customer demand. In just over a year, full-time staff declined by nine per cent, while the proportion of casual workers increased by a comparable amount.

As well, management is trying "to get control of the labour rate." Commission staff are now not seen as civil servants when it comes to determining salary and benefit levels. Rather, the relevant comparison group is increasingly seen to be the comparable occupations and industries of the private sector — especially the food, beverage, and retail sectors — although it is recognized that a wage premium can be justified because employees have the responsibility of dealing with a controlled substance. In general, the approach seems to be to regard privatization not so much as a threat but as a stimulus to do things as efficiently as possible, and in ways that resemble private sector adaptations, so that governments and the public will conclude that privatization is unnecessary, as it would not really result in any improvements.

To fully implement its approach, the Commission now recognizes that it needs to provide more in-house training and to look for new employees with higher levels of education. The computerization of much of the Commission's operations has created a new category of employees in charge of the computer systems. In addition, the demands of the new technology, the push toward customer service, and the emphasis on decentralized decision-making has underlined the need for more on-the-job training for staff such as store clerks and managers. The Commission pays for 100 per cent of job-related training, and tries as much as possible to conduct the training on a decentralized basis by having trained staff within a unit responsible for training fellow workers.

Fewer jobs are now available than previously because of downsizing, and those who are hired need better social skills for customer service and better technical skills (such as the operation of computers). Whether or not the Commission will succeed in sufficiently improving its service standards to ward off privatization, only time will tell. But there is no doubt that the Commission now looks and acts much more like a supermarket than a government office. The main lesson we can draw from the Commission experience is that organizational change is driven by incentives, competition and technology, not by the legal status of an organization (i.e. whether it is publicly owned or not). When an organization faces greater competition (whether implicit or explicit) and has similar hard technology available, both public and private firms have often reacted with similar soft technology strategies: decentralization of decision-making, employee empowerment, down-sizing, and increased use of part-time workers.

We did not observe much organizational change in the military, but then again, the military does not have to worry about some other organization or firm taking over its functions. Effective competition can take many forms — in the Commission's case, it is effectively in competition with public expectations of what the private sector could provide. In a sense, however, the liquor commission case is an easy one for governments, since selling alcohol is not a core function of government, and the threat of privatization is a highly credible way of getting the organization to reform itself. The tougher issue is how to build into the core functions of government the same type of pressures for improved performance. The issue is especially tough because although the private sector may need an efficient public sector to generate jobs, one of the reasons why some sectors are publicly operated in Canada is because Canadians do not want a private market allocation of some types of goods and services.

"General Hospital" — Changing Technology and Social Rigidity

Canadians are justly proud of the medicare system. There is a widespread consensus that we do not want a market-driven system of health care, as in the U.S., because in a market system those without money go without treatment. Many Canadians believe that access to needed health care is a basic human right and the criterion for care should be medical need, not wealth. As well, Canadians have become aware of how much more efficient a "single-payer" public health care system can be. Partly because Canada saves the administrative costs of thousands of private insurance plans, which all try to itemize expenses and offload costs onto "someone else," the Canadian medicare system provides universal health care at significantly lower total cost. In 1993, Canada spent 10.1 per cent of GDP on health care, while the U.S. spent 14.4 per cent of GDP — a considerable saving, since 4.3 per cent of GDP is worth $32 billion to Canadians.[1]

The lower cost of the Canadian health care system is a major financial advantage for Canadian firms, who avoid having to pay for health insurance for their employees. The outputs of the system — healthier workers — are also a significant attraction for investment. Canadians want to preserve these advantages, but an aging population and increasingly expensive medical technology threaten to escalate health care costs, at a time when governments are being pressured to bring their deficits under control. How can government react to expanding demands and contracting resources?

Because health care spending is such a large share of the provincial budget, the increasing needs of an older population and the rising costs of new technology threaten to overwhelm it. Reducing the growth of health care expenditures has therefore become a major priority. Hospitals have received the message that they can no longer expect to dominate the health care field as they have in the past. In Nova Scotia, the Royal Commission on Health Care has argued for community-based alternatives to institutional care, and for preventive measures such as lifestyle changes. In addition, technological innovations have changed the nature of the demands on hospitals. For example, many procedures (such as simple hernia operations) which used to require hospitalization can now be undertaken on an out-patient basis or in doctors' offices. Less invasive forms of surgery have also contributed to shorter stays in the hospital for many patients.

As a result, persons who are in hospitals now for any length of time are likely to be more seriously ill, and more in need of institutional care, than was the case in earlier years, when hospitals catered to a much more diverse range of patients. Ten or fifteen years ago, a typical patient might be a high school football player with a broken arm (basically a healthy person who could eat everything the hospital had to offer); but now, such a person would normally be treated on an out-patient basis. Since it is the more seriously ill with more complex problems who are now the current patient population, and since they require more specialized care, hospital administrators are under severe pressure to do more with less.

In the province as a whole, there are essentially three kinds of hospitals: (a) community hospitals, (b) regional hospitals that have some areas of specialization, such as nuclear medicine and ultrasound, and (c) tertiary hospitals in Halifax/Dartmouth with advanced specialties, such as the capacity to undertake brain surgery and organ transplants.

"General Hospital" falls in the regional hospital category. It serves a primary catchment area of approximately 40,000 individuals with in-patient nursing and out-patient services. It provides some specialized services to community hospitals located in neighbouring towns, but it also refers some cases to Halifax for tertiary treatment. Its role in the health care system is flexible at the margins — on the one hand supplying anaesthetist services to a community hospital (without which the latter cannot perform surgery), and on the other hand possibly taking over surgery services from the community hospital. General Hospital has also taken over some functions that used to be performed in tertiary hospitals, as the technology required has become more widely, and more cheaply, available, and as the workload in the metropolitan-area institutions has become more than can be efficiently handled.

As hospitals go, General Hospital is relatively small. It has 168 general hospital beds, 103 beds in an associated nursing home, 65 in a home for the mentally handicapped, 60 in a detoxification centre, 19 in psychiatry, and a school of nursing. Each of these units is a separate legal entity, but all are controlled by the same board. The hospital is best seen as a mini-conglomerate, composed of five separate subsidiaries. (There is, as well, a legally separate charitable foundation which handles the proceeds from fund-raising drives and purchases "extras" over and above the regular budget.) Since the hospital administrator's job depends on his ability to balance the budget, he has to behave as an entrepreneur. His "markets" are the various programs (such as alcohol and drug detoxification and care for the mentally handicapped) that are paid for by the Department of Community Services and the Department of Health, as well as (occasionally) by possible federal grants.

In addition, the hospital performs laboratory services and provides physician services to other hospitals. It also rents office space to twenty-two physicians as well as to organizations such as the Department of Public Health, Drug Dependency, Hearing and Speech, and the Red Cross. Some full-time employees from General Hospital work in other hospitals. The Hospital has been quite entrepreneurial in diversifying its functions to meet a wide variety of health care needs beyond the traditional hospital role, and in the process it has diversified and maximized its revenue base. As the administrator of the hospital pointed out, this represents quite a change from the situation fifteen years ago, when the role of the hospital — to provide in-house medical services — was quite narrow. The uncertainty of the environment facing the institution has increased, as has the need for the organization to adapt to rapidly changing conditions.

The provincial Department of Health has asked all hospitals in the province to implement a management information system (MIS) which will identify cost items by medical ailment, as is now done by many health maintenance organizations in the United States. The system will tell administrators (both local and system wide) what the average cost and variance of cost is for treating patients with particular kinds of health problems at each location where the procedure is routinely performed (such as the cost for repairing a broken leg in terms of the time required, the resources used, and so forth). Each hospital's, and each doctor's, cost can then be compared to the average both within and between hospitals. Funding can then be tied to the average number of hours to be spent on a particular kind of patient with a particular kind of ailment.

The new MIS will, in effect, introduce a significant increase in the element of competition in hospital care, since the Department of Health (which already has the power to transfer procedures between competing hospitals) will have the information base to better justify such transfers. A hospital that is out of line in its costs will lose functions to neighbouring hospitals. Within hospitals, doctors who are out of line with their costs of treatment will face substantial financial penalties, since they will lose access to the hospital beds and operating room time on which their income depends.

Within specialties, the practice of medicine is very collegial. All the heart surgeons in a particular area, for example, know each other quite well and have to cooperate in the use of the same operating and test facilities. Doctors who are out of line in their costs will be pressured by their peers, who will not want to lose the right to perform specific types of procedures. With the new MIS, there will be much greater pressures on the providers of specific services within the hospital not to contribute to the hospital deficit, and hospitals will face the sanction that they may lose functions to lower cost competitors.

In addition to the MIS just described, a new system involving the measurement of the acuity of care required by a patient is being implemented so that manpower levels can be adjusted accordingly. In effect, new management information systems are creating, within hospitals, the same micro pressures for cost containment that the market has provided to private firms. The positive side of those new information systems is the identification of waste and the pressure that will be brought to bear on doctors whose patient care costs are unjustifiably high. The downside is the increased percentage of professional time spent on record keeping, rather than on patient care.

To the public, the more visible means of coping with the money squeeze are through the closing of beds in the hospital, especially in the summer, both to save money and to accommodate staff shortages due to vacations; reduced services such as building cleaning and maintenance; the education of hospital staff and the general public about the proper use of health care facilities; and the adoption of computerized software to monitor inventories and to improve collections and cash management.

Apart from management-related technology and practices, the adoption of other kinds of health-related technology also can be part of a strategy to reduce (labour) costs, as well as improving the quality of health care. In the last ten years, the hospital has added ultrasound technology, nuclear medicine, and an artificial kidney unit. All were adopted more than five years ago, but the technology has since been significantly upgraded. New technology tends to be adopted on a piecemeal, incremental basis. New tests and procedures are continuously becoming available — for example, a special brain scanner in nuclear medicine, new drugs that eliminate the need for surgery on ulcers or thyroid glands, and laser technology.

The new health technologies make work for the professional staff more complicated and often more interesting. They also improve the effectiveness of the hospital. As one of our respondents put it, "Patients bleed less, they drain better and the lab tests are much improved. Everything is so organized; we hardly ever have infections any more resulting from surgery." The new technologies require higher levels of education and training, in terms of how to operate the new technology, how to build in quality control, maintenance and calibration, running dummy tests, and so on. In general, the new technology tends to modify existing jobs rather than requiring the employment of new persons, unless new functions are being added to the responsibilities of the hospital.

If the new technology has labour-saving effects (something which is especially true in the laboratory), it used to be handled through attrition and by constraining the growth of future employment. Technological changes such as computerization tended to free up people to do other things, or permit them to do more (in terms of quantity or degree of sophistication) without having to increase staff. There was, for example, a particularly large expansion in demand for diagnostic lab services (doubling in the last ten years), and the new technologies assisted the hospital in coping with this increased demand. Beginning in late 1993, however, the financial crunch on the provincial government has escalated to the point where attrition was not enough, and lay-offs have rippled through the hospital system.

At the lower end of the occupational order, technological changes are less pronounced (for example, new washing machines in the laundry which are more high tech but easier to operate, and new and more efficient potato peelers for the kitchen). Housekeeping and cafeteria staff now need more reading and thinking skills — for example, to understand the more particularized diet specifications necessary in a hospital that needs to provide more individual and sophisticated care for people with kidney or gastro-intestinal problems. In maintenance, the hospital could operate satisfactorily with general handymen thirty years ago, but it now needs more specialized, qualified personnel since the sophistication of the building has increased (with air conditioning systems, biomedical equipment, communications technology, and so forth). Hospital administrators now need to engage licensed carpenters, electricians and boiler operators, and they are thinking of employing a professional engineer to head up the maintenance department.

The administrator of the hospital maintains that, on the whole, employees are not reluctant to adopt new technologies. They were, in fact, quite keen on it, except for a few individuals in the older age categories whom he described as being at the tail end of the non-technological age, looking forward to retirement. Hospital administrators have been careful, however, not to link the introduction of new technology with the transfer or lay-off of employees, because such a connection would seriously undermine acceptance of innovations. Instead, the emphasis is on retraining and upgrading, with the reduction of employee numbers through attrition seen as a last resort.

The hard technology of equipment and drugs is thus changing rapidly in hospitals, but are there equal changes in the soft technology of motivation and organization? In universities, we noted how an ethic of professionalism can maintain standards of excellence within an occupation, but disciplinary boundaries can impede coordination and change for the organization as a whole; the same is true, only more so, for hospitals.

Hospitals have a caste-like social organization. Doctors are the top layer and at the top of the top, there are the senior specialist surgeons. Supporting professionals like physiotherapists and nurses are next, followed by non-medical professionals like pharmacists and social workers. Technicians, in the laboratory or x-ray department, are a lower order, but they outrank nursing assistants and secretaries, while cleaners, porters and other support staff are clearly at the bottom. Hospitals employ a whole set of specialized professionals, in areas ranging from pastoral care to nutrition to audiology, and each profession has its own narrow area of responsibility. There is little or no mobility between groups, and there are substantial barriers to the reallocation of work, in the form of licensing, credentialism, and restrictions to practice.

Because hospitals now cater to patients that are, on average, more seriously ill than has been the case in the past, occupational groupings such as nurses, physiotherapists, occupational therapists and speech and language specialists have been able to emphasize their perceived need for four-year degree programs. These specialized occupational groups argue that more junior personnel, such as physiotherapy aides and certified nursing assistants, should be restricted in what they are able to do in the hospital setting. Our interviews revealed considerable resentment arising from "professionalization" for example, physiotherapists who refused to supervise physiotherapy aides in the hospital on the grounds that the proposed work needed to be done by a fully trained health professional.

Similarly, the CNAs (Certified Nursing Assistants) spoke with bitterness about not being able to perform the range of tasks that were once the norm. While CNAs used to perform tasks such as catheterizations, doing complex dressings with tubes, setting up intravenous feeding on their own, and doing patient teaching, new recruits are now limited to more simple tasks such as arranging bed backs, doing simple dressings, and helping people in and out of bed. In the view of the CNAs we interviewed, a CNA can only carry out fifty per cent of their workload because the Registered Nurses Association has put up roadblocks in order to protect their own practice. It is now more difficult for a CNA to become a team leader, and increasingly they need to report to the nurse on duty and seek instruction there, even if the nurse is a recent graduate and doesn't have nearly the extent of experience that the CNA has on the hospital floor. While they have always worked with nurses as part of a team, we were told that newer nursing graduates are taught never to ask a CNA questions and are discouraged from serving as a "buddy" for incoming student nurses. In the words of one of our respondents: "It is nice to have people in the hospital with higher levels of training, but CNAs could be doing more under proper supervision."

The CNAs do recognize that the new hospital environment demands more skills, in part because of a more complicated patient population. As we have seen, there are new treatments, new drugs and medications, and new technologies — all of which have to be handled properly and all of which require a higher skill level. CNAs, however, are not permitted to exercise the skills that they presently have and are frustrated in gaining access to longer and more sophisticated training programs. At the moment, their training is limited to a ten- to twelve-month community college program, which includes a period of ten weeks working on the job in the hospital setting. They would like to see the program extended to eighteen months and to include a more substantial and clinical hospital-based component. In fact, some would prefer to have the hospitals take over the training entirely, for they feel that the vocational school program is behind the times in terms of technology, and the instructors have not changed their way of doing things for the past ten to fifteen years. Their job security, it is alleged, is not shaken by student complaints.

The CNAs we interviewed felt stuck in their positions. They claimed that there were no promotion opportunities and they regretted the fact that a person could not work her way up either by training or by seniority. "To become a Registered Nurse would be really nice, but the minimum required is to take a diploma program. In principle this could be done, but it would require saving up money for two years of living expenses. I wish there were bridging steps, and recognition for prior learning as a CNA."

The prospects for the CNAs to qualify as nurses are further reduced as the emphasis shifts to the mandatory requirement for a four-year nursing degree. Unless arrangements can be made for a decentralized degree program locally, achieving such a credential would mean leaving the area to study for four years — a requirement that imposes significant barriers for CNAs who have families.

In all of this conflict over professional turf, the patient is often the forgotten element. As doctors become more pressed for time and nurses have to work harder to cope with more seriously ill patients, it becomes more difficult for them to spare the time to listen to the fears and concerns of their patients, much harder for them to attend to the emotional part of the healing process. As job duties become more specialized and job divisions become more rigid, each occupational group becomes more clearly responsible for a particular part of the patient, but not for the patient as a whole person. Yet healing is not just a technical, specialized process. Many studies have shown the importance of emotional nurturance, optimism, and caring for the recovery process. Although the channels of influence between emotional and physical health are not precisely understood, it is abundantly clear that people are much more than simply a collection of body parts.

More rapid recoveries would, of course, also mean lower costs. Hence, General Hospital is another example of the four-cornered interdependence of cost, quality, soft technology and hard technology. Although the hard technology of equipment and drugs is modern and efficient, and although new management information systems hold the promise of containing costs, the social rigidities of the hospital, when combined with the increased pressure of work, are a real barrier to the overall quality of care (and ultimately, to reducing costs).

In some hospitals, there is a conscious attempt to build up a team approach to patient care, but these are usually teams of professionals only. Team membership is a jealously guarded indicator of professional status, i.e. nurses can belong and speak up during "rounds," but it is assumed that a CNA has nothing useful to say (despite perhaps having as much or more personal contact with the patient than the doctor). The ethic of professionalism within each occupation helps to maintain standards of quality in the performance of specialized functions. However, the competing demands of professional groups for status and responsibility also mean a fragmentation of patient care, and a rigidity of work roles that is unhealthy, both for the hospital as an organization, and for its patients.

Overall, General Hospital provides an interesting example of a public sector institution adapting to financial, demographic and technological pressures. While it is a major employer in its region, and while it provides stable employment for a limited number of workers with relatively low educational and skill qualifications, it does not hold out hope for a work environment of expanding employment, whether measured in terms of the number of positions available to such workers or in terms of jobs that promise a future of expanding skill and occupational mobility. Its main problem internally is the fragmentation and rigidity of narrow occupational specializations.

Recently, the provincial government has announced a move to decentralize the administration of health care, by dividing the province into four health care regions. Resource allocation decisions are to be made locally, instead of in Halifax. Implicitly, this will intoduce another layer of comparisons and competition. With improved management information systems, doctors can be compared in terms of how quickly patients with a certain ailment recover, or how often specific remedies are prescribed. Hospitals can be compared in terms of cost per bed-night, average length of stay, number of complications, and so on. And with regional health zones, administrators can make decisions about whether to put resources into preventive public health measures or after-the-fact hospital cures, and be judged on the results. Within health care there is, therefore, substantial change in the soft technology of organization, with a theme familiar from the private sector of decentralization of decision-making within a common management information system.

"Rockland School Board" — Rural Isolation and Population Decline

Our final case study in the public sector was of special interest because of what it produced, and where it was located, as well as its being an example of changing employment patterns. A recurring refrain in our case studies is the importance of education and the limited jobs available for school dropouts; hence, in examining a school board, we were interested in both its employment patterns and its educational role. As well, since a number of our case studies have illustrated the general shift from rural to urban areas; this school board is also an example of the response of the public sector to changing demographics.

"Rockland School Board" is located in a rural and relatively isolated region of the province. It is a region of forests, lakes, seashore, and small towns that depends heavily on fishing and forestry-related activities. Fishing and fish processing are severely handicapped by sharply reduced quotas. In forestry, the only options are to supply wood to a pulp and paper mill in an adjoining county, or to work there for wages. In the service sector, small local stores have lost out to the malls of the regional service centre (which are outside the county), where doctors, dentists, and lawyers also prefer to settle. The region has continuing problems attracting resident health professionals, even when subsidized facilities are offered.

As with many other rural areas of Canada faced with the erosion of their employment base, the county is losing its population, especially the younger and more educated. During our interviews, we heard many expressions of despair at the prospect that in ten years time the county's population will be predominantly elderly and retired. The school system is, therefore, important both because it is one of the few large employers in the county, and because it provides the education that may equip young people with the credentials they need to get a job when they leave the county.

In carrying out both roles, the Rockland School Board is strongly affected by demographic changes that have sharply reduced the size of the school-age population. In 1985, the School Board had an enrolment of 2,800 to 2,900 students in Grades 1 to 12, a number that had dropped to 2,500 in 1990 and that is forecast to drop further to 2,000 students by 1995 — and even this figure assumes that the major fish plant in the area, which is experiencing serious economic problems despite substantial public assistance, will continue to operate.

Declining enrolment has combined with the provincial policy of school consolidation to eliminate many local schools in favour of regional consolidated schools. Student numbers in the county have simply not been sufficient to keep a large number of local schools viable, and the twelve schools in the county in 1985 were reduced to eight in 1990. The loss of local schools is more than just a symbol of population decline; the local school is part of the heart and soul of small rural communities — as long as the school is still there, the community can remain an attractive location for young families — and its closing threatens the very survival of these communities.

Closing schools also means fewer teachers are needed. The number of teachers has been reduced largely through attrition, so that until the provincial government offered healthy financial inducement to early retirement there were hardly any new hirings and then only for the occasional teacher with a highly specialized background. School administrators were acutely conscious of the presence of some older "burnt out" teachers in the schools and of the importance of bringing in new, younger teachers with enthusiasm and awareness of the latest ideas in education. But in a shrinking system, this is difficult to accomplish.

One implication of school consolidation has been the creation of jobs for a new occupational category: bus drivers, now the second largest occupational group employed by the school board. These positions do not require a lot of education, so credentialism is not a barrier. But there is little prospect for the further expansion of this occupational group because school consolidation cannot proceed much further, since some children already spend over two hours a day on the school bus.

From an educational standpoint, the consolidation of rural schools is a mixed blessing. Its advantage is that it reduces the social isolation of students and exposes them to a wider range of influences. There are several small black communities in the county whose children formerly attended small segregated schools. School consolidation has provided them the opportunity to attend larger schools with a richer mix of educational offerings and resources — and a mixed racial population. On the minus side, children can now spend up to $1\frac{1}{4}$ hours each way on the bus, which both exhausts the children and rules out any participation in extra-curricular activities.

Approximately half of the high school population graduate and go on to post-secondary education, while the other half either do not complete secondary school or do not pursue further studies. To obtain a better picture of the educational program and prospects facing the "the bottom half," we interviewed teachers of industrial class students (a separate stream from the standard academic classes).

In an impoverished county in a relatively poor province, it is remarkable that "the system" has produced the resources needed to give special attention to those students who are in greatest danger of dropping out. This special education is expensive because these students need the personalized attention that is only possible with a low student-teacher ratio. The county can afford to pay for it because the provincial government has a system of equalization grants to school boards which roughly balances the resources available for students in different counties, despite wide variations in local property tax assessment. The province can afford these grants because it receives, in turn, equalization grants from the federal government, which helps to ensure that provinces can provide an equivalent level of public services at comparable rates of taxation. These transfers between governments are not directly observed by most Canadians, but they are the financial underpinnings of our attempts to provide greater "equality of opportunity."

In this way, Rockland School Board has been able to find the resources to maintain a low student-teacher ratio for disadvantaged students, and has attracted teachers who seem genuinely committed to their students' progress. The teachers are strong advocates of the concept of special classes for students who have experienced a succession of failures, and who may also have had significant behaviour problems in primary school. They argued against the trend to integrated classrooms on the grounds that relative success is central to maintaining the self-esteem of their students. They maintain that breaking the expectation of failure is one of their most important tasks; if their students remained within the regular classroom environment, the continued experience of relative failure would mean that they would drop out of school at the earliest opportunity.

Both the potentials and pitfalls of special education were also on display among the teachers we interviewed. One spoke self-depreciatingly of the need to "ego massage" his students in order to build up their sense of self-esteem. On the day we visited, his curriculum included Arnold Schwarzenegger movies to keep up the level of interest of the students. He noted that, in an area where a trip to Halifax is a major event, it is mainly the children of teachers who have been outside the county — and it is teachers' kids who win all the school prizes.

However, another interview provided an example of a teacher who saw herself as needing to provide a positive role model to motivate the students. She spoke movingly of how much more some students need their teachers now than they used to. Families are much smaller these days, so students often do not have brothers and sisters to talk to. The percentage of single-parent families in the rural counties of Nova Scotia is not much different than in the city, so there is often only one parent available; but in rural areas there is the additional problem that children are isolated by distance from other children or other members of the extended family. This teacher noted that the fixed patterns of family life — such as sit-down meals at specific times — which she grew up with were no longer typical. As one of the few black teachers on staff, she may have felt a special responsibility to "be there" for her students, but she also described a general pattern in which many students need to talk, about deeply personal things, to an adult who is important in their lives — and increasingly the only available adult is the teacher.

Despite some differences in style, however, both of these teachers agreed that the "industrial" group of students have different needs, both intellectually and emotionally, from those in the academic stream. Both spoke of the difficulty in motivating students to take school seriously, in an environment where there are very few people with higher education who might function as living testimonials to the idea that education pays. It is often remarked that students from disadvantaged backgrounds cannot see any connection between their course work in school and "real life." In this rural county, people depend even more on the family and school environment to make this connection than is the case in urban areas, since there are few nearby who would personify the education-income link.

In an environment of few jobs and few role models, one might expect that absenteeism would be a problem, but it isn't. Because of the lack of employment and entertainment opportunities, there is simply nothing else to do and no better way to see one's friends than to go to school, quite apart from the merits of school attendance as a means to learning and getting ahead in life. As an illustration of this phenomenon, we were told that the school bus drivers could not count on non-attendance as a factor in planning the size of bus to run on different routes — that is, one cannot schedule a fifty-seat bus on a fifty-two student bus route in the expectation that some students will typically be absent, since in fact they all do attend. In contrast to the national attention being given to the problem of lack of school attendance and high drop-out rates, this was simply not an issue any more in the county where our case study was located.

In the days when jobs were available in the local fish plant, dropping out of school at sixteen used to be fairly common. Back then, after two or three years seniority one could expect to get fairly steady work and, since there is little differentiation of earnings in a fish plant and no premium for education, nineteen-year-old workers could easily make as much as their parents. The town has a grocery store, a gas station, a laundromat/restaurant, and the school. The fish plant is the only employer of any size. When jobs were available in the fish plant, dropping out of school was an economically rational decision for those who intended to remain in the area, and in the 1986 Census, only thirty per cent of adults in the county reported that they had graduated from high school.

However, those days are long gone. The fish plant has not hired new workers in years; in fact, it has been forced to lay off several hundred of its experienced workers, who now have first claim on any jobs that might open up. As a consequence, very few students now drop out of school before finishing Grade 12. The drop-out rate for the province as a whole is now far lower than it was in the 1970s (see Chapter 6) and the school withdrawal rate of Rockland County is substantially below the provincial average. School teachers gripe about the fact it was easier to teach in the old days, when the students who stayed in school were those who were more intrinsically interested in their courses. But they also acknowledge that high school completion is essential if their students are to have any sort of chance in the outside labour market.

For those who do drop out of high school, there are few alternatives. Although one of the objectives of the Nova Scotia government in setting up the community college system was to provide a set of training opportunities for those not inclined or destined to go on to university — particularly those who did not complete high school — all our respondents argued that the community college system has deserted this constituency. There are many applicants for places in programs offered by the community colleges, and the colleges have responded by "skimming" the population of applicants, selecting only those who have high school graduation or better, and those with the highest marks. Because access to the community college system is rationed by educational credentials, those who find the academic stream difficult but who might well have excellent aptitude for practical vocational skills are shut out.

The vagaries of federal-provincial relations in Canada do provide a partial escape route for some because Human Resources Development Canada sponsors a learning centre that accepts a few high school drop-outs every six months. As a result, although the provincial educational system fails to serve fully the training needs of high school drop-outs, this is partially compensated for by federal training programs. But such programs are vulnerable in an era of federal retrenchment.

In our interviews at Rockland School Board, the dual roles of the public sector competed for attention. We were interested in the role that the school board played as an employer, and in how it had adapted to changes in educational methods and to the money squeeze facing the public sector. For this particular school board, the main story was the extreme difficulty of implementing change while contracting. In part, the difficulties arise from the soft technology of organizational behaviour — a shrinking work force means less hiring, more older workers and fewer opportunities for job rotation and renewal. In response to declining opportunities, many people are emigrating, and the county is depopulating, but the children of those who remain still have a right to an education. The geography of the county does not make it feasible to reduce further the number of schools.

Given these difficulties, we were also interested in the other role that the public sector plays: as provider of one of the key inputs — educated labour — that the private sector requires. It was clear that, for a combination of reasons, Rockland School Board is delivering upper level high school education to a growing portion of its school-age population. Because high school completion is an important credential for the many youth who will have to leave the county in order to find employment, it is essential for the long-run structural adjustment of the Canadian labour market that rural school boards, like that of Rockland County, have the resources needed to provide a generally acceptable educational credential to youth. Although vocational education after high school may be more problematic for the disadvantaged, and although it is undeniable that the local employment situation in Rockland county is pretty bleak, there were also some grounds for optimism at Rockland School Board.

A much higher percentage of rural youth is staying in school in the 1990s, compared to their parents, and some rural schools provide a good quality of education. Nova Scotia has a system of standardized achievement tests at Grades 3, 6, 9 and 12, and the availability of standardized test scores builds in an element of competition among schools and school boards. Some small rural high schools can be found near the top, and some near the bottom, of the provincial rankings. The fact that provincial comparisons indicate that it is possible for small rural schools to do well increases the pressure on school principals and board administrators in the schools that do poorly in the annual comparison of standardized test results.

Conclusion

The public sector is important because of both its direct and indirect impacts on job creation. The public sector is a major direct employer, and it also affects employment indirectly through the quality of services it provides and the level of taxation it demands. Our case studies illustrated the fact that the days of an expanding public sector have been over for some time, and the public sector will not be a large direct creator of jobs in the foreseeable future. Some have argued that although the recession of 1990–1993 produced significant declines in private-sector employment, the "public sector recession" is only just beginning, as governments at all levels cut back employment in an attempt to eliminate budgetary deficits.

Although the general cash squeeze of deficit reduction affects all aspects of the public sector, our case studies illustrated some of the different sorts of pressures that impinge on it. Our case studies of the military and of a county school board illustrated the problem of structural change within government. Essentially, Canadian society wants less of what these two organizations produce — political changes (the end of the cold war) have decreased the need for military security, and demographic changes (emigration and a declining birth rate) have decreased the demand for schooling in some rural areas. The case study of a Provincial Commission was an illustration of the greater questioning of public sector roles and responsibilities — the threat of privatization was the driving force underlying its organizational change. In our hospital case study, increasing demand for health care has collided with the decreasing financial resources available to government, to produce a new emphasis on managed competition within the public health care system.

If the private sector is going to be successful at creating jobs, it will need an effective public sector that provides needed services at reasonable cost. Some public-sector organizations are undergoing substantial changes. We were interested to learn, for example, that although both the hospital and the school board we studied were in isolated rural areas, both had recently hired new senior administrators from outside (British Columbia and Alberta), because of the different outlook and experiences they would bring to the job. We were also interested to observe the ways in which new types of information, such as the hospital's management information system, or the standardized testing program in schools, are creating new pressures not to fall behind. The soft technology of the public sector is clearly changing — in some of the same ways as that of the private sector.

6

Education and Training Policy

The focus of this book has been on the structural changes in the job market that emerged during the 1980s and early 1990s, and whether or not these recent changes imply a continued trend to greater inequality and poverty in Canadian society. A recurring theme of our case study interviews, and of econometric analyses of the labour market, is that in today's labour market education is crucial for higher earnings and better chances of employment. This chapter will emphasize the pay-off to investment in education, but will also emphasize that investment in education is investment *for the long term*.

In thinking about education, it is important to take the long view, because someone starting school in the mid-1990s can reasonably expect to be still working in the year 2050. Today's students can expect a lifetime of change. One way of appreciating the extent of those changes is to think of the changes older workers have experienced during their working lifetimes. Workers who are nearing retirement in the mid-1990s were born in the early 1930s, and left school in the late 1940s. In those days, it was a rare event to complete high school. Primitive computers had just been invented, and air travel was a rarity — no one imagined the revolution in information processing and the globalization of trade that has since occurred. The 1930s generation entered a labour market in which most work was manual, most workers were male, and unemployment was 2.4 per cent (1951). Social change has been just as dramatic as economic change.

Labour market reality has altered dramatically over the last forty years, and there is no reason to think that the pace of change will slow in the next forty years. The rapidity of change means that learning is a life-long process. But it is still the responsibility of the school system to provide the base competencies in mathematics, language, science and social skills upon which further training and retraining can be built.

Furthermore, Canadians have become accustomed to earning wages well above the international average wage, and would like this fortunate situation to continue. In order for it to do so, Canadians will have to offer skills that are similarly above the international average. An "average" quality of schooling will not be good enough. Since educational levels around the world are rising, the quality of Canadian education will have to improve, if Canadians want to continue to succeed in international competition.

However, although better education has a long-term impact, re-forms to the educational system may not be able to solve short-term problems. Although many people feel that an inadequate educational system is part of the cause of Canada's current economic problems, educational reforms cannot hope to provide a quick fix. Given the complexity of the educational system, it will inevitably take time to think through the innovations required in education, to design new curricula to implement these ideas, and to train teachers in their delivery. However, even if the best possible educational system in the world could be implemented in time for next year's opening of school, it would still be decades before it could have a major impact on the average quality of the Canadian labour force.

If the world's best educational system was put in place next year for the entire primary and secondary educational system, next year's graduates would have one-twelfth of their education under the new system, but eleven-twelfths of their education has already taken place under the old system. As time passes, more and more students would go through a reformed system, and its impact on students would increase, but it would be twelve years before any Grade 12 graduate had had all their education under the new system.

Furthermore, the benefit of a new system would be the difference between its quality and the quality of the present system. Most newspaper stories making international comparisons of educational achievement focus on the fact that students in some other countries do better than Canadian students — but *how much* better? Since almost everyone is still in school at age thirteen, comparisons of average education quality at that age are particularly relevant. In tests of science knowledge among thirteen-year-olds, Korean students scored highest in international comparisons — their average score was thirteen per cent higher than Nova Scotia students. There is a debate over whether this test-score differential corresponds to a similar differential in knowledge, differences in the quality of education and thinking skills, or differences in the acquisition of the type of knowledge that can be easily tested for in multiple-choice examinations. However, suppose that the test-score differential measures a real differential in educational quality and that the best possible educational system could eventually increase achievement levels by even more — say 15 per cent. In phasing in a new educational system, students have to be prepared for the tasks they will encounter at each stage — there is no point in asking a Grade 10 student to do calculus if they have not already had algebra. But even ignoring this problem and assuming that the impact of educational reforms is proportional to the time spent in the reformed system, in the first year after reform graduates would only have had one-twelfth of their education under the new system. Hence the impact on their average skill level would be about 1.25 per cent (i.e. 15 per cent divided by 12). The impact of educational reforms on the skills of graduates clearly increases over time, since graduates two years from now will have had two years exposure to the new system, and so on, but it would take a full twelve years before the impact of educational reforms on the skills of high school graduates has its full effect (i.e. 15 per cent).

In addition, the number of high school graduates is, each year, only about 2.5 per cent of the labour force. Hence even if, next year, an educational system could be put in place which immediately increased the quality of Canadian primary and secondary education by more than the differential in average science achievement between Canadian junior high students and those of the highest scoring country (Korea), twelve years from now this reform would only have affected the 30 per cent of the labour force who graduate in these dozen years. The average impact on graduates (given that most of these people are already in school) would be an improvement of 7.5 per cent, but since they would be only 30 per cent of the labour force, the impact on the average quality of the labour force as a whole would be an improvement of 2.25 per cent (= 7.5 per cent x 0.3). The "bottom line" is that reforms to primary and secondary education can only have slow impacts on the average quality of the labour force.

This is not an argument against educational reform, but it is an argument against the expectation that educational reform can provide quick fix, miracle cures for the current problems of the Canadian economy. It is essential for the long-run health of the Canadian economy, and the long-run quality of life in Canadian society, that Canadians students receive an education that is just as good as, and preferably better than, that provided anywhere else in the world. Investments in education will pay off, both socially and economically, for many decades to come. A failure to invest in educational reform will mean that Canada will inevitably lose its ability to compete in the knowledge-intensive industries of the future. In addition, since new knowledge is continually being discovered and new teaching techniques are continually being evaluated, educational reform is a never-ending process. However, it should be recognized that investment in education is investment for the long term. Since it is simply not possible for reforms to primary and secondary education to have a huge impact on the average productivity of the Canadian labour force within the next decade, Canadians should not turn in disillusionment away from educational reform when it fails to provide immediate solutions to the current problems of the Canadian economy.

It is very clear that more years of education mean, on average, higher pay and a lower chance of unemployment. Data for the year prior to the recession (1990) show that people with a university education earned about thirty-eight per cent more than high school graduates, over and above the differences associated with age, occupation, industry, marital status, and so forth. (In Atlantic Canada, education earns a slightly higher premium than in the rest of the country.) In 1990, high school graduates earned about 17 per cent more than people with an elementary education who had similar characteristics (similar age, industry of employment, size of employer, and so on). In 1990, university graduates in Canada had an unemployment rate of 3.8 per cent, compared to the 7.7 per cent unemployment rate among high school graduates. This differential in unemployment widened in the recession to 5.5 per cent for university graduates compared to 10.8 per cent for high school grads in 1992.[1]

During the recession of the early 1990s, unemployment went up for all types of workers, but less so for the better educated. Partly because of the skills they have learned in school, and partly because of the credential value of education, those with more years of education tend to go to the front of the queue for jobs. Education is partly "human capital" and partly a signal to employers that people who succeed in school have more of the underlying traits (such as social skills, intelligence and work discipline) that tend to produce success in both school and work. When there are not enough jobs to go around, as in the early 1990s, employers can be picky. A general surplus of job seekers means that firms can escalate their hiring standards and hire university graduates for jobs that high school graduates used to do. High school graduates then have to compete for the jobs which those with elementary schooling used to do, and as we have seen in our case studies, such jobs are increasingly unavailable.

Part of the greater earnings and lower unemployment of the more educated is therefore due to the fact that, when jobs are scarce, the more educated "bump" many of the less educated down the job hierarchy and into unemployment. As Chapter 7 will emphasize, only a resurgence of growth in the economy as a whole will turn this bumping process around. A resurgence of growth will create more jobs for the disadvantaged directly, and it will also increase their access to jobs indirectly, by creating opportunities for the more educated to move into jobs which use more of their skills, thereby opening up vacancies for those unemployed who have less education. However, if the economy does not grow rapidly enough, job scarcity will continue to dominate the labour market as a whole, and some university graduates will be underemployed, displacing high school graduates from jobs, and not actually using much of the training that they acquired in school.

All the same, an education lasts for a lifetime, and there is abundant evidence that the long-run trend in developed nations is towards an occupational structure that increasingly demands high-level educational skills. One of the big labour market trends of the 1980s in the United States was a substantial increase in the financial return to education, and this has a straightforward demand-and-supply explanation: Partly because of rapidly increasing tuition costs, the proportion of young Americans going to college stagnated in the 1980s. Although the supply of university graduates remained fairly constant, the demand for graduates increased, and the result of greater demand and contracting supply was a significant increase in the real earnings of university graduates. On the other hand, for the increasing number of U.S. high school graduates who did not go on to university, shrinking demand produced a significant decline in real wages through the 1980s.[2]

Canada has largely avoided this trend to increased inequality of wages because in Canada a similar increase in the demand for university-educated workers was matched by an increase in supply. (Between 1986 and 1991, the number of university graduates in Canada increased by a dramatic 26.6 per cent.) Throughout the 1980s, the real cost of post-secondary education in Canada remained heavily subsidized by government. With relatively low tuition fees, (at least by U.S. standards) the cash cost of continued education remained manageable. Canadian students also realized that with high unemployment, they were not giving up much in the job market if they continued in school, and the participation rate in post-secondary education increased steadily.

In the "Information Economy" age, one of Canada's real strengths has been, therefore, the relatively high level of accessibility of the Canadian post-secondary education system. In the 1980s, this accessibility enabled the supply of university graduates to keep up with increasing demand for high-level skills, thereby preventing the widening of earnings differentials. In the recession of the early 1990s, the accessibility of the post-secondary education system has, in effect, enabled many people who would otherwise have been unemployed to invest in their human capital. As they graduate into a high unemployment labour market, they have real difficulties in finding employment and they displace high school graduates from jobs. But although high unemployment means that many of the graduates of post-secondary educational institutions do not now use all the skills they have acquired, those skills are available when economic growth resumes.

It is also essential to recognize the strengths of Canada's primary and secondary educational system. This recognition is necessary in order to in turn focus attention, and resources, on areas of weakness. Canada cannot afford (even if it were possible) to reform every aspect of its educational system, and it would not be desirable to do so, since there are elements of the present system that are worth preserving.

Over the last decade, for example, the school system has succeeded in retaining a dramatically higher percentage of students through the completion of high school. Table 1 presents annual data on the Grade 12 retention rate in Atlantic Canada — the percentage of Grade 7 students who, five years later, are still in school. Between 1980 and 1990, for example, the Nova Scotia Grade 12 retention rate increased from 57 per cent to 82 per cent, and in the two following years the retention rate increased by a further 12 per cent to 94 per cent.[3] Since some students drop out later in their Grade 12 year,

Table 1				
HIGH SCHOOL RETENTION RATES† **FOR THE ATLANTIC PROVINCES**				
Year	**Nova Scotia**	**New Brunswick**	**Prince Edward Island**	**Newfoundland††**
				Grade 11	**Grade 12**
1992	94%	91%	106%	96%	90%
1991	87%	95%	96%	94%	88%
1990	82%	92%	94%	88%	79%
1989	81%	87%	95%	81%	77%
1988	79%	83%	89%	79%	74%
1987	78%	85%	89%	81%	72%
1986	73%	81%	86%	77%	71%
1985	70%	82%	81%	77%	68%
1984	72%	81%	79%	73%	66%
1983	69%	80%	82%	69%	64%
1982	63%	74%	77%	72%	**
1981	58%	73%	73%	71%	**
1980	57%	69%	69%	69%	**
1975	53%	62%	60%	64%	**
1970	52%	n/a	56%	68%	**
1965	33%	n/a	46%	50%	**

† Retention rates are obtained by dividing the enrolment in Grade 12 by enrolment in Grade 7 five years previous. Rates may be overestimated as there is no record of the number of students returning to Grade 12 after dropping out for a period of time. During downturns in the economy, more students are likely to return to school.

†† Before 1983, high school graduation in Newfoundland was after Grade 11, with Grade 12 being a university preparatory year. Beginning in 1983, students were required to complete Grade 12 to graduate.

Source: Provincial Departments of Education

retention rate statistics overstate the high school graduation rate. Furthermore, the 1991–92 retention rate will be overstated to the extent that some people returned for a second year of Grade 12, because there were no jobs available or because they wanted to improve their high school marks. Nevertheless, the advantage of looking at retention rates is that comparable statistics have been collected for a long time and there is no doubt that the improvement in school retention has been dramatic — the Grade 12 retention rate in 1965 was only 33 per cent.[4]

Someone who left high school in 1965 at the age of 16 was only 46 in 1995 — the educational achievement of Nova Scotia youth today is dramatically higher than the educational achievement of their parents. One of the reasons for this difference is that in the 1960s, jobs for high school drop-outs were still available in the fishery, in mining and in the service sector. Since many of these jobs (such as those of fishplant workers) earned the same rate of pay, with or without high school graduation, there was not much economic return then to staying on in school. In the 1980s, however, it became clear that there were very few job alternatives for high school drop-outs — a fact which is very well known by today's teenagers.

As Table 1 indicates, there has been a dramatic change in the high school retention rate in Atlantic Canada over the last dozen years. As well as the teenagers who are now staying in school until Grade 12, many adults return to school to get their GED certificate of Grade 12 equivalency. Over the 1989 1991 period, GED graduates made up about 15 per cent of average Grade 12 enrolment in Nova Scotia. Since the Grade 12 retention rate overstates the high school graduation rate and since the high rate of adult achievement of Grade 12 equivalency reflects in part the high rates of school drop out in previous years, the GED graduation rate and the Grade 12 retention rate cannot simply be added together, but it is clear that the eventual rate of completion of high school is now much higher than it was in the 1960s.

Since there has been a great deal of discussion of illiteracy, Table 2 presents some comparative information on literacy skills in Canada and in Nova Scotia. The Statistics Canada survey on which this table is based measured "functional" literacy, defined as the ability to both decode chunks of written text *and* use that information to solve practical problems. It is presented in terms of levels of literacy skills since there is a continuum of literacy skills, from those who can

Table 2
LITERACY SKILLS – CANADA AND NOVA SCOTIA

	ALL AGES		OVER 35		AGE 16-34			
	Canada	N.S.	Canada	N.S.	Canada	N.S.	Rural N.S.	Urban N.S.
% Level 1	7	5	8	6	1	2	2	1
% Level 2	9	10	13	16	5	4	5	4
% Level 3	22	28	24	31	20	23	23	24
% Level 4	62	57	53	46	73	71	70	71

NOTE:
Level 1 - Canadians at this level have difficulty dealing with printed
materials. They most likely identify themselves as people who
cannot read.
Level 2 - Canadians at this level can use printed materials only for limited
purposes such as finding a familiar word in a simple text. They
would likely recognize themselves as having difficulties with
common reading materials.
Level 3 - Canadians at this level can use reading materials in a variety of
situations provided the material is kept simple, clearly laid out and
the tasks involved are not too complex. While these people
generally do not see themselves as having major reading
difficulties, they tend to avoid situations requiring reading.
Level 4 - Canadians at this level meet most everyday reading demands. This
is a large and diverse group that exhibits a wide range of reading
skills.
Source: Statistics Canada, special tabulation from "Survey of Literacy
Skills Used in Daily Activity" (1989).

barely write their own names to those whose daily work involves
complex literary and mathematical expression.

As might be expected, given the substantial increase in school
attainment in recent years, there is a very significant difference
between the literacy skills of older and younger cohorts of Canadians. The difference is particularly marked for the two lowest literacy
levels — among Canadians aged over 35, 21 per cent either cannot
read or have difficulty with common reading materials, but less than
one third of this number (6 per cent) of Canadians aged 16 to 34 are
reading at similarly low levels. Furthermore, as Table 2 indicates,
there is essentially no difference between Nova Scotia and Canada
as a whole, or between rural and urban areas of Nova Scotia, in the
percentage of youth at low literacy levels.

Readers will note that we are avoiding categorical statements such as "X per cent of Canadians are illiterate." The issue, for functional literacy, is whether or not an individual has the level of literacy needed to solve the problems actually encountered in his or her own daily life. Without reference to the need for literacy skills, it makes no sense to talk of "illiteracy." Those people who have found niches in the labour force that do not depend much on written communication, or who have retired, may not possess the ability to decode complex written text, but this may not cause them much of a problem in daily life in the workplace.

The main lesson of Table 2 is that it is essential to distinguish between the literacy problems of Canada's youth and the literacy problems of its older population. Problems of low literacy skills are concentrated among people who had relatively few years of education and who have been out of school for many years. As our case studies illustrate, limited literacy skills are not always a barrier to continued employment. Multiburger has deskilled its labour requirements to the point where a worker only has to push a coded cash register button and say, "Have a nice day." At Joe's Machine Shop or at Sally Servant, steady work is available for those who are willing to work hard for limited wages. People may need to get help occasionally with written instructions, but as long as they do so, they can cope. The social problem of illiteracy is, however, more pressing for workers at risk of job loss (like those at Family Sawmills), because their lack of literacy will create future problems in locating a replacement job. For those who have to adapt to significant technical change (as at Coal Mine Company), lack of literacy is a problem of the present, since both productivity and safety depend on being able to understand the manuals, and the principles of operation, of new equipment.

Literacy is a problem for one segment of the population, but the Canadian educational system is expected to produce both basic literacy for everyone and Ph.D.-level scientists who are as good as any Ph.D.s trained anywhere in the world. Although the direct employment of research scientists will always be a relatively small percentage of the labour force, this does not mean that the post-graduate university sector is unimportant, but that its influence on total employment levels is indirect.

In the long run, Canada needs an internationally competitive research effort if Canadian firms are going to tap into rapidly changing developments at the frontiers of science. Since Canada is a relatively small country, and since the expansion of scientific knowledge is occurring world-wide, the big issue for Canada's economic development is not how much new knowledge is discovered in Canada, but how much of the world's new knowledge Canadians can put to work. If Canada has only a small percentage of the world's scientists, it is unreasonable to expect Canada to produce a large percentage of the world's research results. But although Canadian scientists may only produce 4 per cent of the world's new knowledge, Canadian industry also needs access to the other 96 per cent.

Access to the world's knowledge depends crucially on the presence, in Canada, of first-rate scientists who know what is going on at the frontiers of science and who can evaluate its significance. It is rarely possible to jump directly from a scientific discovery to the complex, practical realities of producing and marketing a new commodity — a long process of adaptation and engineering is invariably essential. In order to choose the technologies that have a chance of eventual success, and in order to make them a success, a sophisticated familiarity with the problems and potentials of the underlying science is needed. Such familiarity cannot, in practice, be expected to come from spectators in the world of research. Basic research in Canada is crucial both for its results and for the access it gives to research results developed elsewhere.

Some of the firms we interviewed have imported state-of-the-art machinery that embodies new technology; for example, the computerized shearer in use at Coal Mine Co., or the machining stations at Aerospace Manufacturing. Other firms, such as Quality Architects, are developing new production technologies in-house. Others collaborate with external research agencies; for example, a joint industry-university research program to enhance the regeneration of fish stocks.

Although there is a variety of pathways for the development of new technology, the big issue, in economic terms, is the rate of adaptation and diffusion of new technology. This process of diffusion of advanced technology throughout the economy depends on both a local research community that operates at the highest international levels of expertise, and a broad base of technological competency that is able to absorb continual innovations in production technology. Firms need a *few* research scientists but they need *many* skilled technicians to take a new idea from the laboratory to low-cost, high-quality production.

			TABLE
			AGES, PARTICIPATION
	Percentage in school	**Mean age**	**Percentage taking Biology**
Australia	39	17	18
Canada (English)	71	18	28
England	20	18	4
Finland	45 (63)*	18	45
Hong Kong	20	18	7
Hungary	18 (40)*	18	3
Italy	52	19	14
Japan	63	18	12
Norway	40	18	10
Poland	28	18	9
Singapore	17	18	3
Sweden	15 (30)*	19	15
U.S.A.	90	17	6

*The figures in parentheses include students in vocational or similar streams which were not sampled.

For this reason, we would emphasise the simultaneous importance of a broad base and a high peak in science achievement. And Canadians should recognize that a major strength of the Canadian educational/training system is the broad base of exposure it provides to Canadian youth in upper level secondary science education. Table 3 presents comparative data on science achievement among senior high school students in the early 1980s. Columns 1 to 5 are included in order to make the point that in Canada a substantially higher fraction of youth remain in school compared to most other countries.

The United States is the only country with a higher rate of school retention than Canada, but because many other softer options in high school education are available, the percentage of 17/18-year-olds

3					
AND TEST SCORES					
of age group course			**Mean Test Score**		
Chemistry	Physics	Biology	Chemistry	Physics	
12	11	48.2	46.6	48.5	
25	19	45.9	36.9	39.6	
5	6	63.4	69.5	58.3	
14	14	51.9	33.3	37.9	
14	14	50.8	64.4	59.3	
1	4	59.7	47.7	56.5	
2	19	42.3	38.0	28.0	
16	11	46.2	51.9	56.1	
15	24	54.8	41.9	52.8	
9	9	56.9	44.6	51.5	
5	7	66.8	66.1	54.9	
15	15	48.5	40.0	44.8	
1	1	37.9	37.7	45.5	

Sources: R.K. Crocker, *Science Achievement in Canadian Schools:
National and International Comparisons*, Economic Council of Canada,
1990, Ottawa (p.27).
I.E.A., *Science Achievement in Seventeen Countries*, Pergamon Press,
Oxford, 1990, pages 51-53.

who take advanced secondary school chemistry or physics is dramatically lower in the U.S. than the percentage of Canadian youth
taking similar courses. Indeed, columns 1 to 5 not only indicate a
major strength of Canada's education system, they also go a long
way to explaining the differences in average test results revealed in
columns 6 to 8 — highly selective school systems (such as those in
England or Singapore) can achieve higher average test scores because of greater selectivity, but the cost of a high average test score
among the elite 5 per cent who take upper level chemistry (as in
England) is greater ignorance of chemistry among the 95 per cent
who have been weeded out.

The International Assessment of Educational Progress project has also tested thirteen- and nine-year-olds in science and mathematics. At these earlier age levels, there is less variation in school attendance rates, hence "skimming" does not inflate the test scores of highly selective systems. At this level, Canadian test scores are quite similar to those of most countries, but in "average percentage correct" Canada lags behind the achievement levels of Korea and Taiwan. (For example, in the test of science knowledge, 69 per cent correct was the average score for thirteen-year-olds in both Nova Scotia and in Canada as a whole, which compares closely with 68 per cent in Scotland, 69 per cent in France, 67 per cent in the U.S., and 71 per cent in the Soviet Union, but lags behind the 76 per cent score in Taiwan and 78 per cent score in Korea.)

However, achievement scores at ages nine and thirteen are primarily useful as internal diagnostics for the educational system; from the point of view of the labour market, the important issue is the skills and attitudes students have when they leave school. The educational system is succeeding in reaching a relatively high proportion of youth with upper-level secondary school courses in mathematics and science. Continual improvement in the delivery of these courses is vital, but reforms which increased the selectivity of mathematics and science education would defeat the objective of a broad base of technological competency.

Furthermore, a persistent refrain we heard in our case studies of high technology companies is the importance of social and communications skills. These skills did not matter much to more traditional employers, since the traditional assembly line did not require much problem solving or teamwork, and the traditional multi-level hierarchy had lots of mid-level supervisors to supervise what workers do — but traditional firms have not been doing too well recently. The traditional objectives of ensuring basic literacy and numeracy are still needed, but they are not enough for high-quality services and high tech manufacturing industry. Organizations emphasizing high-quality production demand high-level social skills, as well as cognitive knowledge.

To meet the needs of these employers, schools are laying greater emphasis on non-traditional skills in oral expression, teamwork, and independent research. Since technology is rapidly changing and the workplace is increasingly organized into self-directed teams, these non-traditional skills are becoming more and more crucial. The school system, from grade primary through Grade 12, has in fact shifted very substantially in the direction of emphasizing communications, teamwork and learning skills, and it would be a retrograde step to shift its emphasis back to the comfortingly familiar curriculum of the 1950s.

Training and the School Work Transition

In some societies, it is considered socially acceptable for educational planners to expect that children will usually follow in the footsteps of their parents in socio-economic achievement. The structure of the educational system in those countries can therefore sort children into streams at a fairly young age. In Germany or Switzerland, for example, children are separated at the junior high school level. A small minority of students are admitted to the academic high schools (the "Gymnasium") which prepare students for possible entry to university and the professions, while the majority are directed into vocational education (the "Realschule"), apprenticeships and the skilled trades. Vocational high schools are focused on the preparation of students for skilled trades, and such schools integrate school work with apprenticeship work. Since students alternate between days of classroom instruction and their work as apprentices, the transition between school and work is relatively easy and the classroom content of upper grades can be closely tied to the specific needs of the workplace.

The German system of apprenticeship and vocational education is justly renowned world-wide, but it cannot easily be transported to Canada. Part of the reason it works so well in these countries is because the comprehensive nature of the welfare state means that much less is at risk when students are being streamed. German workers have substantially more social benefits, and there is a considerably more equal distribution of after-tax income than in Canada.[5] In Canada (as in the United States) the emphasis historically has been on educational policy that promotes "equality of opportunity," rather than social policy that increases "equality of results." Since economic rewards are more unequally distributed in Canada than in Germany or Switzerland (especially at the bottom end), there is a greater cost here to being placed early on in an educational stream that only prepares students for manual occupations. Because the social safety net is weaker, Canadian parents have good reasons for insisting that their children should, as long as possible, have a chance at society's better jobs. Faced with this parental pressure, Canadian educational planners have been reluctant to stream students at an early age into fundamentally different types of schools — and it is hard to see that reluctance changing as long as parents want an "equal opportunity" for their children, in a society with very unequal results.

It is not until they are young adults, at the post-secondary level, that Canadian students encounter a clear differentiation between the community college system, whose mandate is job-relevant training for immediate applicability in the workplace, and the university system, whose educational mandate is much broader.

Community college systems differ greatly across the country. In some provinces (British Columbia, for example), they are well integrated into the university system, and students can easily use their course credits to obtain advance standing if they transfer to university. In other provinces (like Ontario), the system is highly differentiated, and some colleges have acquired excellent reputations for training in unique specialties. In Nova Scotia, the community college system was built on the basis of a network of vocational high schools, but as a community college system, it is of relatively recent origin. Originally, its objective was to provide a career path for students who did not complete high school, and many community college courses nominally still only require Grade 10 completion for admission.

However, this focus has been overtaken by events. Since most people are now graduating from high school, there has been a shift upward in the educational qualifications of the community college clientele. High unemployment during the 1980s has also led many students to look for job-relevant training and has produced new demands for retraining. The result is a long queue for admission to community colleges and an escalation of the de facto entrance requirement for community college courses. Although there is substantial variation in the popularity of different community college offerings, our interviews with the administrators of community colleges indicated that over 60 per cent of entrants now have high school graduation, or more. The admission requirement for some specialized courses may be, in practice, a 75 per cent or higher average on Grade 12 graduation, plus completion of specific mathematics and science subjects. This increase in the de facto entrance requirements means that community colleges increasingly exclude many of the people whose training needs they were intended to serve.

In our interviews with firms, a major theme was the speed of change in technology and in market conditions. To cope with these external changes, firms must constantly change the ways they do business — which necessarily implies changes in job duties and in job availability. Since the demands of the labour market are always changing, and the aim of community colleges is to provide job-relevant training and to place graduates in jobs, community colleges need to work closely with employers to design training courses that are relevant and timely. A good community college also wants to sell its product, and the best colleges go to considerable lengths to locate permanent employment for their students after graduation. Close ties between the colleges and the labour market are obviously essential.

An invaluable part of good vocational training is on-the-job experience. The colleges need good contacts with employers in order to place students for practical sessions of on-the-job training. If a community college course involves a lot of "practicum" placement with employers, it can in practice end up looking not terribly different from a German apprenticeship, since the German system also involves a substantial component of classroom training, as well as work placements.

In Canada's complex society, the diversity of training needs means that community colleges must work with an enormous variety of employers. A single community college we visited had courses ranging from the cradle to the grave (for daycare workers and for morticians), and covering every type of industry, from agricultural mechanics to bookkeepers to machinists to disc jockeys. Which courses should the community colleges offer? How should they offer them? What mix of classroom and on-the-job training works best?

A number of detailed forecasts of occupational growth are available for educational planners — sector studies by industry groups, input/output-based forecasts such as the Canadian Occupational Projection System (COPS) of Human Resources Development Canada, etc. However, employee-needs forecasting is a very risky business. For example, in 1981, the federal government predicted that, because of high energy prices, the construction of a series of energy megaprojects would cause a shortage of construction labour in the mid-1980s; however, when oil prices collapsed, so did the mega-projects, and the 1980s and 1990s have seen chronically depressed demand for construction labour. Even the best of the forecasting models have many uncertainties; national or provincial projections always have to be tailored to fit the specific reality of local labour markets. In all this uncertainty, the one thing sure about the community college curriculum is that the courses needed in 1997 will not be the same as those needed in 1996; constant change and adaptation of the curriculum has to be the name of the game.

If the labour market is continually changing, the issue in planning vocational education is not "what courses will be needed in 1996?" The more important question is, "what institutional structure will best ensure that training institutions teach the courses society will need in 1996, 1997, 1998, and each subsequent year?" Since training needs are continually changing, the problem of course curriculum is not going to be solved once and for all — but a system can be created that will solve the problem anew, each year in the future.

In a very real sense, the problem for community colleges is similar to the problem our case study firms faced. In the private sector, managers often speak of the speed of change in the markets to which they sell. They emphasize the specialized nature of customers' needs and the necessity to stay closely in touch with customers in order to respond quickly to changing demand and new opportunities. The strategy adopted in many of the businesses we interviewed is to create an organizational structure that devolves authority and responsibility to the lowest feasible level. A strategy of empowerment of local managers needs a common management information system to enable senior managers to keep track of the performance of each unit, but the emphasis is on helping local management to solve problems, by bringing them the management tools and information they need to make effective operational decisions.

In some jurisdictions the community college system functions very successfully in this sort of decentralized, autonomous manner. When the vocational school system was originally established in Nova Scotia, the intent was to make the schools responsible to local boards and to allow them to design their curriculum to suit local needs. However, fear of course duplication, and a centralized approach to cost control, has meant that the system has become rather centralized. In Nova Scotia, some community colleges have retained local community advisory boards to help them keep track of the needs of their local labour market and to smooth the flow of their students into jobs, but there has been a high degree of centralized control within the Nova Scotia community college system.

At one community college we visited, for example, instructors complained strenuously about the department's decision to shorten the training course for machinists from two years to one. Although both instructors and local administrators agreed that local employers wanted the level of skills that a two-year machinist training program could provide, the decision had been made in Halifax — all such training programs within the province must be a maximum of one-year's duration. Standardization of courses has benefits, in the sense that credentials become more portable — but it also has costs, because courses can no longer be tailored to meet local needs, and because the process of curriculum revision to meet changing markets and technologies is inevitably slower in a standardized system.

At another community college we visited, we saw state-of-the-art computer-controlled machine tools, spacious facilities and hundreds of students. Yet we also heard staff members comment, when speaking of major local employers, "I haven't been there in years, mind you." As it turned out, one of those employers was a case-study firm we had earlier interviewed. While at the firm, we heard personnel and production managers complain about the quality of graduates from this particular community college. Although a special training facility had been set up and equipped with expensive modern machinery to prepare students especially for employment with this particular firm, in recent years the firm had not hired any graduates from the local community college. Community colleges in New Brunswick and Cape Breton had made the effort to market their graduates and to respond to the firm's perceived needs for training. No comparable result had occurred locally. At the firm's initiative, a committee had been set up with the local community college to discuss training issues, but after meeting once the initiative fizzled. From the firm's perspective, the local community college was not selecting students carefully enough, was not emphasizing the right mix of manual and intellectual skills, and was not effectively marketing its graduates — hence they hired the labour they needed from schools outside the area to do the job they wanted.

When we discussed this issue within the department, we encountered a uniformly defensive response — the problem had either never existed or had been solved long ago (which would have been news to the firm). It appeared to us the root of the problem was that local managers at the community college had relatively little decision-making discretion and knew that their budgets depended primarily on the internal allocation of funds within the department, and as reasonable people, their tendency had been to emphasize the internal politics of budget allocation, at the expense of their external contacts with the business community.

Inflexibility and central control can be costly. If their training is to be relevant, community college students must work with the equipment they will use on the job. Community colleges must always be investing in up-to-date capital equipment in each of the occupational training programs they provide. An alert administrator can often save money by purchasing almost-new equipment (good enough for training purposes) from a friendly local firm — but this is much harder when the purchasing procedures of the provincial government require that expenditures of more than $300 be centrally approved, and when there is an inflexible, and time-consuming policy of open tendering. If equipment-purchase budgets were large, schools could perhaps afford the inflexibility and delay produced by centralized purchasing approval — but the combination of restricted budgets and slow decision making is doubly costly.

Since community college courses are short, the student population turns over fairly rapidly. There is, therefore, a much shorter lag in the impact of educational reforms on the quality of community college graduates than is the case for the primary and secondary educational systems. As well, community colleges are important for the retraining of older workers, in addition to the initial training of high school graduates. A significant proportion of the labour force can be affected by an improvement in the delivery of community college courses within a five- or ten-year time horizon. Furthermore, the specificity of the skills taught in community colleges means that there is a close link between improvements in the educational curriculum and improvements in the productivity of workers on the job. For all these reasons, we see improvement in the community college system as a priority.

We do not think it would be particularly useful to make specific training recommendations — to say (for example) that because jobs are available today for trained undertakers, community colleges should provide more courses for morticians. Change in the labour market is continuous, and recommendations for specific courses can become out of date between the time they are penned and the time they are printed. However, it is useful to stress that community colleges need a decentralized organizational structure that makes them aware of needs in the local labour market, and gives them the ability to respond.

Conclusion

We believe that investment in education, and continual improvement in education, is essential for the long-run prosperity of Canadian society, but we do not believe that the short-run problems of the Canadian economy are due to the failures of the educational system, or that educational reform can, in a few years, solve those problems.

Education lasts a lifetime and it is often useful to draw a distinction between the general role of education and the specific aims of training. Education can be thought of as a broadening process whose objectives are the instilling of high-level values (like tolerance or cooperation), the formation of general skills (such as literacy or numeracy), the acquisition of useful habits, (such as dependability or punctuality), and the learning of broadly applicable knowledge (such as how to take a partial derivative in calculus). These attributes are useful to people in a wide variety of contexts over the whole of their lives, and the increasing sophistication of our society has produced a steady escalation of the general skills demanded by the world of work.

For most people, the general education they get early in life has to serve as the basis on which their training, and future retraining, is built. Training aims at providing specific, directly useful skills. It builds on the basic attitudes, such as adaptability to change, and the general skills, such as literacy, that a general education provides. However, because job duties are constantly changing, training and retraining is a never-ending process.

The dividing line between education and training is not exact but we draw the distinction in order to make the point that the major problem area for Nova Scotia, and for Canada, is not primarily the educational system, but rather the training system. At the primary and secondary level of education, Canada's system delivers a broad base of general skills, comparable in quality with that in most other developed countries, and with the significant advantage of a relatively high penetration of science education in the youth population. At the post-secondary level, Canadian colleges and universities compare well internationally in quality. Accessibility has also been a major strength of the Canadian university system, as enrolment rates have continued to increase throughout the 1980s (in contrast to a decline in college participation rates in the United States). However, one of the troubling trends of the 1990s is the extent to which universities are being forced to raise tuition to solve their budget problems, putting at risk the accessibility of post-secondary education.

Many of the problems faced by older workers in today's labour market stem from the fact that the Canadian educational system did not always perform so well. Because it was so common for people to drop out of school in the 1950s and 1960s, many older workers

lack a high school education today. However, the current performance of the educational system is much improved.

In our interviews with employers, we probed repeatedly for any
problems experienced by employers due to inadequacies in the educational or training system. As far as general skills go, the most
frequent criticisms concerned inadequate writing skills among high
school graduates (not in the sense of the writing skills needed to write
a book, but rather in the sense of the writing skills needed in business
correspondence). There has also been widespread concern, primarily
among educators, that advanced mathematical skills (such as calculus) are not introduced sufficiently early in the Canadian curriculum.

We would stress that these generic skills are important because
they increase the adaptability of workers to new situations and because it is difficult to anticipate changes in labour market that will
demand new types of skills.[6] Furthermore, we would repeat that it is
not good enough for schools in Nova Scotia and in Canada to be
"average" in comparison to schools in other countries if Canadians
wish to retain above-average wage rates in the long term.

These important issues need to be faced in improving the quality
of the educational system. However, given the large number of people with good general skills who cannot get work in today's labour
market, and the broad level of satisfaction expressed by employers
with the general skills of most young workers, we think the more
pressing issues are (1) job availability (see Chapter 7) and (2) training
and retraining.

It is not very realistic to think of importing a European system of
apprenticeship and vocational high schools to Nova Scotia, or to
Canada. Unless the returns, in pay and job security, of employment
in the skilled trades improve noticeably, parents are likely to continue
to resist limiting the options of their children so obviously and so
early. Sparsely populated rural areas (of which there are many in
Nova Scotia) would also find it extremely difficult to offer a separate
vocational stream in high school. Despite drawing students from a
radius of an hour or more on the bus each way, rural high schools
may have only two or three classes in each grade. Such schools
already find it difficult to offer a full range of senior high school
electives. Furthermore, the escalation of industries' needs for general
academic skills and for non-traditional social skills means that vocational education increasingly has to be built on a deeper educational
foundation.

Since our focus throughout this book has been on the question, "What has happened to the sort of jobs that high school graduates used to get?", we have not paid much direct attention to the university system, except to note that when jobs are scarce over all, university graduates will tend to displace high school graduates in the labour market. We have emphasized the community college system because of its original mandate to serve the training needs of those not proceeding to university and because of its important role in retraining.

Our conclusion is that the community college system needs more attention, more resources and a more responsive plan of governance and accountability. More resources are needed because more spaces are needed. But the issue for community colleges is not just to provide enough training spaces to meet student demand, but also to continuously adapt those courses to the needs of business. The performance of community colleges is crucial, both because they provide the initial job-relevant skills that many high school graduates need, and because they are a crucial source of retraining for older workers (often under contract to Human Resource Development Canada).

We would argue for a substantial devolution of managerial authority and responsibility within the community college system, a strengthening of the sense of responsibility to the local community through local boards of directors, and a wholesale re-thinking of the role of central administrators. Local administrators need to be able to assess their own performance, in comparison to the performance of other community colleges. They need access to the latest information on labour market trends and the latest developments in curriculum design. They need, in other words, the knowledge, the responsibility and the authority to respond to the needs of the local labour market. Central administrators have a crucial role to play in establishing a managerial culture of responsiveness and service to the community, of adaptability to change and best possible education practice — but the general strategy ought to be the empowerment of local managers.

Jobs

The Crucial Role of Labour Demand

In many ways, having a job in today's labour market is like having a seat in a lifeboat. There are only a few lifeboats (firms) in the water and a lot of people are trying to get into them. Since the sea is storm-tossed, some lifeboats occasionally sink and their occupants have to swim for safety. Indeed, lifeboats that are in danger of sinking have been known to throw some of their occupants overboard. Once in the water, people have to swim for the nearest available boat — some people make it, some people don't and some keep treading water, in the hope that a lifeboat will appear.

The crucial issue then is, "Are there enough seats in the lifeboats for all the people who need them?" New entrants to the labour force are continually trying to find a place, and new lifeboats (firms) are always being launched. The number of lifeboats varies, since bad weather (i.e. a recession) means that more lifeboats sink and fewer are launched, and the total number of places (jobs) available shrinks. Some lifeboats have higher sides than others and are much safer — but they are also harder to get into. To get into the best lifeboats, people have to have special training and strength — or a helping hand from someone inside.

If, at any given time, one looks at this scene and asks, "What kind of person is in a lifeboat? What kind of person didn't make it?", the answer is that those who made it to safety are those who were stronger, those who had swimming lessons, or those who knew someone who threw them a line and pulled them in. In the labour market, it has long been clear that those with more training, more ability and better personal contacts have better chances of getting a job. But although it is true that the better swimmers make it and the poorer swimmers do not, it does not necessarily follow that lives will be saved if more people get swimming lessons.

If there are plenty of lifeboats, swimming lessons will save lives. The faster swimmers will fill up the closer lifeboats first, but if there are lots of lifeboats available, even slow swimmers will eventually make it to safety. However, if too many lifeboats are sinking and if not enough new lifeboats are being built, there simply will not be enough spaces available. Swimming lessons (job training) will help some individuals get to safety faster than others — and in the labour market everyone, as individuals, is vitally interested in who wins and who loses in this competitive race. But if there are not enough spaces available, those who are relatively slow will not have a chance of finding a place. The key issue is the number of places available, i.e. how many jobs the labour market is producing compared to the number of unemployed.

In Canada's current debate on social policy, it is sometimes asserted that "Many Canadians are unemployed today. But there are also many jobs available. Too often, people who are unemployed don't have the skills that these jobs require."[1] This leaves the impression that the basic problem with the Canadian labour market is that Canada's unemployed do not have the skills that available jobs demand. If there really were many vacancies available, then Canada's unemployment problem could be termed a "structural" one, since the basic problem would be a mismatch between the skills the labour market is demanding and the skills that workers are capable of supplying. The appropriate remedy would be changes to training programs and social policy, to provide the skills that are needed. Of course, "many" is a vague term. One might describe 15,000 or 20,000 vacancies as "many," and one would certainly describe 1.3 million unemployed as "many." The crucial issue is how many available jobs there are in the Canadian economy, compared to number of available workers.

In our case studies, we found lots of evidence for the permanent disappearance of some types of jobs. The fish plants that have closed, the lay-offs due to greater mechanization in textile mills, the closing of bank branches, and the disappearance of jobs as draftspeople or switchboard operators — these are all examples of permanent structural change in the Canadian labour market. However, we found no evidence whatsoever for the existence of any comparable number of job vacancies. Both at the time of our interviews during the recession, and in following up with our case studies during the recovery, we found a few firms who were expanding employment, but the number of vacancies was nowhere near the number of lay-offs. (And employ-

ers had absolutely no problem in filling those vacancies with qualified people.)

Our case studies are, of course, a small sample, drawn from one
part of the Canadian labour market. However, the impressions of our
case studies are entirely consistent with macroeconomic evidence on
the extent of unused capacity in the Canadian economy, and
econometric evidence on the quantitative importance of job availability in the Canadian labour market.[2]

In this book, we have considered the experiences of a range of
individual firms, both because we were interested in whether or not
there really are "many" job vacancies that remain unfilled due to the
lack of available skilled workers, and because we were interested in
the strategic choices of firms that might help them to survive the
rapidly changing demands of modern technology and the global
market place. We have tried to draw out some of the common
elements of successful adaptation and some of the factors that have
inhibited change. In terms of the lifeboat analogy, even if the core
of the problem is that there are not enough lifeboats, it is still important to know the factors that determine whether an existing lifeboat
(firm) will sink or survive.

Chapter 6 also discussed the role of education and training policies
in smoothing the path of structural change. However, it is essential
to recognize that although these policies can be very important for
individual workers and firms, they work by influencing the characteristics of potential workers — their motivation and training — and
they can be likened to the swimming lessons that will improve the
chances of survival of individuals competing for lifeboat places.

If jobs are available, "supply-side" policies that improve the speed
with which individuals locate them, or their ability or motivation to
fill them, can be very valuable. However, the policies of government
also have a crucially important influence on the number of jobs —
the demand side of labour markets.

In the short run, the demand side of labour markets is dominated
by the business cycle. Like the storms that sink thousands of boats
at a time, recessions can destroy hundreds of thousands of jobs in the
space of a few months. However, recessions are not simply "acts of
God" like the weather. If the Bank of Canada tightens monetary
policy and raises short-term interest rates, investment and consumer
expenditures will fall, firms will go bankrupt, and jobs will disappear. Although Canada is unavoidably affected by economic trends
elsewhere (particularly those in the U.S.), Canadian macroeconomic

policy — on interest rates and government spending — has a major impact on job creation.

In the long run, the structural policies of government can also have a major impact on the number of new jobs created. Governments may not be particularly good boat-builders themselves, but they can play a major role in making it profitable for the private sector to build the quantity and quality of boats that are needed. Governments set the context in which individual workers and firms must operate. Basic decisions by government can, for example, affect the quality of the education Canadian workers receive, and in the long run the average skill level of the Canadian labour force is crucial to our ability to compete internationally. However, although structural policy decisions can in the long run influence the number of jobs available, and condition the chances of success of individual firms, the short run is dominated by macroeconomic policy decisions on short-term interest rates, the exchange rate and government spending and taxation.

The problems that motivated this research project — increasing unemployment, the polarization of incomes, rising poverty, and greater dependence on transfer payments — all have their special complexities, but there is also a root problem, a lack of jobs. The fundamental problem facing the Canadian economy in the 1990s is the fact that it is functioning well below its potential productive capacity.

The rate of unemployment is an especially important factor in poverty, economic inequality, and dependence on social assistance, because marginal workers are at the back of the queue for jobs. When firms find that sales are slow, or when governments face deficit pressures, hiring is cut back. New entrants to the labour market (especially youth and older women) compete for the shrinking number of vacancies with those workers whose jobs have disappeared, through plant closing or lay-off. The fiercer the competition for jobs, the less reason there is for employers to take a chance on a worker with poor educational credentials, a poor work history or an "unsuitable" age, race or gender.

Employers are now opting for greater use of sub-contractors, casual employees and temporary help agencies. As the Economic Council of Canada (1991) noted, these "non-standard" forms of employment accounted for 44 per cent of the employment growth of the 1980s. Some workers prefer the instability of such non-standard employment, but they are a minority; most casual workers would prefer the security of permanent employment. However, given the limited number of permanent jobs available, employers are able to find high-quality temporary employees, and hence have no incentive to provide greater employment security to their workers. This ready availability of replacement workers is the crucial factor underlying the increased casualization of Canada's labour force and the cycle of dependence on transfer payments it entails. Our interviews at Retail Clone, Sally Servant and Temp Help provided prime examples of this trend.

One objective of this research project was to understand the impacts that structural changes in the Canadian labour market, such as the increase in non-standard employment, might be having on inequality of earnings in Canada. However, it has become clear that issues of structural change and poor macroeconomic performance are strongly intertwined. A high rate of unemployment means that there is a large pool of people willing to work in casual or temporary jobs at low rates of pay, and this in turn makes it profitable for employers to change their employment strategies. The change in the structure of employment and the shift to low-paid jobs then produces greater inequality in the distribution of earnings.[3]

High unemployment also affects training. In Chapter 6 we emphasized the importance of close links between employers and schools for good vocational training. We emphasized the importance of employer feedback on needed skills for curriculum design, and the crucial role of on-the-job training for the school-to-work transition, as well as for the transition from social assistance to employment. However, all this is pointless if employers have no jobs to offer.

We are far from the first to note the low level of investment in training by many Canadian employers,[4] but we would stress the link between high unemployment and the training decisions of firms. Employers who are laying off skilled workers (such as Coal Mine Co.) have no need for training programs to increase their supply of skills. Employers who have a queue of qualified workers available (such as Nova U) have no incentive to bear the cost of training. Although our case studies indicated that a few firms (for example, Telecom Company) continue to invest heavily in the skills of their workers, such employers are relatively rare.

In the long run, it is widely recognized that Canadian productivity, and Canadian jobs, depend upon the skills of the Canadian labour force, which depend in turn on both the adequacy of the educational and training programs offered by government and on the training initiatives offered by employers. However, it is pointless to bewail the lack of a "training culture" in Canadian industry if the maintenance of high unemployment, for prolonged periods of time, means that employers become accustomed to having a ready supply of well qualified job applicants for almost any vacancy. It should not be particularly surprising that employers do not usually bother with the expense of an on-going training program, if the skills they need are easily available on the open market.

A useful way of categorizing economic policies is to think of them as operating on either the supply side or the demand side of labour markets. However, as the great English economist Alfred Marshall observed over a century ago, the two basic principles of economics, demand and supply, are like the two blades of a pair of scissors. Separately, neither demand nor supply can do much, but together demand and supply can explain a great deal. In the long term, the supply of a skilled, healthy and highly motivated labour force is essential to long-run labour productivity and to higher wages and employment, but the demand for labour is also crucial. If jobs are not available, society's investment in producing a trained and healthy work force will not have a chance to pay off. If there are not enough jobs, encouraging more people to look for work will only add to the length of the queue for jobs.

Increasing the demand for labour in the economy as a whole would directly provide some jobs for disadvantaged workers, but the indirect impacts would be equally important. As we have noted, a generalized surplus of labour has meant that workers with university credentials are willing to take jobs that do not really use their skills, and those with poorer credentials have been pushed into marginal employment, or into unemployment. A higher rate of growth of labour demand would reverse this process. As university graduates moved into better jobs, the vacancies they left behind would be filled from the ranks of the marginally employed/unemployed. A tighter labour market would also mean that firms would run the risk of not getting needed labour if they only hired on a "just-in-time" basis; some firms would find it profitable to smooth out their production and offer more stable employment. Firms would also find it more profitable to invest in training, since they would not be able to depend on already-trained unemployed workers always being available. A tighter labour market would also mean that there would be jobs waiting at the end of training courses for the disadvantaged and some pay-off to more effective job search by social assistance clients.

The aggregate unemployment rate is, therefore, crucially important for a whole range of labour issues. The unemployment rate can be brought down, if governments make it their priority. In the short run, the monetary policy decisions of the federal government can have a major impact. The level of short-term interest rates and the foreign exchange rate are crucial to the level of demand firms face, and the number of jobs they can provide. In the longer run, the productivity and profitability of firms, and their long-run demand for labour, also depends crucially on the quality of education and training, and the labour market institutions that regulate industrial relations, as well as on the physical and social infrastructure. But in order to get to the "long run," we first have to go through the "short run."

Since health, education and industrial relations are areas of provincial jurisdiction under the constitution of Canada, many of the crucial "framework" policies for the long run are necessarily set at the provincial level. In Chapter 6, we discussed education and training policy, noting that even if the provinces were to adopt immediately the best possible set of educational and training policies, these policies could only gradually affect the labour market, since new graduates are always only a small percentage of all workers. Over time, changes in educational and training policies can have a major impact, but that impact mounts only gradually as the proportion of recent graduates in the labour force increases. Provincial governments cannot, therefore, typically provide the "quick fix" in employment creation or economic prosperity many of their voters desire. Similarly, social policies, such as counselling, retraining, or transitional employment for social assistance claimants, have the potential for long-term structural benefits, but whatever their long-term potential, they can easily be frustrated if the short-term environment is unfavourable. There is simply no point in trying to train the unemployed, or in trying to motivate social assistance clients to look hard for a job, when there are not enough jobs available.

In the short run, federal government decisions have the biggest impact. Through its monetary policy decisions, the federal government can influence the level of short-term interest rates and the foreign exchange rate, with major implications in the short run for economic activity and for unemployment. When interest rates are high, consumer demand for such things as housing and automobiles falls, and the investment projects of business become less profitable. Tight money also means that foreigners who want to get high interest rates on Canadian bonds will bid up the exchange value of the

Canadian dollar, which hurts the exports of Canadian goods and services. Demand therefore falls for consumer goods, and for investment projects and exports — hence employment also falls, and unemployment increases.

High unemployment dooms many provincial programs to failure. If firms do not, in the short run, have enough demand for their product, they simply will not hire workers. Without placements for their graduates, retraining programs will fail. Without jobs to go to, social assistance clients will remain dependent on transfers. The short-run macroeconomic policies of the federal government have, therefore, major impacts on the success of the long-run structural adaptation policies of the provincial governments.

It is essential for the success of long-run policies of structural adjustment that short-run macroeconomic demand management should stress economic growth and job creation. If the long-run goal is to move people from transfer dependence to productive employment, such a long-run readjustment of the economy can only be reached by going through a succession of short runs. Short-run macroeconomic policy must make it possible for long-run adjustment to succeed.

The High Costs of High Unemployment

The "output gap" is the difference between what the economy is producing and what it could produce. High unemployment means output is lost because both labour and capital are unnecessarily idle. Economists have long recognized that a lower unemployment rate produces a more efficient utilization of capital, as well as attracting back into the labour force many discouraged workers who had given up looking for work. As a result, output increases rapidly when the unemployment rate declines. The "Okun's Law" approximation is that each 1 per cent decline in the unemployment rate results in a 2.5 per cent increase in total output.

How low could unemployment get before there is a worrisome resurgence of inflation? Many recent estimates have put the long-run "natural" rate of unemployment at about 7 per cent.[5] When economists use the term "natural rate" of unemployment they mean the rate of unemployment normally expected, given the age, location and skills of the labour force and the institutions (like Canada Employment Centres, unions or unemployment insurance) which affect the labour market. If Canada adopts more effective educational, training and social policies, the natural rate of unemployment will fall, since the capabilities of unemployed individuals will be matched more effectively to the needs of employers. However, without an improvement in the demand for labour, such policies would only add to the gap between the natural rate of unemployment (7 per cent), and the actual rate of unemployment.

Between the time of writing this book, and the time it will be read, the actual unemployment rate may change, but readers can get a rough approximation of the output gap (the difference between what the economy is producing and what it could produce at the "natural" rate of unemployment) by multiplying 2.5 per cent of Gross Domestic Product times the difference between current unemployment rates and 7 per cent. When the unemployment rate is 10 per cent, the "Okun's law" approximate estimate of the output gap is about 7.5 per cent (= 3.0 x 2.5 per cent) of GDP. (Large, multi-equation econometric models, such as the Informetrica model, produce the same estimate of output gap.) Since GDP in Canada was $766.4 billion in 1994 (fourth quarter), an unemployment rate of 10 per cent means that Canadians are foregoing approximately $57 billion per year in output, lost due to excess unemployment.

Fifty-seven billion dollars is an unimaginably large sum of money. It is, for example, far larger than the "poverty gap" — the amount of money required to raise the incomes of all poor people in Canada above the poverty line — which the National Council of Welfare estimated as $13.4 billion in 1991. Furthermore, since lay-offs and low wages have increased the number of poor people and the depth of their poverty, a return to 7 per cent unemployment would, in itself, pull many people out of poverty. Lower unemployment would therefore not only provide $57 billion in additional output, it would also shrink the poverty gap by approximately one-third. The remaining poverty could be entirely eliminated by a tax rate of about 13 per cent on the increase in output achieved by a return to 7 per cent unemployment.

We are not arguing that the problems of poverty can or should be solved entirely by simply writing larger government cheques. There is great diversity in the needs of the individuals who are now dependent on transfer payments, some of whom need counselling, training and other services just as much (if not more) than they need cash transfers. However, we *are* arguing that macroeconomic performance is so poor — lost output of $57 billion — that it has become the crucial factor now determining the availability of resources for the social policies that will reduce poverty. The loss of output due to poor macroeconomic performance is so large that a return to 7 per cent unemployment would also imply that other problems — such as the budget deficits of federal and provincial governments — could also be much more easily eliminated.

In Canada, a growth rate of five per cent a year for five years is entirely feasible (see Pierre Fortin, "Diversified Strategy"). Since more rapid growth would mean a rapid decline in UI and social assistance payments and an increase in tax revenues, the best route to eliminating governments' deficits is to encourage enough growth to eliminate the output gap. Closing the output gap does not mean increasing government spending; instead, the way to close the output gap (and eliminate the deficit) is to use monetary policy — lower short-term interest rates. With lower interest rates and a lower foreign exchange value of the Canadian dollar, the private sector would find it profitable to expand production, increasing the number of jobs in manufacturing, resources and services. As our case studies have illustrated, employers have been cutting jobs in order to increase labour productivity. As a result, firms can now produce the same level of output with fewer workers. If they are to begin to expand employment, the demand has to be there for more output.

The Jobs That Won't Come Back

Macroeconomic policy can have a major effect on the number of jobs that are created, but these jobs will not necessarily be located where unemployed people now are. Although it is possible to increase the money supply in Canada, and thereby decrease short-term interest rates and the exchange rate, the new offices and factories that open up as investment spending and exports increase will not likely be located near the fishplants that have closed in Atlantic Canada. For generations, Canadians have been highly mobile geographically and there is no indication that the need for mobility will decrease in the future.

Some Canadian communities have had essentially only one economic reason for existence. The mining towns of northern Ontario, British Columbia, Manitoba and Quebec have always known that when the ore runs out, the town will die. Many small farming communities in Alberta and Saskatchewan sprang up before the First World War, when farms were small and the maximum range of a shopping trip was the distance a horse drawn buggy could travel in a day; many of these communities have disappeared as the number of farms has shrunk and highways have enabled easy access to regional shopping centres.

For generations, rural Atlantic Canada has been part of this process of emigration. Out-migration is now being accelerated by the widespread closure of the fish processing plants that have been the largest source of employment in many rural communities, but it has been going on for decades.

As we interviewed the inhabitants of rural areas and the bureaucrats who administer government programs of community renewal and rural development, we encountered again and again a curious dualism of hope and despair. On the one hand, one heard the modern buzz words of the trade —"community economic development," "small business job creation," and "local initiative." And there were some examples of small-scale local firms that had managed to open and to survive. However, although there are examples of new initiatives in eco-tourism, new bed and breakfast operations or shops for tourist curios, it takes a very large number of such employers to replace the 300 to 400 jobs that are lost when a fishplant closes. The scale of job creation through new small businesses in rural Nova Scotia is an order of magnitude smaller than the job loss that has occurred.

Although the people we interviewed could, with one breath, try to be hopeful, with the next breath they would go on to say that there simply are no jobs in the local area and that young people inevitably have to move away to find employment. Among the bureaucrats administering the community and rural development programs whose ribbon cutting ceremonies are invariably a "photo opportunity" for local politicians, there were some who questioned the value of their role. Some wondered whether they were being "dream merchants." They wondered whether they were encouraging unrealistic hopes and leading people to hang on and stay in the hope that prosperity would return, and whether government programs may simply be delaying the inevitable and increasing the pain of the eventual transition.

Although we found some useful examples of initiatives, such as aquaculture, which can generate some new employment in rural Nova Scotia, we found no indication in either our case studies or our quantitative analysis that there will not be a continuing need for large-scale emigration from rural Nova Scotia. We think that government can and should recognize the necessity for migration and, if necessary, assist with relocation expenses.

The Industrial Relations Framework for Long-Run Adjustment Policy

Much of the debate on unemployment in Canada has focused on the educational, training and social policy choices that influence the availability of trained and motivated workers — the supply side of modern labour markets. Earlier in this chapter, emphasis was placed on the macroeconomic policies of the federal government and their importance for the success of supply-side provincial policies. However, provincial government policies also condition the labour relations climate at the workplace, influence the rate of diffusion of technology, and shape the infrastructure that surrounds an individual firm. These factors can be crucial for the long-run success of job creation strategies.

Labour relations are especially crucial because it is clear from all our case studies how important cooperation can be to the productivity of individual firms. However, it is unclear how labour relations can or will change to foster such cooperation. Changes in technology and changes in the social relations of production are happening rapidly throughout the economy. Giving workers a say in the social relations of production and providing them with a share of the economic benefits of cooperation is what collective bargaining is all about. It is very hard to see how collective bargaining can remain unaffected by the new modes of organization of work, but the development of new relationships is greatly impeded by the anti-union attitudes of some employers and by the widespread mistrust of employers that many unionists feel.

It is easy (but not very useful) to point fingers and to assign blame in industrial relations. We interviewed a number of employers (at Family Sawmills and Joe's Machine Shop, for instance) where managers clearly felt that workers should, basically, shut-up and do as they are told. Since unions might get in the way of this, such employers are dead set against unionization. We also visited firms (such as Aerospace Manufacturing) where union avoidance was more sophisticated and more subtle. We found firms whose unions felt that they had been suckered by management rhetoric on cooperation — as when a big lay-off followed close behind the signing of a collective agreement (as at Telecom Company). On the other side, we also visited union offices in which a history of bloody-mindedness by both management and labour had produced inflexibility and a failure to recognize the imperatives for change (Coal Mine Co. was a classic example). Among some unionists there is an attitude of pervasive mistrust and the feeling that any change must be a management plot. However, although it is essential to understand the history, and the depth of feeling, underlying the attitudes of both management and labour, it is not particularly productive to assign blame.

The discussion of changes in industrial relations is a minefield of rhetoric. One person's "mutual cooperation" or "reasonable compromise" can well be another person's "sell out" or "betrayal." Some terms that describe organizational change have also become loaded and emotive. The idea of "industrial democracy" gets a negative reaction from many managers, because in it they perceive a threat to their own ability to get their jobs done in the future, as well as an implicit criticism of how they have done their job in the past. The phrases "team production" or "worker/management cooperation" irritate many trade unionists, because they see the power that management often wants to retain behind these terms' facade of worker involvement in decision making.

One union organizer gave us the example of a work group that studied, for a year, whether or not to adopt a new piece of machinery, only to find out (by accident) that the machinery had already been ordered, eighteen months previously. He was angry at the waste of everybody's time, but he saw it as inevitable that companies make engineering and financial decisions, and some of these decisions have long lead times. He thought it a hoax to expect meaningful worker input into such decisions, and a mirage not to realize that the interests of firms and workers can differ.

However, the same organizer also was concerned about the number of industrial disputes that have their origins in pure misunderstandings, due to workers' lack of reliable information. In a number of European countries (Germany, for example), workers gain access to financial information on firms through the requirement, imposed by legislation, that elected worker representatives have seats on company boards of directors. In these countries, large union federations can also afford the research expertise to evaluate carefully economic and technological trends. In this way, shop-floor workers have access to high-quality information, which they can trust, on the need for organizational and technical change.

Canadian business may not be ready for a comparable degree of worker participation in decision-making. The Canadian union movement is also relatively fragmented, since it must bargain separately for each individual bargaining unit and must operate under slightly different legislation in each province. Individual unions rarely have the resources needed to invest in background research. The Canadian union movement must also, unlike many of its European counterparts, operate with the knowledge that its position is not fully secure — an influential segment of the Canadian business community has never accepted the legitimacy and permanency of the trade union movement.

For all these reasons, the unionists we interviewed distrusted talk of a "new paradigm" of workplace organization, and preferred to advocate "good industrial relations practice," and gradual change in workplace relationships. However, when unionists are asked exactly what "good industrial relations practice" actually is, the answer is a management that pays fair wages and is responsive to worker concerns with workplace equity, safety and quality of working life — which is not too different from the concerns of the "new paradigm" of workplace organization. As well, there is nothing inherently anti-union in the idea of a "team." Many workplaces have long been organized in production teams, and this is not felt to be in conflict with union objectives.

Furthermore, although managers may react negatively to phrases such as "industrial democracy," managers have also tended to like the idea of workers who are "self-starters." There is now much greater managerial emphasis on work teams that allocate responsibilities and tasks, without referring the issue up the hierarchy — i.e. worker decision-making on important aspects of the work process is not inherently in conflict with all management objectives.

There is, therefore, some reason for optimism that firms and unions can resolve practical issues of adaptation to change, if both sides can get beneath the rhetoric. And it is worth emphasizing that there is no simple correlation between unionization status and organizational change. We interviewed some non-union firms that were socially and technologically dynamic (such as Aerospace Manufacturing) and some non-union firms that were organizationally rigid and technically backward (such as Family Saw Mills and Joe's Machine Shop). There was also a wide range of outcomes in the process of technical and organizational change among unionized firms. Diverse Construction, International Hotel, Telecom Company and Provincial Commission were all examples of unionized workplaces in which the union had clearly not been an impediment to organizational change. In some other instances (for example, Coal Mine Co.), union-management relationships remain a major issue. But the important point is that there is no single stereotype of the union-management working relationship. Unionization is not inherently incompatible with dramatic change in workplace relationships. But unionization does tend to mean that *some types* of reorganization are more difficult.

A particularly important issue is job security. Although we interviewed a number of workers who thought it was only reasonable for everyone to pitch in together to get the job done, regardless of job classification, it was understandable that this willingness to be flexible tended to disappear if it might also mean a loss of their own job. Individual workers obviously differ substantially in their personal desire to "buy into" new methods of work organization by acquiring cross training or being flexible in their work assignments, but from a union's perspective, the crucial issue is the "bottom line" on pay and security. Whatever its other problems, the seniority/job ladder system now in place in most firms does maintain security of employment and income for senior workers.

Firms that switch to a flexible team mode of production want to keep their teams intact, even in periods of economic downturn, because the cohesion of the team is hard to maintain if there is high turnover or unequal sharing of burdens. Hence, they tend to prefer to cope with lean periods by instituting short-time working for all employees. Many unions have been accustomed to protecting the interests of established workers through a system of detailed job descriptions, with lay-offs for low seniority workers during slack times and "bumping rights" for high seniority workers. This system creates inflexibility in work assignment, but the underlying reason is that senior workers need some degree of security of employment and income. Switching to a team mode, with flexible job assignment and work-sharing, means that those who are now protected by seniority get treated just like anyone who has been newly hired — and older workers are quite aware that they often have less mobility and poorer educational credentials than younger workers.

Issues of job security are also especially important to workers when new jobs are hard to find. High unemployment increases the cost of being laid off by decreasing a worker's chances of finding a new job, and therefore tends to increase the incentives for rigidity in protecting existing systems of job allocation. The federal government therefore plays a major role in shaping the environment for change in industrial relations, through its control of macroeconomic policy, and also through its control over unemployment insurance regulations on worksharing. However, since the constitution assigns responsibility for labour relations to the provinces, it is provincial governments who must play the dominant role in shaping a new consensus framework for industrial relations.

Canada needs to develop a new model of labour relations, which builds on the common real interests of workers and management, and which maximizes the total gains of cooperation and change. Effective communication is essential to this process. European countries, such as the Scandinavian nations, Germany or Switzerland, have long recognized that statutory provision for works councils and the inclusion of worker representatives on boards of directors can be an effective way of minimizing misunderstandings and creating a sense of common purpose. Some Canadian managers probably need to be convinced that the sky will not fall if they reveal financial information to their employees, and some Canadian unionists probably require reassurance that sitting at the same table with "the bosses" does not mean "selling out." Canada may need a somewhat different institutional framework than that in Europe to ensure that communication and cooperation are effective. However, one of the benefits of living in a federation such as Canada is that each province can learn from the success (or failure) of other provinces' initiatives in labour relations. The industrial relations system in Canada has changed much less over the last fifty years than the world of work; it is time for provincial governments to look at new patterns of industrial governance, and new institutions.

Physical and Social Infrastructure

Canadians are familiar with the important role physical infrastructure plays in job creation, in part because its contribution is so visible. It is obvious that firms need dependable electrical power to produce goods and that they need roads, bridges and railways to move those goods to market. As the pace of production has quickened in recent years, the quality of this infrastructure becomes increasingly important. Our interviews with Aerospace Manufacturing and Megabank provided concrete examples of how the success of "just-in-time" manufacturing and high-quality service production depends on rapid, dependable movements of parts, paper and people — i.e. the quality of the transportation infrastructure.

However, one of the themes of this book is the interdependence between the hard technology embodied in capital equipment and the soft technology of organization and motivation. A high level of organization is needed in order to keep physical infrastructure useful.

In a very real sense, when the production process becomes more tightly coordinated, the efficient operation of the private sector becomes much more dependent on an efficiently functioning public sector. The success of just-in-time manufacturing depends on parts arriving exactly when they are needed, but that dependable delivery requires both the existence of a good highway network and a public works department that clears the road quickly and dependably after every winter snowstorm. The transportation, communication, water and power infrastructures need both capital investment and an efficient public service, if they are to be effective.

However, our concept of the social infrastructure goes beyond those organizations connected directly to the design and operation of physical infrastructure. Economic markets necessarily operate within a social framework, and their efficiency can depend heavily on that framework. The social framework within which business operates includes some organizations (such as the Chamber of Commerce) that represent the interests of business in general, and others (like the Cape Breton Tourism Association) that represent the common interests of a specific segment of industry. Although large firms have the internal resources to provide their own services and to market their own reputations, small business is especially dependent on the quality of its institutional links to suppliers, customers, labour and government.

As our case studies of small and large business have indicated, customers demand dependable supply and a reputation for quality. An association of small producers may be able to satisfy these demands, but it is often not feasible for individual small businesses to do so alone. In the service sector, for example, major hotel chains can advertise heavily and establish a reputation — indeed the slogan of one chain is "no surprises." An individual motel operator cannot afford similar advertisements and cannot credibly guarantee to strangers the quality of its accommodations. In this sort of situation, government- or industry-association-certified standards can provide a real service; for example, in Europe small hoteliers can compete more effectively because strict grading standards for accommodation allow potential customers to know exactly what to expect in one-star, two-star or three-star hotels.

Currently, Nova Scotia, like other provinces, is only beginning to institute a similar grading system for restaurants or hotels, probably because of the political pressures that a grading agency could expect from those who are disappointed with their grade. What Nova Scotia

does have, which other provinces do not, is the CHECK-INNS service for long distance hotel reservations, which enables small hotels
to link up with potential customers who otherwise would not have
known of their existence. A central data base of available rooms is
linked to terminals in all tourism information booths and a toll-free
long distance line. Tourists are saved the anxiety and bother of
searching for a room, and small motels and bed and breakfast operations have access to a potential pool of customers they could not have
reached otherwise. Since superior access to information is key to the
success of major hotel chains, the shared reservation system is a
major aid to the small business sector.

We use this as an example of the potential role for government,
since providing this service was beyond the financial capability of
any single small business. The service was initially started by a
government initiative, but its operation has since been taken over by
the local industry association. Since there are, in the area of information and the setting of standards, substantial set-up costs and
economies of scale, the role of government in this case was to enable
small business to gain access to economies of scale in information
processing.

However, the area of training provided a less happy example from
our case studies. Since it is beyond the capacity of the relatively small
textile firms we interviewed to design and mount the training programs their employees need, and since there is no effective industry
association to help design training programs or to lobby training
institutions for improved service, we heard constant complaints in
that sector about the difficulties of training.

Our interviews at Multiburger and Sally Servant provided examples of how, if an operation can be standardized, the private sector
can provide the accounting, advertising and technology development
services small business needs. To some extent, the franchise system
already functions as a way of centralizing marketing strategies and
the development of technology, while keeping the production efficiency advantages of small business and local ownership. Government intervention is not needed in areas like fast food, where the
private market is already operating effectively.

However, small business start-ups in more specialized areas, such
as eco-tourism or machine shops or aquaculture operations, have
valid common interests which need an organizational framework.
They also have competitive individual interests, which the market
process will sort out. But the role for public policies is to help ensure

the success of an industry as a whole. In Nova Scotia, there already are a number of industry associations, but we could see substantial room for improvement. We would urge that governments look carefully at the positive role they can play in helping to organize industry to help itself.

8

Conclusion

This research project originated in our concern with the increased inequality, widespread unemployment and greater poverty that began to emerge in Canada in the 1980s. We wanted to know why traditional "good" blue collar jobs were now so scarce, and whether the anxieties that many Canadians feel about the future living standards of their children had any foundation. We started with the hypothesis that these trends were heavily influenced by international trade — especially the opening up of Canadian markets to American competition in the Free Trade Agreement (FTA) of 1988 — and by the relentless advance of computer technology.

In the end, our case studies and our reading of other evidence lead us to de-emphasize the importance of the FTA. Certainly, the agreement was very important for some firms. However, over 70 per cent of the labour force works in the service sector, where the impact of the FTA was relatively small. Among firms in the goods sector, many were essentially unaffected either because they had always exported most of their output to international markets or because their industrial sector had, like automobiles or aerospace, long operated tariff free or nearly so. And although we interviewed in our case studies some firms that had been heavily affected by the FTA, some of those were in fact managing to adjust.

Although we end up de-emphasizing the role of the FTA, we do emphasize how tough the competition is for jobs. Sometimes local plants must compete for new product lines with other plants within the same firm, while sometimes the competition is between local firms and other Canadian firms from outside the region. Local firms may also find that foreign producers have begun to penetrate previously uncontested markets. It may once have been the case that regional or local firms could rely on a local market for their goods, but decreasing costs of transportation and communication have largely eliminated the barriers of isolation and distance that once used to provide some shelter to local producers.

In this increasingly competitive world, our research has given us a new appreciation of the role and complexity of "technological change." The impact of technological change on job creation is complex and subtle, because there is both a technology of things and a technology of people. Throughout this book, we have tried to underscore the interdependence between the hard technology of capital equipment and cognitive skills, and the soft technology of organizational structure and motivation. Both are important because there are very few "easy rides" left in the labour market of the 1990s. Canada has always been, and still is, a very fortunate country, but we are certainly not the first to notice that Canada's advantages are shrinking. There was a time when the abundance of this country's natural resources, and the fact that Canada was spared the devastation of World War II, meant a lot. In "the good old days," Canadians could expect (without question) good jobs and rising incomes; but the certainty of those expectations has largely disappeared.

In the private sector, employers now face a tougher, more competitive market place. In the public sector, there is a relentless pressure to restructure, reform, and do more with less. Whatever the reason for these new pressures on employers in both the public and the private sectors, employers are trying to get the most output possible from their labour force. In almost all our case studies, it is clear that the pace and intensity of work has increased.

Employers are becoming very analytical about the soft technology they use. Many are using the new information technology to plot very carefully their peaks of labour usage, in order to restructure their labour force into a core group of permanent employees and a contingent group of part-time or short-term workers who are called in only when necessary to meet surges in production. Employers are also examining carefully the roles of middle managers, and (even if reality often falls short of the rhetoric) there is a new push to decentralized decision-making and team building.

Most employers have made major changes in the way they do business and are continuing to do so. However, there also remains a group of low-tech laggards who continue to be locked into their old technologies and their old strategy of minimizing their investment in their labour force. As well, firms that have attempted to change their ways of doing business face new problems.

In their attempts to instill and to manage an "ethic of professionalism," firms want to create the internalized norms of excellence of autonomous professionals, yet they also want to avoid the turf wars of competing professional groups. They want to promise their employees upward mobility, but to do that they have to avoid the blockage to mobility that comes with a hierarchy of professions. Employers also want to build on their employees' pride of individual workmanship and their independence and personal initiative, while at the same time they want their workers to be team players (multiskilled and multi-tasked), who shift flexibly from role to role in accordance with the overall goals of the organization. Clearly, some of these new expectations are inconsistent. If these expectations are to be balanced, employers must recognize that the new world of team building and employee motivation demands a higher level of management skills than simply bossing people around.

Unions also face an identity crisis in the 1990s. Unions are very aware of the competitive pressures facing private-sector employers and the budget crunch of the public sector. The experience of collective bargaining imposes a certain realism and practicality on union leaders — they know that employers have to make a profit if they are to continue in business and continue to pay wages. They also know that fine statements of principle do not mean much if there is no practical mechanism of implementation. However, the collective bargaining experience also leaves many unionists with a lot of cynicism about the true motivation of management and scepticism about the truth of the "facts" management supplies. In all too many cases, there is a residue of bitterness about past injustices and an apprehension that management would, if given half a chance, get rid of the union all together.

In this mixture of cynicism and realism, unionists have to try to figure out what their role is going to be in the workplace of the 1990s. How can unions find the dividing line between co-optation and cooperation? How can unions find the balance between the needs of their members for job security, decent income, and fair treatment at the workplace, and the new demands of employers for job flexibility and lower labour costs? The old seniority system imposed significant rigidities and inefficiencies, but it also provided some security in an increasingly insecure world. Any replacement system must also provide some basis for security.

Government has to be part of any change in the industrial relations system, because governments write the labour law that provides the structure within which the industrial relations system must operate, and because the broader policies of government, especially in job creation and social policy, crucially affect the job security and incomes of workers. It is easy for policy analysts in governments or academia to look around the world and see the benefits of industrial relations reform. Industrial relations practices that increase the flow of credible information to employees and that provide a meaningful channel for their participation tend to encourage the cooperation on which effective implementation of new technologies depends. However, given the history of mistrust and the adversarial structure of collective bargaining in Canada, it has not been easy to demonstrate leadership in changing the system of industrial relations.

Leadership is also needed if businesses are to help themselves by helping each other. We have emphasized the importance, especially for small business, of the social infrastructure. Industry and trade associations that set industry standards, cooperate in designing and implementing training programs, exchange technologies, and share the costs of market development can have major benefits. Governments have a role to play in ensuring that such associations do not become mechanisms to reduce competition, and governments can reasonably expect such associations to pay their own costs; but governments can also play an important facilitating role in helping firms to help themselves.

In many areas, the public sector has much to learn from the new private-sector models of delayering, decentralization, and team building. But such strategies will not work if they are just cost-cutting exercises. New types of expenditure are also needed, since the local administrators of a decentralized system need to have an information base if they are to learn from their own past experience and that of others. Such an information base often does not yet exist. Since there have been little data available, there has been little rigorous research or analysis of program effectiveness. There are, for example, costs to finding out exactly what is happening to community college graduates or social assistance clients, and why. However, the long-run savings in improved policy design and delivery will likely vastly outweigh the short-run costs of data gathering and analysis.

In the social policy area, the same theme of decentralization and improved analysis can help to meet the specific needs of particular disadvantaged workers. People have labour market difficulties for very different reasons and training and counselling for individuals needs to be tailored to their specific needs and their local realities. But since all children have a need for, and a basic human right to, health, education, and a decent standard of food, clothing and accommodation, the customized delivery of remedial services to adults should be combined with the universal delivery of medical care, daycare, primary and secondary education, and child allowances.

Some of these things are already provided, on a universal basis, to Canadian children — but others are not. The cash crisis of Canadian governments means that it would be essential to balance the universal availability of such services with taxation of their value. By consolidating the value of services people receive from government programs and counting it as an addition to taxable income, the work disincentives that are now built into our uncoordinated system of transfers and services, as well as the administrative costs now created by separate bureaucracies, would be substantially reduced. It is possible to reform social policy in a way that increases both efficiency and equity, but real reform cannot just be a cost-cutting exercise.

However, although there is no doubt that money alone will not solve the problems of poverty and inequality of opportunity, these problems cannot be solved for free either. Can Canada afford to spend more to improve the equality of opportunity for all children and to reintegrate marginalized adults into the community? If Canada as a whole continues to throw away nearly $60 billion a year in lost output by operating the economy at less than full employment capacity, the answer will likely be "no." Although the poverty gap (at 2 per cent of GDP) is much less than the output gap (7.5 per cent of GDP), Canadian governments are cutting back on anti-poverty spending. If they continue to do so, one cannot expect the problems of poverty and inequality to miraculously "solve themselves."

However, the cash crisis of Canadian governments is basically due to our slow growth. Depressed tax revenues from a stagnant economy, and the cost of unemployment insurance and social assistance payments to the jobless (plus the interest costs of past debt) have created deficits at all levels of government. These deficits are, today, the strongest single constraint on effective anti-poverty policy.

Although the issues raised by long-run structural change in the economy are important, they are dominated by the day-to-day reality of the lingering aftermath of the recession. In this research project, we followed the fortunes of a cross section of companies over three years (1990 1993). Since our series of interviews at each company took quite a while, they were spaced over this three-year period and, as we went through our cycle of interviews, we maintained contact with each of the firms in our sample, up to the date of final revisions to the manuscript — March 1995. It was depressing to see how many of them have had no choice but to engage in major lay-offs despite, in most cases, having made major internal changes to improve their productivity and competitiveness.

The fundamental fact is that although individual firms can, with best practice technology and salesmanship, often increase their share of the market, it is very rare that an individual firm can increase very much the size of the market as a whole. An individual hotel can, for example, vastly improve its attractiveness and quality of service, but if there are fewer people travelling on business or pleasure, there will be fewer hotel rooms sold. Even an increased share of the market, if the market as a whole is collapsing, may still not provide enough business to avoid closure. Individual firms are doing their best to improve their productivity and competitiveness, but all these micro-economic responses can be frustrated by bad macroeconomic policy. For the past decade, macroeconomic policy in Canada has empha-sized high interest rates to control inflation and program expenditure cuts to control the deficit. The result has been slow growth, rising unemployment, and increasing poverty. Canada needs macro-economic policy that stresses growth.

In writing this book, we were influenced both by our interviews of our case study firms and by our econometric analysis of labour market data done in the course of this and other research projects. We were influenced, as well, by the series of interviews we did in the late 1970s with firms and workers as part of the "Marginal Work World" research project of the Institute of Public Affairs, Dalhousie University. In several cases, we re-interviewed the same firms in 1991–92 that we contacted previously in 1979–80. It was striking to observe the substantial changes that firms have made in both the hard and soft technology of production, but it was also striking to observe a substantial change in employer attitudes to social policy. In the late 1970s, there was a vehement and consistent critique by employers of the excessive generosity of unemployment insurance. Employers who could not get the workers they needed often blamed UI for encouraging excessive unemployment and undermining the effort of those who continued to work. However, since the 1970s there has been a series of amendments to unemployment insurance which have progressively made benefits much less generous and eligibility more difficult. There has also been a significant increase in the unemployment rate.

Our 1990s interviews with employers were notable because employers almost never mentioned unemployment insurance (or social assistance) as an issue in their labour problems. Since we were interested in their opinions of social policy, we often raised the subject, but even if we pushed for some comment on the connection between unemployment insurance generosity and unemployment, we heard little suggestion that UI generosity was excessive, or caused unemployment, in other than a minority of workers. Even among the employers whose levels of pay were closest to the income levels available on social assistance, there was little criticism of social assistance. That is not to say there was *no* criticism of social assistance, but because employers now have no difficulty in attracting workers — indeed they typically face a queue of willing and qualified applicants for any vacancy — and because hard times have continued for a while, there was some recognition among the employers we talked to that in today's labour market, people will take work if they can get it.

There has also been a significant change in the nature of low-wage work. Our 1970s research on labour market segmentation was informed by the theoretical perspective of the time, which argued that there was a "secondary labour market" in which low-wage employers were typically small, informal, low-technology establishments, offering insecure work with little prospect for advancement. In the 1990s, a significant fraction of the labour force also faces low-wage, insecure work with little prospect for advancement, but those jobs are often found *within* large, sophisticated, high-technology corporations. When a multibillion-dollar corporation with thousands of franchises employing minimum-wage workers has manuals for its supervisors with sections on "Manipulative Flattery — How and When to Use It," it becomes clear that big business and sophisticated personnel policies have come to the world of low-wage work.

In the 1990s, we still found a few of the small, informal, low-technology employers that dominated the world of low-wage work in the 1970s, but the big dividing lines of the 1990s are those within firms. The adoption of a core worker/contingent worker strategy has been a pervasive response to the market pressures faced by the private sector and the cash crisis faced by the public sector. And although part-time, short-term and contractual employees face the greatest uncertainties, those with jobs often worry about their future. Economic insecurity has become pervasive throughout the labour market.

Nowhere is anxiety about the future greater than in the small rural communities whose livelihoods depended on resource sector jobs. The crisis in the Atlantic fishery has only accentuated the problems of rural job loss created by the closure of mines and by labour shedding in forestry and agriculture. Since the emerging jobs of the information sector tend to be city jobs, the decline of resource-sector employment creates cruel dilemmas for many tightly knit rural communities. Those people within commuting range of an urban labour market can hope to combine the benefits of urban pay cheques and rural housing costs. However, isolated communities that have lost their economic function cannot pretend that their problems will disappear at some future time.

Even if the federal government adopts macroeconomic policies (such as lower interest rates and a lower exchange rate for the Canadian dollar) that create jobs and growth in the country as a whole, the problems of isolated rural communities will remain. The danger is that a fig leaf of rhetoric about "community development" will conceal a cynical policy of inaction which leaves these communities to die a slow death. After all, mobility grants or industrial assistance programs cost money. Governments may think it cheaper to "warehouse" older, poorly educated rural workers where they are, rather than attempt to retrain them for new jobs elsewhere.

In today's labour market, employers can get all the skills they need by careful selection from the pool of the unemployed. The fate of their rejects is not something that directly concerns any individual employer — even if they do eventually face higher tax bills to finance the transfer payments that enable contingent workers to survive intermittent unemployment.

In the current reality of labour markets, firms are not limited in production by the lack of workers with high-level cognitive and social skills — as long as they choose carefully from the queue of the unemployed. The danger is, therefore, that governments — despite their rhetorical commitments to training and equal opportunity — will not in fact want to pay the costs of improving the skills of all Canadians. The fate of the inner cities of the United States should be a constant reminder to Canadians of the very high costs society as a whole bears if one section of the community is ignored and written off. But at the political level in Canada there is also a widespread unwillingness to face the fact that investing in people costs money.

Right now, only a minority of employers have adopted high technology production methods. However, as more and more employers do so, and as the technology of production continues to evolve, one can expect the demand for workers with high-quality social and cognitive skills to increase. Unless Canadians have invested effectively in the social and educational policies that create a motivated and skilled work force, the unavailability of skilled workers may become a constraint on future growth. Investment in the skills and opportunities of all Canadians is, in the long run, crucial to both the efficiency and the equity of the society in which we live. Canadians have major choices to make about the sort of society we want to live in. We believe that Canada can be a society that is both fair and prosperous, but this requires public policy that puts full employment and investment in people at the top of the agenda.

Appendix

Research Papers Produced as Part of the Research Project
(partial list)

Erksoy, Sadettin, Osberg, Lars and Shelley Phipps. "The Income Distributional Implications of Unemployment Insurance." Paper presented at conference of Canadian Economics Association, Calgary, June, 1994.

Grude, Jan. "Education and Entrepreneurship." Paper presented to the Business Education Conference on Entrepreneurship, April, 1992.

Grude, Jan, Osberg, Lars and Fred Wien. "Disadvantaged Workers in a Competitive, Technology Driven Economy: Firm Case Studies from Rural Nova Scotia." Paper presented to the Annual Meetings of the Canadian Sociology and Anthropology Association, Queen's University, Kingston, Ontario, June 4, 1991.

———. "Achieving Competitiveness: Three Lessons from Firm Case Studies in Nova Scotia." Paper presented to the Baddeck Symposium, Halifax, May, 1992.

Lin, Zhengxi and Lars Osberg. "Short-Run Intertemporal Substitution of Labour Supply in Canada." Working Paper No. 92-07, Department of Economics, Dalhousie University, Halifax, September, 1992.

MacPhail, Fiona. "Has the 'Great U-Turn' Gone Full Circle?: Recent Trends in Earnings Inequality in Canada 1981-1989." Working Paper No. 93-01, Department of Economics, Dalhousie University, Halifax, January, 1993.

Osberg, Lars. "Unemployment Insurance and Unemployment — Revisited." Paper presented to the conference on "Unemployment: What is to be Done?," Sudbury, Ontario, March 26/27, 1993 and Working Paper No. 93-04, Department of Economics, Dalhousie University, Halifax, March 1993.

———. "The Economic Role of Education with Special Reference to Atlantic Canada." Working Paper, No. 94-01, Department of Economics, Dalhousie University, Halifax, January 1994.

————. "Social Policy and the Demand Side." Paper prepared for the Canadian Employment Research Forum Workshop on Income Support, Ottawa, September 24, 1993 and Working Paper No. 93-13, Department of Economics, Dalhousie University, Halifax, December, 1993.

Osberg, Lars, Erksoy, Sadettin and Shelley Phipps. "Unemployment, Unemployment Insurance and the Redistribution of Income in Canada in the 1980's." Working Paper No. 93-07, Department of Economics, Dalhousie University, Halifax, Truro, 1993, forthcoming in The Distribution of Economic Well-Being in the 1980's: An International Perspective, B. Gusfafsson and E. Palmer (ed.) Cambridge University Press, 1995.

————. "The Distribution of Income, Wealth and Economic Security: The Impact of Unemployment Insurance Reforms in Canada." Paper presented at the Memorial Conference in honour of Aldi Hagenaars in Leyden, the Netherlands, August 28/29, 1994, forthcoming in The Distribution of Welfare and Household Production: International Perspectives, S. Jenkins, A. Atkinson and A. Kapetyn (ed.) Oxford University Press.

————. "Labour Market Impacts of the Canadian and U.S. Unemployment Insurance Systems." Working Paper No. 94-12, December, 1994.

Osberg, Lars and Shelley Phipps. "Labour Supply with Quantity Constraints: Estimates from a Large Sample of Canadian Workers." Oxford Economic Papers, Volume 45, April, 1993, pp. 269-291.

Wien, Fred. "The Implications of the Changing Economic Base for rural Communities in Nova Scotia." The Class of 1944 lecture given at the Nova Scotia Agricultural College, Truro, N.S., March 17, 1992.

————. *The Role of Social Policy In Economic Restructuring* (Halifax: The Institute for Research on Public Policy, 1991).

Students who based their thesis work on data generated by our research project include:

Ahmed, Nina. "Job Mobility and Wage Determination." Department of Economics, Dalhousie University, Halifax, M.D.E., 1994.

Audas, Rick, "Factors Influencing the Probability of Dropping Out of School." Department of Economics, Dalhousie University, Halifax, M.A., 1994.

Erksoy, Sadettin. "The Distributional Effects of Disinflation and Unemployment in Canada, 1981-1987." Department of Economics, Dalhousie University, Halifax, Ph.D., 1992.

Lin, Zhengxi. "Three Essays on Intertemporal Labour Supply." Department of Economics, Dalhousie University, Halifax, Ph.D., 1992.

MacDonald, Maureen. School of Social Administration, Ph.D. (in progress), Warwick University, England.

MacPhail, Fiona. "Three Essays on Trends in Poverty and Inequality in Canada." Department of Economics, Dalhousie University, Halifax, Ph.D. (in progress).

Selby, Todd. "A Study of the Labour Supply of Single Mothers in Canada." Department of Economics, Dalhousie University, Halifax, M.A. 1992.

Zeman, Lucie. "The Effects of Disability on the Labour Market Activities of Canadians." Department of Economics, Dalhousie University, Halifax, M.A., 1994.

Notes

Preface

1. Lars Osberg and F. K. Siddiq, "The Acquisition of Wealth in Nova Scotia in the Late Nineteenth Century," *Research on Economic Inequality: Studies in the Distribution of Household Wealth*, vol. 4 (Greenwich, CT: JAI Press, 1993), 181-202.
2. Nova Scotia Department of Advanced Education and Job Training, *Career Options* (Halifax: Planning and Evaluation Division, 1992).
3. See Appendix.
4. See, for example, L. Osberg, S. Erksoy, and S. Phipps, "The Distribution of Income, Wealth and Economic Security: The Impact of Unemployment Insurance Reforms in Canada," Working Paper No. 94-08, (Halifax: Dalhousie University, Department of Economics, September 1994).

Chapter 1

1. S. Ostry and M. Zaidi, *Labour Economics in Canada*. 2d ed. (Toronto: Macmillan Canada, 1972), 82; 1991 *Census of Canada*.

Chapter 2

1. People from outside Nova Scotia do not often think of textiles as being an important industry in the province. Nova Scotians still recall with considerable amusement the public remarks of a federal Minister of Industry who came to the province a few years ago and boldly proclaimed that Nova Scotia did not have a textile industry at all. The news photo caught the moment perfectly, as the provincial Minister for the Department of Development rolled his eyes to the heavens.

Chapter 4

1. Statistics Canada defines service-producing industries to include: transportation and storage, wholesale trade, retail trade, finance and insurance, real estate and insurance agents, business services, government services, educational services, health and social services, accommodation, food and beverage services, communications, and other services. Goods-producing industries include: agricultural and related industries, fishing and trapping, logging and forestry, mining, manufacturing and construction, and utilities.

2. For an extended discussion, see L. Osberg, E.N. Wolff and W.J. Baumol, *The Information Economy: The Implications of Unbalanced Growth* (Halifax: Institute for Research on Public Policy, 1989).
3. See, for example, *Employment in the Service Economy* (Ottawa: Economic Council of Canada, 1991).

Chapter 5
1. Health Canada, *National Health Expenditures in Canada 1975-1993* (Ottawa: June 1994), 11.

Chapter 6
1. For a fuller discussion and the detailed regression results on which these estimates of the return to education are based, see L. Osberg, "The Economic Role of Education, with Special Reference to Atlantic Canada," Working Paper No. 94-01, (Halifax: Dalhousie University, Department of Economics, 1994).
2. See Gary Burtless, "Earnings Inequality Over the Business and Demographic Cycles," *A Future of Lousy Jobs? The Changing Structure of U.S. Wages,* (Washington: Brookings Institute, 1990) 77-117, and R. Morissette, J. Myles and G. Picot, "What is Happening to Earnings Inequality in Canada," *Research Paper No. 60,* (Ottawa: Statistics Canada, Analytical Studies Branch, 1993).
3. The percentage of Grade 7 students who attend Grade 12 is somewhat greater than the percentage who graduate from high school five years later, but the trend in both statistics is similar, and as a measure of long-run trends there is some reason to prefer the statistics on grade 12 attendance, since some fraction of the student body (varying over time) has been in programs (such as vocational education), which did not get a grade 12 certificate. For a fuller discussion of measures of attendance/completion see Nova Scotia Department of Education, *Departmental Working Paper on Dropout Related Indicators,* (Halifax: Statistics and Data Entry Section, Planning and Research Division, June, 1993).
4. The sorry state of educational statistics in Canada means that national figures comparable to Table 1 are not available. Indirect survey evidence (from the Census or the Labour Market Activity Survey) is available on educational attainment by province and by age group that indicate the improvement in self-reported educational attainment in central and western Canada happened earlier than in Nova Scotia. (Saskatchewan and Quebec showed particularly big improvements in the 1970s.)
5. See T.M. Smeeding, "Cross-National Comparisons of Inequality and Poverty Position," L. Osberg, ed., *Economic Inequality and Poverty: International Perspectives* (Armonk, N.Y.: ME Sharpe Publishers, 1991).
6. For example, who would have predicted that physics PhDs would find employment with investment bankers and stock brokerages? Yet it turns out that the mathematics background of a physics education is highly useful in analyzing the risk structure of new financial instruments such as swap and option calls in the derivatives market.

Chapter 7

1. Human Resources Development Canada, *Have Your Say,* October 1994: 6.
2. See, for example, L. Osberg, "Social Policy and the Demand Side," Working Paper No. 93-13, (Halifax: Dalhousie University, Department of Economics, December 1993); L. Osberg and S. Phipps, "Large Sample Estimates of Labour Supply: Results with Quantity Constraints," *Oxford Economic Papers,* 45, (April 1993): 269-291; P. Fortin, "A Diversified Strategy for Deficit Control: Combining Faster Growth with Fiscal Discipline," (Montreal: University of Quebec at Montreal, Department of Economics, August 1994).
3. For a fuller discussion, see L. Osberg, "Concepts of Unemployment and the Structure of Employment," *Economie Appliqué* XLVIII(1): 157-81.
4. G. Betcherman, "Are Firms Underinvesting in Training?" *Canadian Business Economics* 1(1): 23-33.
5. For a full survey, see Fortin, "Diversified Strategy." A recent estimate of the IMF is even lower, at 6.8 per cent — see L. Bartolini and S. Symansky, "Unemployment and Wage Dynamics in Multimod," *Staff Studies for the World Economic Outlook* (Washington, D.C.: International Monetary Fund, December 1993): 79. Fougère presents two estimates of the "natural rate" of unemployment for Canada in 1994 — his structural model produces an estimate of 6.5 per cent, while the reduced form estimate is 7.5 per cent. See Maxime Fougère, "Why the Unemployment Rate is Higher in Canada than in the United States," Department of Finance, Fiscal Policy and Economic Analysis Branch, paper presented at the Annual Meeting of the Canadian Economics Association, Montreal, June 1995.

Selected References

Betcherman, Gordon. 1992. "Are Firms Underinvesting in Training?" *Canadian Business Economics.* Vol. 1, No. 1.

Burtless, Gary, ed. 1990. *A Future of Lousy Jobs?: The Changing Structure of U.S. Wages.* Washington, D.C.: The Brookings Institution.

Canadian Institute of Advanced Research. 1988. *Innovation and Canada's Prosperity: The Transforming Power of Science, Engineering and Technology.* Toronto: The Canadian Institute of Advanced Research.

Dertouzos, M., Richard Lester and Robert Solow, et al. 1989. *Made in America.* Cambridge, MA: MIT Press.

Dollar, David and Edward N. Wolff. 1993. *Competitiveness, Convergence, and International Specialization.* Cambridge, MA: MIT Press.

Economic Council of Canada. 1987. *Innovation and Jobs in Canada.* Ottawa: Minister of Supply and Services.

———. 1991. *Employment in the Service Economy.* Ottawa: Minister of Supply and Services.

Fortin, Pierre. 1994. "A Diversified Strategy for Deficit Control: Combining Faster Growth with Fiscal Discipline." Mimeo. University of Quebec at Montreal.

Mahon, Rianne. 1987. "From Fordism to ?: New Technology, Labour Markets and Unions." *Economic and Industrial Democracy.* Vol. 8.

Osberg, Lars, ed. 1991. *Economic Inequality and Poverty: International Perspectives.* Armonk, N.Y.: M.E. Sharpe.

Osberg, Lars, Wolff, Edward N. and William J. Baumol. 1989. *The Information Economy: The Implications of Unbalanced Growth.* Halifax, N.S.: The Institute for Research on Public Policy.

Piore, Michael, and Charles F. Sabel. 1984. *The Second Industrial Divide: Possibilities for Prosperity.* New York: Basic Books.

Premier's Council. 1988. *Competing in the New Global Economy,* Vols. I and II. Toronto: Queen's Printer for Ontario.

Premier's Council. 1990. *People and Skills in the New Global Economy.* Toronto: Queen's Printer for Ontario.

Royal Commission on Employment and Unemployment. 1986. *Building on Our Strengths.* St. John's: Government of Newfoundland.

Summers, Lawrence H. 1990. *Understanding Unemployment.* Cambridge, MA: MIT Press.

Index